This volume was inspired by the work of the American Marxist Robert H. Langston, whose untimely death interrupted his path-breaking work on the labour theory of value. A unique collaborative effort between an international team of contributors from a broad range of disciplines has been brought together by ERNEST MANDEL, the foremost Marxist economist of today whose widely acclaimed works include *Marxist Economic Theory*, *The Second Slump* and *Late Capitalism*.

About the contributors

EMMANUEL FARJOUN is Professor of Mathematics at the Hebrew University of Jerusalem and joint author, with Moshe Machover, of *Laws of Chaos*.

ANWAR SHAIKH is Professor of Economics at the New School in New York and has contributed extensively to the debate on value theory, reflected in his essays in *The Value Controversy*.

HECTOR GUILLEN ROMERO is Professor of Modern Studies in the Department of Economics in the autonomous Metropolitan University of Itzapalapa in Mexico. His most recent work is *Origenes de la Crisis Económica en México 1940–82*.

PAOLO GIUSSANI is an Italian Marxist who has been working on the Marxist interpretation of National Income Statistics. His papers include *The Anti-Okishio Theorem* and a study on the reduction of skilled to unskilled labour.

PIERRE SALAMA's book *Sur La Valeur* is one of the established French reference texts on the question. He is a professor at the University of Paris. He has just co-authored, with G. Mathias, *L'Etat surdéveloppé*.

JESUS ALBARRACIN GOMEZ was Professor of Economic Structure and Theory at Madrid University until 1981 and is now an economist with the Bank of Spain.

SUNGUR SAVRAN was lecturer in economics at the University of Istanbul until 1983 when he resigned in protest at the repression of Turkish universities. He has contributed frequently to *Capital and Class* on value theory.

ALAN FREEMAN is editor of the weekly *Socialist Action* and author of *The Benn Heresy*.

**Robert Langston**
**Emmanuel Farjoun**
**Anwar Shaikh**
**Hector Guillén Romero**
**Paulo Giussani**
**Ernest Mandel**
**Pierre Salama**
**Jesus Albarracín**
**Sungur Savran**
**Alan Freeman**

**Verso**

# Ricardo, Marx, Sraffa
## The Langston Memorial Volume

*Introduced by Ernest Mandel*
*Edited by Ernest Mandel*
*and Alan Freeman*

**British Library Cataloguing in Publication Data**

Ricardo, Marx, Sraffa: the Langston memorial
    volume.
    1. Economics
    I. Mandel, Ernest   II. Freeman, Alan
    330.1          HB171

First published 1984
© Langston Foundation 1984

Verso
15 Greek Street, London  W1

Filmset in Times Roman by
Mid-County Press, London

Printed in Great Britain by
The Thetford Press, Ltd,
Thetford, Norfolk

ISBN 0 86091 078 4
        0 86091 778 9 pbk

# Contents

This book is dedicated to Robert H. Langston, revolutionary socialist, whose untimely death interrupted the pioneering work which inspired this volume. Its appearance testifies that his work and memory survive through the international socialist movement to which he dedicated his talents. It is our contribution to furthering his efforts towards the conquest of ignorance, the eradication of exploitation and the abolition of humanity's enslavement by outmoded economic forms.

# Introduction
## Ernest Mandel

Ever since the third volume of *Capital* appeared, a debate has been raging around Marx's solution to the so-called transformation problem: the transformation of values into prices of production and of surplus-value into profit. A critical balance sheet of this debate, which has gone on for more than forty years, would fill a book.

The first major turning point in the discussion came with the publication, in July 1907, by the Prussian statistician Ladislaus von Bortkiewicz, of an article entitled 'Zur Berichtigung der Grundlegenden Theoretischen Konstruktion von Marx im Dritten Band des Kapitals' (*Jahrbücher für Nationalökonomie und Statistik*). This drew attention to an alleged 'feedback' failure in Marx's presentation of the transformation of values into prices in the third volume of *Capital*. Here, inputs to production are represented by value magnitudes, while outputs are calculated in terms of prices of production.

Von Bortkiewicz used Marx's reproduction schemata in the second volume of *Capital* to establish a logical contradiction, pointing out that if the inputs to such a schema are represented by price of production magnitudes, a solution to the transformation problem can be derived which differs from Marx's. From this he inferred that Marx's own calculation should be corrected.

This approach has informed the great bulk of subsequent work on the transformation problem. Successive authors, by studying the distribution of the total product of society between different branches of the division of labour, have under various assumptions devised methods of calculating prices and values which produce results differing from Marx's to a greater or lesser degree.

Heinrich Dietzel, a now largely forgotten German author, tried to expand the debate in his book *Von Lehrwert der Wertlehre und vom Grundfehler der Marxschen Verteilungslehre*, 1921, by establishing a dichotomy between Marx's alleged theory of distribution — the theory of wages, rent and profits — and his theory of value. Anticipating Sraffa, he tried to prove that the labour theory of value was unnecessary to sustain the theory of distribution.

He could achieve this, however, only by starting from the physical quantities of products and their interrelationships. He thus abstracted from the very problem Marx tried to tackle, namely the regulation of commodity production and circulation by private, unplanned exchange in the market.

I. Rubin, the most brilliant of the Russian Marxist economists, answered that if one does not start from the social relations of production that underlie commodity production, one will fail to understand why value analysis is needed. If the division of labour in society were regulated purely by the gross exchange of the total product of society between different branches of the division of labour, a completely different economic system would have to be involved, without private property and without commodity production. All labour would immediately be recognized as social labour, and one would no longer have a system in which private labour is recognized as social only through exchange. Behind value there is abstract labour, and behind abstract labour lie the specific social relationships which regulate the behaviour of private owners of the means of production exchanging the products of their labour under conditions of approximate equality, without which the social division of labour would collapse.[1]

This argument has by and large not been followed up. The same cannot be said of von Bortkiewicz's critique, which was developed by Paul M. Sweezy in *The Theory of Capitalist Development* (1942), a book which triggered a long and detailed discussion, notably in articles by J. Winternitz in 1948 and F. Seton in 1957. This had two important consequences. The first was a generalization of von Bortkiewicz's analysis from three departments (Means of production, consumer goods, and 'luxury' goods) to an arbitrary number of industries, each producing a more or less homogeneous commodity, and each consuming the product of other industries in proportions which, it was soon to be argued, were 'technically' determined by the means of production employed in each industry. This treatment connected the study of the transformation problem to that of 'input–output' models of both capitalist and post-capitalist economies, developed by Wassily W. Leontief in his work *The Structure of the American Economy 1919–1921*, published in 1941, and in subsequent publications. Authors in the 1940s and 1950s were able to apply the techniques of matrix algebra to study the properties of such input–output models.

A second turning point in the debate followed the appearance of Piero Sraffa's *Production of Commodities by Means of Commodities* in 1960. Unlike Leontief, whose pioneering work had a strong empirical and statistical component, Sraffa used input-output equation systems to construct a theoretical critique of neo-classical marginalism. In his models, however, the relation between prices and physical magnitudes was entirely independent of values — a result already indicated by Seton.

Though Sraffa himself made no explicit attack on Marxist analysis, the conclusions implicit in this work were rapidly drawn, and the debate moved away from a technical critique of Marx's value constructions towards an attempt to show the labour theory of value is unnecessary for economic analysis and should be discarded.

This in turn precipitated a long and rich debate, some of the main phases of which were articles by A. Medio, E. Wolfstetter, A. Garegnani, Benetti and others, and Michio Morishima's book *Marx's Economics*, the latter drawing also on linear programming techniques suggested by the cybernetician John von Neumann.[2] A watershed in the debate came with Ian Steedman's book *Marx After Sraffa*, which not only summarized and synthesised the preceding debate but forcefully asserted the thesis which now characterizes the post-Sraffian school: namely that the accumulated inconsistencies and problems revealed by this debate are now so great that Marxist value theory as a whole must now be scrapped.

Sraffa's book is thus important, not merely in its own right, but in the general history of economic theory. It marks the beginning of a current of economic thought widely referred to as neo-Ricardianism. This current has dealt neo-classical marginalism a staggering blow, especially in the field of capital theory. However, its mainstream authors question Marx's contribution to economic theory by reabsorbing him, so to speak, into a general theory in which — as in Ricardo — distribution is analysed in terms of the division of a surplus between and within classes. At the same time basic aspects of the labour theory of value — shared by Ricardo and Marx — are abandoned and prices explained purely as a function of so-called 'technical conditions of production' and the division of the surplus product between the two main classes in society.

Until now the response of Marxists to this challenge has been rather inefficient. It has either been dogmatic ('X is true because He said so') or purely ideological and political ('the neo-Ricardians are wrong because objectively they undermine the proletariat').

Before his untimely and deeply regretted death, our friend and comrade Robert H. Langston spoke to me and to our common friends Emmanuel Farjoun and Anwar Shaikh about a new approach which, he felt, should answer the neo-Ricardian challenge. He intended to settle down in Europe for a lengthy stay in order to work on this project with us. However, his sudden death left us with only preliminary notes. The opening article in this volume is based on these notes, as edited by Emmanuel Farjoun. Like the other contributors to this book, his intention was vigorously to defend Marxist economic theory against the onslaught directed against it in recent years.

Langston sought to break free of a crippling constraint imposed on the study of value-price transformation by von Bortkiewicz type models, as generalized by later authors, if used to model a real capitalist economy: namely that they abstract from economic movement in time.

Several authors have commented that despite neo-Ricardianism's critique of the marginalist element in neo-classical theory, both schools share an equilibrium approach. They do not, therefore, furnish the tools to study one of capitalism's most essential features: the uneven and combined character of capitalist development, distinguished by the constant movement of capital, the never-ending disequilibriation and re-equilibriation of the prices, profits and differential rents of independent producers.

Langston's attempt to develop the study of value-price relation-ships without falling into this neo-Ricardian trap connects up to Rubin's earlier, and as yet unrefuted response to von Bortkiewicz and Dietzel. The uneven development of capitalism, its ceaseless and unplanned fluctuations, result precisely from the private character of production and exchange: from the fact that producers do not, and cannot plan. The neo-Ricardian approach is a profoundly unscientific starting point for the study of capitalism, because it abstracts from the very feature which distinguishes capitalism from all other economic systems.

The defence of classical Marxism undertaken by Langston and the other contributors to this book is not, therefore, merely a reaffirma-tion of a believer's faith. Though combined with a moral and political dedication to the cause of the emancipation of the working class, the exploited and the oppressed, it is a scientific endeavour of a fully investigative nature.

First of all the authors consider, to apply the best of all scientific tests, that the validity of Marx's basic hypotheses and his analysis is confirmed — more dramatically in recent years than ever — by all the available empirical evidence and by the real history of the capitalist system. This is not to say that Marxism has closed the book of empiricial study. On the contrary, the new statistical methods that have become available through the use of input-output models can be used to examine empirical issues within a Marxist theoretical framework in a degree of detail probably not previously possible. In this volume Anwar Shaikh in particular combines an exposition of the formal inconsistencies of neo-Ricardian methods with a practical demonstration that many of Marx's central hypotheses are empirically confirmed by input-output data.

The authors approach the argument that Marxist theory is logically flawed in this light. Marxism's (unchallenged) empirical superiority to neo-Ricardianism suggests that its theoretical conquests cannot be discarded cavalierly or arbitrarily. The authors maintain that any criticism of Marxist economic theory, as well as its defence, must understand its inner coherence and hence the key role played by the basic categories of social labour, abstract labour, value, exchange-value, money, capital and surplus-value in explaining how commodity production in general, and capitalist commodity production in particular, function, what their laws of motion are, how they came into being and why they are condemned to disappear. The book sets out to combine a defence of Marxism from its own vantage point — by demonstrating that the logical inconsistencies attributed to it by the neo-Ricardians do not exist — with a counter-attack exposing the inner contradictions, inconsistencies and evasions of neo-Ricardianism itself.

A thoroughgoing piece by Emmanuel Farjoun refutes the principal accusations of inconsistency made by the neo-Ricardians. He not only rebuts but inverts the charge that labour values cannot cope with 'joint production', bringing to light devastating contradictions in the Sraffian's own solutions. Both he and Savran deal with the charge that Marxist analysis gives rise to negative values. They show it is the product, among other things, of a failure to understand the role of 'individual values' in Marx's analysis, and its relation to value and to exchange value.

Pierre Salama concentrates on the interrelation between these three concepts, and both his piece and my own study the connection between value, exchange value and money (gold) in the emergence of prices and price problems — in other words, in the transformation problem and its solution.

Farjoun, Giussani and Albarracin take the charge of inconsistency into the camp of the neo-Ricardians, not only laying bare some of their more obvious contradictions but suggesting which of their underlying assumptions are responsible.

These studies of neo-Ricardianism's inconsistencies, finally, relate to a third aspect of our defence of Marxism. The inner coherence of Marxist theory means that you cannot arbitrarily remove this or that conceptual foundation from the system without making the rest of it meaningless and condemning it to collapse. We now have the benefit of more than sixty years of discussion and theoretical development to answer the question: can von Bortkiewicz's 'corrections' to Marx, and the neo-Ricardian approach in general, be assimilated within Marxist class analysis, as writers such as Sweezy and Meek argue, or does it presuppose a fundamentally different theoretical framework? In an overview which also serves as a useful introduction for the non-mathematical reader, Hector Guillen studies the relation between Sraffa's system and neoclassical theory on the one hand, and Marxism on the other. He systematically expounds the conclusion, formally demonstrated by several other contributors — notably Guissani — that the analytic weaknesses of the neo-Ricardian approach not only divorce it from Marxist theory but from class relations as they actually develop under capitalism. A summary piece by Alan Freeman, which also tries to develop Langston's approach, draws together the arguments shared by the contributors to try and show why the logical structure of Marx's labour value theory as a whole offers a far more coherent foundation for studying capitalist political economy.

While all contributions share a defence of Marxist economic theory, and therefore share most of the arguments in one way or another, even if approaching them from different analytical points of departure, there are some differences between the authors which have not been ironed out, despite several fruitful conferences made possible by the generous aid of the Robert M. Langston Foundation.

I would like to point out one of them, which I feel is the most important. Pierre Salama and I argue that the main theoretical purpose of Marx's solution of the transformation problem in the third volume of *Capital* was to uphold a combined identity which the neo-Ricardians have challenged, the identity of both the sum of values equalling the sum of prices of production, and the sum of surplus-value equalling the sum of profits. I feel that this double identity flows from the basic assumptions of Marxist economic theory: that no value can be created except by living labour in the process of production; that the expenditure of living labour in that same process of production is the sole source of surplus-value; and that no profits can originate from anywhere else but from surplus-value. When the neo-Ricardians challenge this combined identity, I feel that they challenge the very essence of Marxist economic theory.

Anwar Shaikh's contribution to the present volume, while sharing the position that value and surplus-value can only be created by living labour in the process of production, and that profit originates in surplus-value, nevertheless concludes that the sum of profit can and generally does differ from the sum of surplus-value. He argues that prices and profits are the circulation forms taken by value and surplus-value respectively. As such, these forms of value are viewed by him as being more complex, as containing more determinations, than their corresponding value foundations. Since he accepts the proposition that by itself circulation neither creates nor destroys total value but merely transfers it from one hand to another, the question for him is to show how exactly these total value-preserving transfers can nonetheless give rise to a quantitative difference between profit and surplus-value.

He contends that overall social reproduction comprises not only the circuit of capital but also a distinct circuit of revenue, which he identifies with the circuit of capitalist consumption at the most basic level of abstraction. This latter circuit originates in the capital circuit in the form of that portion of surplus-value which the capitalists receive as income, but it ends in the personal consumption of the capitalists, so that value and price magnitudes associated with this revenue circuit do not feed back into the circuit of capital. It is precisely because there are two circuits, he argues, that the strictly limited transfer of value between one and the other can give the illusion that profit is independent of surplus-value, whereas it is in fact merely the slightly changed outward form of the latter. Shaikh's argument, it should be noted, is conducted primarily in terms of comparisons between money prices proportional to values (direct prices) and money prices of production. One should remember that for Marx, prices of production are the 'regulating averages' of market prices.

These disagreements should not obscure the great underlying similarities of approach. The important question is: what flows from these divergences and what does not? It is an important task for future investigation to pursue this question, and it is fitting and proper that the issues themselves are presented as clearly as possible. The debate around the transformation problem is certainly not over.

But the unity of the contributions to this volume is rather striking: all the more so given the differences in academic training and specialization of the authors, as well as their differences in nationality.

When I finished writing *Marxist Economic Theory* more than twenty years ago, I stressed the urgent need to internationalize Marxist theory not only by extending the empirical data and the problems with which it traditionally dealt beyond the all too narrow framework of Western capitalism and Western society, but also by involving thinkers from all over the world in the further development of the theory. The fact that the contributors to this volume come from countries as far apart as Belgium, Britain, France, Israel, Mexico, Italy, Pakistan, Spain, Turkey and the United States, is an encouraging sign that we are approaching that goal. But for the pressure of time, this volume would also have included contributions by Marxists from Brazil, Germany, Japan, and Scandinavia. And it will not take too long to extend the list to Eastern Europe, the People's Republic of China and the USSR. For, to the utter dismay of professional anti-Communists, Marxism is beginning to revive there too, albeit mainly among the younger 'dissidents' rather than among those who uphold the establishment. Let those who speculate about the crisis of Marxism get on with their wishful thinking. Creative, critical and open Marxism is alive and kicking, more alive than ever before. This volume is only one example among many of that essential fact of life.

# A New Approach to the Relation Between Prices and Values

## Robert H. Langston

*The following piece is based on notes concerning the transformation problem left by the late Robert Langston. Just before his sudden and· untimely death he was engaged in an attempt to break new ground on this question by discarding the traditional concept of price as a fixed numerical magnitude. At that time I was an interlocutor to his ideas while occasionally giving him technical mathematical advice. Unfortunately he did not have the time to pursue his work or to prepare his notes for publication—which end abruptly. Therefore in writing up this piece some degree of interpolation was inevitable. All the same I have tried to stay as close as possible to the original notes.* (Emmanuel Farjoun)

The reality of prices has not yet found a satisfactory theoretical counterpart in any modern labour theory of values. The traditional concepts such as prices of production, while capturing part of that reality, are riddled with well-known theoretical difficulties. I view the famous transformation problem as the problem of formulating within the labour theory of value a concept which will strengthen our theoretical hold on the phenomenon of 'price' and its intrinsic relations to value. By considering critically neo-classical and Sraffian positions I am led to a concept of price which reflects the volatile, chaotic and ever-changing nature of observed market prices. In doing so, I attempt to show that the ceaseless movement of real market prices—while irreducible to a single, deterministic matrix of ideal prices—is limited within certain determinate bounds. Let me begin by comparing the concepts of price and value.

### Sraffa's Distributive Prices

Prices in both the neo-classical theory and Sraffian framework are determined by a certain norm for the distribution of the net product:

the net product itself is assumed to emerge somehow out of the various social production processes. The physical composition of that product and of the processes themselves in terms of machines, raw material, type and amount of labour and technological make-up are assumed to be given. Once these are given each commodity that emerges out of these processes is assumed to acquire a certain ideal price or value—which is supposed to regulate the exchange of commodities against each other.

In both frameworks the basic concept behind the formation of these prices is that of appropriate rewards or appropriate distribution of the net product. It is taken for granted that the two main factors of production, capital and labour, must be rewarded according to their real contribution in order for the equilibrium to be maintained. In neo-classical theory capital is rewarded for its abstention from consumption, as a function of the amount of capital it has dedicated to the specific process. Labour is rewarded for the labour-time given up by the worker for the sake of production. In the Sraffian framework, moreover, rewards are exactly proportional to the capital invested, in order to guarantee that there will be no flow of capital from one branch to the other so that, in the words of Sraffa, 'day after day, production continues unchanged.'

Up to this point Sraffa travels together with neo-classical theory in formulating what I shall call *distributive prices*, prices which are so formed as to guarantee a certain mode of distribution of the net product as rewards to the factors of production. From here their ways part, for neo-classical theory goes on to make a much stronger claim than Sraffa. It claims that in addition to prices of commodities, theoretically it can also capture the rate of profit, or the exact size of the rewards themselves, and not only the mode of distribution between capital and labour. The neo-classical concept of an ideal equilibrium attempts to reflect the inner logic of free market competition. This concept of equilibrium allows for the assessment of rewards from the contribution of each factor. Once the contribution of capital is assessed, profits can be derived from the so-called production function of the particular process.

It is here that Sraffa raises a basic question. How can one measure the contribution of capital? He points out that capital as a huge collection of physical goods has no natural economic measure except as prices. But capital itself must be regarded not as abstract money but as a concrete collection of physical commodities—for example, machines, energy, raw materials. When this is taken into account, the rather strict framework that Sraffa shares with the neo-classical theory does not allow for the complete determination of prices independently of that of wages and profit. Thus the assumption that the contribution of capital as a numerical measure can somehow be assessed before a precise mode of distribution is assumed is shown to be inconsistent with the basic tenets of distributive prices which, as I said, neo-classical theory shares with Sraffa. Under Sraffa's assumptions, the size of capital itself depends crucially on the exact proportion of the division of the value of net product between the providers of labour services and providers of capital services. Thus it is impossible to assess objectively even under ideal equilibrium conditions the economic contribution of capital to the process of production. The whole theory of profits and prices built carefully by neo-classical theory to account for the size of profit falls to the ground.

The algebraic equations and theorems used by Sraffa serve mostly to show that the value of capital cannot be assessed even from a very detailed knowledge of capital's physical composition and the production conditions under which this physical capital is reproduced. On the contrary, economic value under equilibrium can move quite freely within a wide margin. Sraffa shows that distributive prices can also move freely without any change in the actual material production process, and hence without any change in the physical inputs of capital or labour.

The upshot is that one cannot assess the contribution of each factor deductively, and thus the claim of the neo-classical theory to be able to determine theoretically the level of profits is shown to be unfounded. Moreover Sraffa shows that within the above concept of prices and profit, the level of the rewards themselves, say the rate of profit, can vary enormously without any change in the technology and method of production, that is without any visible change in the production processes themselves. This is a decisive blow to the neo-classical theory of prices and profits. Its two central concepts of the level of contribution and the appropriate level of reward are shown to be without any objective economic foundations. All this is done without any change of framework, simply by regarding capital as a physical object composed of the very commodities that it produces with the help of labour.

**Values in the Sphere of Production**

In the framework of the labour theory of value, values as distinct from prices arise exclusively in the sphere of production. They are determined by the level of development of the forces of production and the social organization of labour. In turn they determine the general parameters of both distribution and exchange. But the exact proportion of the distribution of the net value or net product has no direct influence on the values of commodities themselves. Moreover, both in theory and practice, a knowledge of the values of all commodities produced for profit in socially-organized production-lines does not by itself allow the exact determination of the proportions of distribution. A given system of labour values is consistent with a whole range of possible distribution methods and outlets of the net product. This property of labour values, namely their relative independence from distribution, is unique to them as values which depend on the sphere of production.

How do changes in value, due to development of new production techniques, new products and better labour organization, influence distribution? This is elementary. For example, real wages, considered as a bundle of physical commodities or use-values, can be significantly raised when certain productive conditions are met. In this case, the value of the formerly inaccessible bundle of goods is reduced, and can thereby be incorporated into the socially recognized workers' standard of life. It is here that the difference between labour values and Sraffa's prices become clear. In the latter, the price of a given commodity, say a car or a computer, may undergo huge reductions simply because for some reason the general level of profit has changed. This may suffice to reduce the prices of machines so much as to allow every worker to buy the most sophisticated machine, without any change in the material production of these commodities. In the framework of the labour theory of value, on the other hand, a formerly expensive commodity can, in general, become accessible to the average worker only when the total amount of social labour-time devoted to its production falls to a certain rather well defined level. Such a reduction is not a result of changes in the distribution of the net product, although it may in consequence bring about such changes.

These initial observations do not imply that the detailed relations between values and exchange ratios of commodities are already understood. This question is still an open one. At the root of the difficulty lies the duality of the capitalist mode of production. One of the main features of the present mode of production is the duality that on the one hand, chaos and fierce competition prevail in the market and regulate relations between the various producers, while on the other hand, strict rationalization of the division of labour and utmost collaboration and coordination among various direct producers prevails within each production unit. Labour values arise out of this rationalization process and they acquire their importance precisely because the amount of labour used up in production is the subject of huge downward pressures. Constant efforts are made to reduce it to the necessary minimum. Out of these processes of production, commodities emerge with a well-defined labour value, the amount of abstract labour-time which is socially necessary for their production under the technologically prevailing methods.

Once these values are shaped, the variations in the ratios of distribution are severely restricted. But the precise ratios of exchange are not yet given, as they are further determined by the various forces of competition and in the chaos of the market. Thus if the value of capital employed for each worker increases, that is, if there is an increase in the organic composition of capital, great pressure downwards will be exerted on the average rate of profit. This pressure may cause the money rate of profit to fall. But it may also be transmitted forward towards a reduction of the value of wages, or even further towards changes in the methods of production which will reduce the value of capital and bring the organic composition back to a more realistic level.

**The Transition to Prices of Production**

One of the main inferences to be drawn from the above discussion is that one cannot compute or deduce, directly or indirectly, the distributive price of a given commodity from the value of that commodity. There is no formula which gives the natural market price of a product in terms of its value. The reason is simple. I have shown how Sraffa deduces that the price of any commodity depends crucially on the precise ratio according to which the total net surplus is divided between the classes of capital and labour. Values, however, do not depend on the ratios of distribution. Had the prices depended functionally on those ratios, then they would also be indifferent to the mode of distribution. In other words, if prices could have been directly computed exclusively from values, they would not change unless values changed. But values do not change whenever there is a change of distribution, while prices do. Thus prices cannot be computed algebraically or in any other way from values. It follows that the traditional search for some formula that somehow transforms values into prices of production has been misguided.

## Ceaseless Motion and Variation

With all its achievements in demolishing the marginalist concept of prices, the decisive weakness of the Sraffian notion of prices is the fact that it depends crucially on a very rigid and unrealistic concept of distribution, namely the uniform rate of profit. There seems to be no way to modify that notion so as to reconstruct it without rigid distributive assumptions. Therefore its real pertinence is in analysing and criticizing other neo-classical theorems which depend on the same axioms of distribution.

But as far as the reality of the market is concerned, and the social and economic logic of that reality, Sraffa's prices have a very limited theoretical salience. The problem is of course that rates of profits are never uniform and never guaranteed, and prices cannot be taken as fixed magnitudes associated with given commodities. Furthermore, one must reject the notion that any essential feature of the system can be understood by considering a hypothetical model 'in which', according to Sraffa, 'day after day, production continues unchanged in those respects . . .' and in which 'no change in output and no change in the proportions in which different means of production are used by an industry are considered . . .'

There is an additional crucial assumption which is common to all input-output models and which must also be rejected. This indispensable assumption is that the same commodities which are used as raw material and machinery inputs in the production process emerge at the end of the production period as outputs. A fixed set of commodities is assumed to reproduce itself, possibly with the help of labour (hence the title *The Production of Commodities by Means of Commodities*). Everyone admits that this is a simplified case. But the following question has rarely been raised: Is it possible to capture the reality in which prices of commodities are in permanent flux, and in which the very nature of commodities changes from one period to the next, and where no complete equalization of rates of profits ever takes place, by assuming the exact opposite: that prices never change, that the same commodities are produced over and over again, and that each and every one of them realize the same uniform rate of profit?

To my knowledge no argument, either economic or mathematical, has ever been presented in support of the view that such an abstraction from the real movement preserves any interesting property of it. In the recent debates around the transformation problem it has been proven time and again (for example by Ian Steedman) that the labour theory of value is incompatible with the above set of rigid idealizations. This was taken by many as a refutation of the labour theory of value. But in truth this incompatibility only shows that the traditional search for some perfect transformation formula was misguided. It does not impy that the basic tenets of the labour theory of value are wrong or incapable of further development. On the contrary, it actually shows that the labour theory of value has an enormous advantage over distributive price theories. This is precisely because the latter are based on a notion of prices and profit which are logically incompatible with the inner nature of the present mode of production. If one could show that the rigid assumptions on price and profit are unable to capture or even approximate to the oscillating and ever-changing magnitudes of real prices and profits, then the labour theory of value could be credited with the early detection of these problems.

Of course it is not enough to be inconsistent with a false theory in order to be right. Far from it. The task of clarifying the formation of prices is still a vast one. But I draw from Sraffa's work the conclusion that one cannot advance one step in this direction by assuming a fixed set of prices and a uniform rate of profit. As I have said I will not address here the difficult question of the precise definition of labour values. It suffices to say the following: within any of the existing input-output models, labour values are well defined. They can be constructed without using any assumptions about prices and profits, for they arise simply out of the presentation of the production process as a physical input-output system. Furthermore one can easily conceive of a labour value under much weaker assumptions. One does not have to assume that the same commodities are produced and reproduced endlessly. Commodities can change from one period to the next, and still labour values will be well defined.

## Time-Dependent Prices

I now want to construct a system of prices of production (or prices, for short) which does not depend on the usual set of rigid assumptions and thus can better reflect the volatile nature of the formation of prices and the realization of profit. Let us take the following steps: First, assume social production is accomplished over a period of time called the period of production, over which inputs are used in the social labour process and turned into outputs whose price is then determined. This is a common assumption to all input-output models. Now divide our economy into branches. Since the nature of commodities within each branch is subject to changes, group them by their value. At each period of production denoted by t the totality of commodities coming out of a given branch $B_i$ were sold for a certain price which depends on the particular period, and may change. This total price is denoted by $P_i(t)$ and we assume that $P_i(t)$ is in general different from $P_i(t+1)$. Being total price, it depends on the volume of production in the branch $B_i$.

In order to get a unit price we divide $P_i(t)$ by the total value of all commodities belonging to $B_i$. We get the price per unit value of a typical commodity of the branch $B_i$ denoted by $\tau_i(t)$:

$$\tau_i(t) = \frac{P_i(t)}{\Lambda_i(t)}$$

where $\Lambda_i$ is the labour value of the output of the branch $B_i$.

We do not assume that the unit price $\tau_i$, which is the price per unit value of $B_i$, remains the same at all times. If one denotes by $t+1$ the production period immediately following, then in general:

$$\tau_i(t) \neq \tau_i(t+1)$$

This inequality means that price is not a numerical magnitude attached to any commodity or a group of commodities (say commercial vehicles). Rather it is a whole series of magnitudes. This series has neither a first element nor a last one:

$$\ldots \tau_i(t), \ \tau_i(t+1), \ \tau_i(t+2), \ldots$$

so that no member of the series is more significant than any other member. The most interesting feature of this series is its oscillation and the most important information carried by it is its mode of oscillation.

Notice that the series takes care of both changes of prices or commodities from one period to the next and changes in the very nature of commodities. I do not attach price to specific commodities but rather to the average unit value emerging from a given branch. I am not trying to follow the price of each and every new product that emerges from $B_i$, but rather the general trend of the realization of values in a given branch at a given time T. Since the absolute level of price of a unit value is of little importance at this stage it is advisable to refer all prices to a standard commodity, of which gold is the most natural candidate for the role. Let $B_g$ denote the gold-producing sector. We have the following expression for prices in terms of gold:

$$m_i(t) = \frac{\tau_i(t)}{\tau_g(t)} = \frac{P_i(t) \cdot \Lambda_g(t)}{P_g(t) \cdot \Lambda_i(t)}.$$

Now of course many factors account for the variation in price from one period to the next. The transformation problem attempts to understand only those influences which arise from the equilization of the rate of profits. I will not assume that at the current prices the rates of profit are in fact uniform or equal in all branches. This is in my view contrary to the very nature of the system and, as argued above, leads to a price theory which has very little, if anything, to do with labour values.

Let us assume however that prices are readjusted from one period to the next so as to try and achieve the general rate of profit. In general these attempts fail, leading sometimes to lower rates, sometimes to higher. Let us denote by $r_i(t)$ the rate of profit realized in the i-th branch at the end of the period. The general rate of profit for the economy as a whole will then be:

$$r = \sum_i \left( \frac{K_i(t)}{K} \cdot r_i(t) \right)$$

during the period and $K = \sum_i K_i(t)$. Assume that r is determined by surplus-value, namely that $r = s/c + v$. For a large economy that is surplus-value, namely that $r = s/(c + v)$. For a large economy this is not a bad assumption since the deviation of prices from value in various branches will tend to cancel each other out, so that the average money rate of profit will be very close to the average value rate.

One can now write the appropriate algebraic expression for the oscillating unit prices. One reason for doing so is to examine the mode of oscillation of these prices. My main contention is that in each branch, so long as production conditions remain approximately stable, prices will oscillate within a rather limited range. Any other behaviour will indicate that something is wrong in the present framework. On the other hand, a series of bounded oscillations of unit price, within a given technological horizon, can very well serve as a theoretical counterpart to the phenomena of market prices within the framework of labour values.

Let $(a_{ij})$ be the technical coefficients in value terms. That is, given i and j, let $a_{ij}$ be the amount of value needed in branch $B_i$ from branch $B_j$ for its output. Thus the total amount of value used in branch $B_i$ is $\sum_j a_{ij}$. If the price of a unit value at the period is, as above, $\tau_j(t)$, then the total prices of inputs in $B_i$ is given by

$$K_i(t) = \sum_j \tau_j(t) a_{ij}.$$

Therefore the price in the next period is set so as to try and equalize the rate of profit:

$$\tau_i(t+1) = (1+r) \cdot \frac{\sum_j a_{ij}\tau_i(t)}{\sum_j a_{ij}} = (1+r) \frac{K_i(t)}{\sum_j a_{ij}}.$$

Of course, if branch $B_i$ calculates its monetary rate of profit in terms of current price it will in general be different from r. But the average of all the rates will still be r, since the various deviations will cancel each other out.

The prices in terms of gold are:

$$m_i(t+1) = \frac{\tau_i(t+1)}{\tau_g(t+1)} = \frac{1+r}{1+r_g} \frac{\sum a_{ij}(t)\tau_j(t)}{\sum a_{gj}(t)\tau_g(t)} \cdot \frac{\sum a_{ij}}{\sum a_{gj}}.$$

Even assuming that the rate of profit in the gold industry is different from the general rate, we find that the above expression leads to bounded oscillation of all prices in terms of gold.

To conclude, the above system of prices shows that once it is agreed that prices need not remain the same from one period to the next, a reasonable system of prices based on the average, value rate of profit can be worked out. This system demonstrates that there is no contradiction between the law of value and the equalization of the rates of profits, an equalization which does not occur simultaneously but over a few periods of production, and is always only tentative.

# The Production of Commodities by Means of What?

## Emmanuel Farjoun

The neo-Ricardian economic school, influenced by Piero Sraffa's clear and relatively tight formalism, appears to have exposed fundamental weaknesses in the traditional labour theory of value. On this basis some argue that the very notion of labour value should be rejected outright. They claim to have shown that even when it can be unambiguously defined, it is worthless in any conceivable formulation of a precise model for generalized commodity production.

Ian Steedman's statement of this challenge is the clearest and most forceful. In this piece I therefore discuss his challenge, mostly on his own ground. My main aim is to show how the traditional concept of labour value can be understood in the most general input-output framework, namely joint production. Careful mathematical analysis reveals that the neo-Ricardian school has missed the most important ingredient for understand both labour values and prices in Sraffa's framework.

Somewhat surprisingly it turns out that precisely in this most general context the advantages of labour values emerge most clearly while neo-Ricardian formulations lose most of their validity and clarity. Sraffa freely admits these problems but his followers seem to have ignored his warnings.

However, neo-Ricardian criticisms are not without a rational kernel. Only by addressing them can some of the real difficulties with traditional labour value theory be overcome. Though Steedman's arguments rest on a narrow foundation, their merit is that the central part of this foundation is shared by all economic schools including, it would appear, traditional Marxism. This is the view that under perfect competition one must assume that the same rate of profit prevails in all production processes. Of course, no one asserts that a uniform rate actually exists. Yet it is claimed that the most fundamental economic analysis can be conducted by assuming that it does.

This assumption plays a different role in different schools. It is essential for Sraffa and far less important in *Capital*. Nevertheless it is taken for granted in the discussion on the formation of prices in the third volume of *Capital*. Thus Steedman can with some justice claim that under an assumption shared by Sraffa and *Capital* Volume 3, many of the numerical results arrived at in the first and third volumes of *Capital* stand on shaky ground. This rational kernel of Steedman's argument is independent of his assertion that the very notion of labour value is inconsistent.

These difficulties can, in my opinion, be resolved only by a systematic and principled rejection of the concept of a 'uniform profit rate' and of simplistic schemata involving a direct numerical relation between 'natural price' and the labour value of individual commodities to which such a concept gives rise. Some of the implications of this latter rejection, which I cannot discuss here in full, are developed in Robert Langston's piece in this volume. I will now turn to Steedman's detailed criticisms.

**Two Major Difficulties**

Steedman's first major criticism is that there is only one solution to the problem known as the transformation problem: a system of prices and profit totally unrelated to the system based on labour values. It is apparently proved algebraically that the famous $S/(C + V)$ formula for the rate of profit will not fit a precise model of capitalist production, that is, it does not fit the mould of an input-output model for a hypothetical economy. It is noted that no way to fit this formula in such a mould was proposed, and that with a uniform profit rate and fixed prices of production, the classical formula cannot be a precise expression for the uniform profit rate, at least without further assumptions.

The second criticism goes further. It is claimed that in the most general framework, joint production, labour values make no sense because values cannot be assigned to individual commodities.

I will show that this second criticism is completely off the mark, being based on a superficial and partial algebraic analysis. Using well-known algebraic results one can show that classical labour values produce far better behaviour than the alternative price-value theories. This does not prove that the labour theory of value, howsoever modified, is economically valid, but it does prove that the second half of Steedman's book, where the above criticism is presented, has a very shaky mathematical foundation. Morishima[1] has developed a similar point of view.

Before making this demonstration, however, I will briefly outline my objection to Steedman's first line of criticism, which poses a problem only if one assumes that commodity production can be analysed by postulating fixed prices and a unique uniform rate of profit in all production processes. An alternative framework embodying the concept of free competition without these assumptions, based on the concept of a probabilistic profit rate perceived as a random variable, has appeared in Emmanuel Farjoun and Moshé Machover, *Laws of Chaos* (London 1983).

## Uniformity—Theory and Reality

In the classical tradition the fundamental organizing principle is that prices are so formed as to guarantee identical rates of profit in all production processes. This uniform rate, it is argued, is the result of free and perfect competition which is assumed to be the motor behind the capitalist economy. It is the mathematical form taken by the famous principle of the equalization of profit rates.

I do not wish to dispute the concept of free competition or the principle that there is a real process of equalization. The problem is whether the economic logic and the algebraic results of this process can be captured by the rigid assumption of a universally prevailing uniform rate. These distinctions may seem pedantic at first sight. But they are as critical as the distinction, for example, between classical and quantum mechanics. The former offers almost no help in analysing atomic phenomena whereas the latter is crucial to understanding any fundamental atomic process.

The concept of uniform rate is neither necessary nor reasonable for understanding accumulation, price formation or profit formation. Indeed, I claim that a uniform rate and free competition are contradictory concepts that cannot be reconciled. I show later that Sraffian models are critically dependent on the very rigid notion of uniformity, which plays a relatively minor role in labour value theory. Therefore all arguments based on it collapse with the slightest relaxation of the assumption. Once this is grasped, all Steedman's examples, which show (very small) numerical deviations between his profit rate and the labour-value rate, are rendered irrelevant. I will further show that even from a purely algebraic standpoint, uniformity of rates cannot be consistently organized.

Sraffa was careful enough to draw attention to the abnormal behaviour of his formal system and the very restrictive and distorting nature of this assumption. After describing a 'reasonable economy' which in his system gives rise to infinite prices, he makes the following remark which has apparently left little impression on his followers:

> It is perhaps as well to be reminded here that we are at all times concerned merely with the implication of the assumption of a uniform price . . . and a uniform rate of profits on all the means of production. In the case under consideration [these conditions cannot be met but] the 'beans' could be produced and marketed so as to show a normal profit if the producer sold them at a higher price than the one which, in his book-keeping, he attributes to them as means of production. (p. 91)

Thus Sraffa is well aware of the purely formal nature of his framework and its weak relation to reality.

Since a uniform profit rate is of such crucial importance to neo-Ricardian theories the concept should be analysed not only from a mathematical but from an economic point of view. There is no such analysis in, for example, Steedman's book. None of the articles of faith published in this vein investigate the relation between uniformity and the long range tendencies of the various profit rates. This relation is far from cut and dried. Here I would like to outline some of the directions such an analysis might take.

First, in the real world of commodity production there is no reason to assume an equal profit rate for all commodities that are regularly produced, even on average over long periods of time. In the United States some 60,000 different chemicals are produced regularly among many millions of other commodities. Can one seriously claim that each of these is so priced as to generate on average, over 'long periods', equal rates? The very question contains doubtful notions—for example, what kind of average must one take?

A whole series of factors inhibits the realization of an equal average, not to mention uniform rate, even under competition: time lags, constant changes in technique, indivisibility of capital, the importance of the mass of profit as opposed to the rate, monopoly, and other conservative forces of all kinds. No one has ever produced even a hint of statistical or other empirical data to demonstrate an equal profit rate, even over a long period, for each and every commodity. For medium or short periods it is patently false.

One might argue that various capitals engaged in sundry branches of the economy would, eventually over a long period, generate an effective average for each branch. But the precise meaning of such a claim is unclear since neither the notion of 'branch' nor that of 'average' has a universally accepted meaning. It is true that the formation of some sort of effective average rate over time and over different economic units is assumed in most classical discussions. But this does not make it true. Moreover, it certainly does not imply the very narrow interpretation that the average rates for *each and every commodity* under perfect competition are identical, let alone their convergence to that narrow average over time.

The only existing statistical studies on profit rates deal with whole groups of industries, each of which comprises tens of thousands of products. Even then one cannot discover any one time in which these 'branches' yield profit rates which are even 'close' (say $\pm 10\%$) to a uniform rate. The long-term tendencies of the average for these large groups of processes are far from clear. Some studies indicate an effective average (say $\pm 20\%$) over twenty to thirty years, while others insist on the opposite tendency, polarization.[2]

'But', Steedman may reply, 'we are not really interested in the present or past confused reality but in a pure hypothetical system in which by definition competition produces a uniform rate'. This may be a perfectly legitimate concern, but the consequence—that no uniform rate argument carries any weight against a theory which does not need this assumption—must then be accepted.

But suppose one accepts a framework in which, for some groups of commodities over long periods, some form of equal average is formed. Can one then proceed to analyse that system by abstracting from the constant movement of rates around that average? This movement never dies. One must show that by imposing a uniform rate on oscillating systems, one still preserves the features of the system. Since the oscillation can never be assumed to converge on the average, it is clear on general grounds that the substitution of a uniform rate for oscillating rates can be expected to obliterate important properties of the moving system. The burden of proof rests with those making this substitution. They must show that the properties they are interested in are preserved by it.

Let us illustrate this with a physical analogy. In the thermodynamics of an ideal gas one can deduce certain results assuming the gas to be made up of particles which move with a uniform speed, since we know the speed of any particle oscillates around an average. But it is well known that a coherent overall theory cannot be developed around the rigid assumption that all particles actually move with this uniform speed, and, indeed, false and contradictory results are produced by this assumption. The moment we assume, however, that the velocity of each particle is given by a certain probability distribution, we are in a far better position to understand the real and theoretical behaviour of gases. In fact the foundation of the theory of ideal gases rests precisely on the non-uniformity of the velocities. It is to be expected that considerations of non-uniformity, and probabilistic considerations, have a great role to play in the further development of economic theory.

## Steedman's Example

We turn now to the second major point raised by Steedman, Morishima, Samuelson, Lippi and many other authors: that the traditional concept of labour values makes no sense in the most general input-output framework of joint production. To substantiate this point, numerical examples are given of a supposedly reasonable economy in which, when one tries to calculate values, one finds that there are no reasonable solutions to the traditional value equations. But a deeper algebraic analysis reveals that all the possible counter examples are unreasonable from an economic point of view, or at least depend on incomplete information about the economy.

This algebraic analysis further shows that in the most general case of joint production it is Sraffian rather than labour values framework that suffer from grave mathematical difficulties.

Let us first recall the numerical example used by Steedman and others to demonstrate that labour values are in general meaningless. Steedman considers a very simple economy with only two main products, say machines and cars, which we will denote by M and C. It is assumed that there are two industrial processes which use certain given technologies to produce machines and cars. Further, each process produces both machines and cars simultaneously. This is a simple case of joint production which is quite common in many industries: consider for example the fact, mentioned above, that about 60,000 different chemicals are produced annually in the United States by only several hundred chemical factories. Clearly many of these are produced jointly for both economic and technological reasons.

Now Steedman assumes that the material flow of production is summed up in the following table, taken from p. 153 of *Marx after Sraffa*.

Figure 1

| | Machines | Cars | Labour units | → | Machines | Cars |
|---|---|---|---|---|---|---|
| Process I | 25 | 0 | 5 | → | 30 | 5 |
| Process II | 0 | 10 | 1 | → | 3 | 12 |

On the left of the arrows we find the inputs while on their right we find the outputs of each process.

At first sight this seems a perfectly reasonable table. In the Sraffian framework it is in fact acceptable, and a Sraffian economy with the above input-output table can function faultlessly. However, it takes only a little calculation to see that one cannot assign any reasonable numerical values to the concept of 'total social labour time necessary to produce one machine' on the basis of the above table. If one tries to do it in the straightforward way one gets no possible positive solution. Some labour values turn out to be negative numbers, which is unacceptable. This example presents a problem to the concept of labour values: at least it shows that they are not well defined under arbitrary circumstances. But is this a drawback or an advantage?

Let us examine this example a bit further. We shall see below that the above economy has a very strange property indeed. If one stops using the first process altogether and applies only the second process then one can increase all the outputs while using a smaller amount of total social labour, i.e. using less than six units of labour.

Let us not forget that the above economic table represents for Steedman a hypothetical economy in a state of ideal equilibrium generated by perfect and free competition. Now under these conditions what company can long survive in the market if it uses process I while a competitor uses process II?

In technical terms the above example of a *production table* is not on the *frontier*. Namely, using exactly the same techniques as are used by other firms, each firm which has shares in process I can increase its output while reducing its input by moving even a small amount of labour to process II. In fact, for each unit of labour moved from process I to process II, we shall get a net product free of charge of two machines and one car. In other words, by a reallocation of labour and without introducing any new production techniques, in Steedman's counter-example one can increase the total net output (the total net product at the end of each production process). If we transfer one unit of labour from process I to process II we shall get the following table of production:

Figure 2

|             | Machines | Cars | Labour | → | Machines | Cars |
|-------------|----------|------|--------|---|----------|------|
| Process I′  | 20       | 0    | 4      | → | 24       | 4    |
| Process II′ | 0        | 20   | 2      | → | 6        | 24   |

Taking the economy as a whole we get:

Process I′ + II′: 20M + 20C + 6 (units labour) → 30M + 28C

This means that for the net social product obtained by deducting the material input from the corresponding material output we get:

Net Process (I′ + II′): 6 (units labour) → 10M + 8C

while if we do the same calculation for Figure 1:

Net Process (I + II): 6 (units labour) → 8M + 7C

Thus in Steedman's economic example a simple reallocation of labour will result in an increase in the net available product for further consumption and investment without increase of inputs and without using any new processes. Further, the rates of profit as computed by him will stay the same!

We can see that the unreality of Steedman's example is best captured by writing down the table for the net output in each process, namely the result of subtracting the input in each commodity from the corresponding output. For the economy as a whole the net material output must be greater than zero for each commodity, but this of course is not the case for each individual process. Since labour is the only factor of production which is not the output of any capitalist production process, we cannot reasonably talk about net output of labour. So using Steedman's first process, the net output is three machines and five cars (5M + 5C). In order to compare various process it is best to calculate the net output for every unit labour input. The above 5M + 5C of net output of the first process is achieved by five units of labour. Therefore, one unit of labour yields in the first process exactly $1M + 1C$. We can write this symbolically as:

Net Process I: 1 unit labour $\rightarrow$ $1M + 1C$

Now let us compare this to the net output per unit labour of process II

Net Process II: 1 unit labour $\rightarrow$ $3M + 2C$

A quick glance at the two net processes then reveals that the second is superior in all respects and that if process II is functional, as we assume it is, the first process will not survive in a free, equilibrium economy. After all, who is going to use process I?

## Labour Values in Joint Production

At this point several questions suggest themselves.

Firstly, is the unreality of Steedman's example an accident? Can one possibly construct another counter example which will be on the 'frontier' in the sense explained above and will nevertheless yield negative labour values?

Secondly, is the problem of the non-existence of value specific to the more complicated case of joint production or does such an example exist in the simpler case where each product is produced separately?

Thirdly, what happens if, in Steedman's example, one cannot transfer resources from the first process to the second for various reasons, say the second is environmentally damaging or uses as an input a very rare resource? What if for some social reason labour cannot be transferred from one process to another?

The answer to the first two questions is definitely negative while the third question brings in the concept of differential rent. Let us begin with the first two questions.

It turns out that the first question really contains as an answer the whole secret of labour values in a general, non-rent, joint-production economy. Using very simple well-known algebraic results (to be detailed later in this paper) about positive solutions to arbitrary linear equations, one can easily show that in every input-output table for which no positive labour values can be assigned, the above phenomenon necessarily arises, namely that by reallocating labour resources one can increase the total net output of each and every commodity while using the same amount of labour. Since the net output is the aim of the production process, such examples cannot be regarded as economically reasonable.

Our basic point is that not every hypothetical production table is acceptable for economic matrix manipulations. Some tables must be regarded as either contradictory or incomplete. One should expect that severe economic physical restrictions will be imposed on acceptable tables of production. To use an analogy from physics: not every interaction table of elementary particles is acceptable. Certain laws (for instance, preservation of energy, or spin) must be obeyed, and the whole of elementary particle theory can be defined precisely as the theory which analyses those restrictions on 'interaction tables' which make them physically acceptable. One cannot consider an arbitrary table to refute the theory of spin or other mechanical measures, just because it obeys some other arbitrary invented 'law' such as 'uniformity of particle speeds'. Our conditions on acceptable tables stem from the category of socially necessary labour-time which should be understood to imply that there is no combination using only existing processes of production through which one can get additional net output without any additional social labour.

For the benefit of those readers who are not put off by a little simple algebra I will give a somewhat technical account of the situation in the appendix. But it is worth noting here that the precise condition under which labour values exist can be understood without any reference to the algebraically confusing question of joint production. We come now to the second question that was raised above. It turns out that the problem of transition from a given input-output hypothetical table to the algebraic calculation of values has very little, if anything, to do with joint production. This problem is as old as labour values themselves and the same difficulties, which were rediscovered by Steedman and others, were encountered and analysed by Ricardo himself. In the context of joint production their analysis necessitates the use of a little algebra.

I shall give an extremely simple version of the kind of numerical and economic problems that those who favoured 'negative value' confronted and surrendered to. The impossibility of jumping directly from raw, physical tables to algebra and the apparent problem of 'non-existence of values' will be shown to occur without joint production. Of course it is better hidden behind the complication of joint production.

Consider an economy with only one product, corn, and two process to produce it: $P_1$, $P_2$. In the process $P_1$, growing in the hills, we need two bushels of corn and two days of labour to produce four bushels of corn. In the second process $P_2$, growing on the plain, we need three bushels of corn and two days of labour to produce nine bushels of corn. Symbolically we get a production table composed of two production processes:

Figure 3

| | corn bushels | labour days | → | bushels |
|---|---|---|---|---|
| $P_1$ | 2 | 2 | → | 4 |
| $P_2$ | 3 | 2 | → | 9 |

The net product table is

| | labour days | | corn bushels |
|---|---|---|---|
| Net $P_1$ | 2 | → | 2 |
| Net $P_2$ | 2 | → | 6 |

Now these are perfectly reasonable physical data but we cannot compute the value of one bushel of corn directly from them! Because according to $P_1$ we need one day of labour for one bushel of corn while according to $P_2$ we need only a third of a day. Nor can Sraffian prices be calculated directly from them. The problem is, of course, not joint production but the existence of alternative production processes for the same bundle of goods. Not every joint production system involves alternative processes, and neither does every case of alternative processes involve joint production.

When confronted with physical data as above, which may be very realistic even in a stable economy in which 'day after day production continues unchanged',[3] we must introduce some independent considerations. The whole theory of differential rent comes in here. It is strange that the neo-Ricardians should miss this, for after all, it was Ricardo who developed his rent theory precisely to deal with such situations.

In general it turns out that *problems arise either in a joint or non-joint production table only if one of the processes used is strictly worse for each and every one of its net products than a combination of other existing processes.* This is the full truth behind Steedman's numerical example. Such a situation exists in the real world because new, better, techniques are developed all the time and because, for example, we cannot always abandon an old oil field even though it is much less productive per unit labour than other fields.

How to deal with such tables has concerned economists greatly and several possible answers exist, as we shall see. However, coming back to the corn-growing economy, if one assumes that in Figure 3 both process can be expanded and contracted at will, no matter how slightly, then of course the table must be considered inconsistent on the grounds that no one in their right mind will continue using process $P_1$ 'day after day'. One would simply transfer some labour days from $P_1$ to $P_2$ thereby getting something for nothing, namely some extra bushels of corn without any extra work or other inputs whatsoever. Assume now that no transfer is possible for lack of land or other reasons. One still may want to assign a definite labour value to one bushel of corn. One way around the difficulty is to take an average. We must know how many days on average are socially necessary to produce one unit of corn taking all the existing processes with their actual relative weight. If only very small quantities of corn are produced on the hills by $P_1$ then the value would be close to $\frac{1}{3}$. One may simply write the actual number of days and bushels:

$$P_1: \quad 2{,}000 \text{ days} \rightarrow \quad 2{,}000 \text{ bushels}$$

$$P_2: 20{,}000 \text{ days} \rightarrow 60{,}000 \text{ bushels}$$

therefore the combined process $P_1 + P_2$ looks as follows:

$$22{,}000 \text{ days} \rightarrow 62{,}000 \text{ bushels.}$$

Thus one bushel is worth $\frac{22}{62}$ days. If we cannot transfer resources from one branch to another, or some commodities cannot be produced at will, then we are already outside the framework of Steedman. But let us consider it briefly nonetheless.

In the real world it may be impossible to expand a given process even minutely, or it may take a considerable amount of time. For example a superior technique may have just appeared on the scene. Values are both still determined for a period by the prevailing less-efficient techniques. In that case the new technique brings in a technological rent to its owner. (That is, she or he appropriates surplus value from the other producers in circulation). If the old less-efficient technique is just a relic of old times, value will be determined by the dominant better one and the owner of the old one will sustain a penalty.

If we have a scarce resource such as oil wells, then according to the classical theory value is determined by the least efficient field, and ground rent is assessed for the most abundant oil fields. At any rate, value will be given by some weighted average whose weights must be determined by information which is independent of the input-output production data, since this data does not contain such crucial information as for instance the availability of oil fields, the temperature in Siberia and the amount of rainfall in the American Midwest. This extra information is crucial to the exact determination of value in these cases.

## Economic Conditions

Within the general framework developed above it is not hard to see why Steedman's discussion of 'negative values' is very misleading. He presents a simple imaginary economic table that seems reasonable at first sight, showing no 'abnormal behaviour' with respect to certain economic norms defined in his 'assumption' section, but to which one cannot assign positive labour values.[5] Steedman imposes on his table a set of assumptions which apparently make his conclusions inevitable. They are nevertheless unwarranted for at least two reasons.

First, Steedman ignores in his book the fact that one can impose a different (and smaller) set of assumptions on a different table of production, perfectly reasonable from a 'physical-data' point of view and yielding positive labour values and profit but to which no positive Sraffian prices and uniform profit can be assigned. Such examples are given below. Thus the situation seems symmetrical. Some tables behave nicely for Sraffian prices only, others for labour values only. So it is then reasonable, in fact necessary, to inquire under what economic conditions one gets a positive solution in each framework.

I have given such a condition on the physical data, a condition which refers to no specific value theory, uniform rate assumption or the like. It is a purely objective condition, namely that the formal table take full account of socially necessary labour-time in the sense that one cannot manipulate the existing processes, without any increase in the intensity of labour in any existing process and without bringing in any new process, to increase net production while preserving total labour inputs. On the other hand, Steedman has never formulated any condition for the existence of meaningful solutions in his own framework. This is a grave omission. When Steedman comes up with a necessary and sufficient condition for Sraffian prices to be positive in a general input-output table, then one can compare the two systems. Until then one must stick with labour values, even from a purely formal algebraic point of view.

On general algebraic grounds Steedman is very unlikely to be able to present such a condition. To see why, consider again his table (Figure 1). That Table, with a real wage level of 3M + 5C for six labour units, gives positive Sraffian prices. But if we raise the wage to 8M + 7C for every six labour units, which is compatible with zero growth, leaving everything else intact, the resulting 'economy' will satisfy all his physical assumptions but the corresponding prices will be non-existent or negative. Not a hint of such a possibility—which is obviously of some interest—can be found in his book. No explanation for why the economy cannot work with a wage of, say, 6M + 6C is given. Thus for Steedman a demand for raising wages from 3M + 5C to 6M + 6C must be considered incompatible not only with the greed of capital but with the *technological structure of production*, even though the higher wage is still smaller than net output.

Consider the following further example. The whole of chapter eleven of Steedman's book could be written, without changing the argument, to establish that the following net product table can represent a stable economy with free movement of capital:

Figure 4

| | labour days | | commodity 1 | commodity 2 |
|---|---|---|---|---|
| Process III | 1 | → | 1 | 1 |
| Process IV | 1 | → | 2000 | 3000 |

Such a big gap in productivity can arise and the two processes can co-exist temporarily. Recall for example the jumps in productivity which occur periodically in the computer industry.

But one misses the very essence of accumulation if one maintains with Steedman that processes III and IV can co-exist in an equilibrium state, in spite of the viability and clear advantage of process IV which may yield exactly the same rate of profit. By applying his strange economic reasoning to extreme cases its weakness and irrationality is exposed. In reality we know that the drive towards increased labour productivity for many well known economic and social reasons is a fundamental motor force in investment considerations in spite of inevitable periodic over-production. Small excess products can always be consumed, sold, hoarded or even change consumption habits. An existing, more efficient technique that yields the same rate of profit will eventually force itself onto the market by reducing unit costs even if in the short, medium or long run it leads to considerable changes. How can a formal framework which is completely and consciously oblivious to that drive give a good account of accumulation, profit, prices, crisis, etc?

It can be proven without difficulty that labour values are the only economic measures which capture the profound similarity from a social and economic point of view between Figure 3 and Figure 4. It is the great advantage of this measure that it does not accept such tables as providing consistent and complete information about a generalized commodity production system.

## Sraffa's Omission

In light of the discussion above it seems legitimate to ask how Steedman, who put so much faith both in Sraffa's model as a reflection of reality and in the purely mathematical discussion of its ramifications, could stop short of raising the fundamental mathematical question associated with his own framework. The fundamental question is: *under what precise condition on the material input–output data does his system of equations have a reasonable solution?* Reasonable, in this instance, means a solution including positive numbers for prices and for the uniform rate of profit. But we should not blame Steedman alone for this omission. This fundamental question is mostly ignored by the Sraffian school as a whole. Steedman however bears a somewhat heavier responsibility, since he has tried to get so much mileage from tables with negative labour values.

This omission is all the more surprising since its resolution leads naturally to the concept of differential rent to which Ricardo, Sraffa's inspirer, gave so much weight. Sraffa's omission is most obvious when one notes that although he opens his discussion of values with some observations about economies without an economic surplus, nowhere does he discuss the general case of joint production without surplus. In the case of joint production, which is the most general, and in which the logical difficulties come to the fore, he jumps directly to surplus economies.

It turns out that the question 'when do positive labour values exist?' has a very simple economic answer which can be given in terms of the input-output data only. On the other hand, it seems that no such conditions can be found for the existence of prices in Sraffa's framework of joint production. In other words, even on pure algebraic grounds, there do not seem to be any reasonable necessary and sufficient conditions on the input-output data which will secure positive Sraffian prices and a positive profit rate. Thus the mathematical situation as far as joint production is concerned is the exact opposite of what Steedman says. While there is a nice theory for the labour value equations, which are linear, there is no such theory for the Sraffian equations, which are not linear, involving as they do the product of two unknowns—prices and profit rates.

## Joint Production in a Subsistence Economy

Once we have made explicit the question of the existence of positive values and prices in joint production and its economic meaning, we can easily fill in the gap left in Sraffa's book concerning the formation of values and prices in non-surplus, subsistence economies. In fact the advantage of labour values emerge precisely when one considers the passage from subsistence to surplus-producing economies. Consider a simple society in which bundles of commodities are produced without surplus by other bundles, the latter including means of production and sustenance for the society.[7]

A typical process would appear as follows:

20 Bushels of wheat + 15 bushels of corn + 10 Kg of iron → 15 Kg of sheep meat + 2 units of sheep skin + 3 Kg of sheep wool + 40 Bushels of wheat + 10 Kg of hay.

Formally, if our commodities are $c_1, c_2, \ldots, c_n$, then the bundle $x_1 c_1 + x_2 c_2 + x_3 c_3 + \cdots + x_n c_n$ is used to produce another bundle $\bar{x}_1 c_1 + \bar{x}_2 c_2 + \cdots + \bar{x}_n c_n$. This we could write as:

$$x_1 c_1 + x_2 c_2 + \cdots + x_n c_n \rightarrow \bar{x}_1 c_1 + \cdots + \bar{x}_n c_n. \tag{1}$$

The same situation would occur in a 'bundle-exchanging' economy in which, for instance,

12 Kg meat + 2 Kg wool + 2m$^2$ skin exchanges for 5 Kg corn + 3 Kg hay.

If the vector of commodities $(x_1, \ldots, x_n)$ exchanges for the vector $(\bar{x}_1, \ldots, \bar{x}_n)$ we shall denote this by the *exchange relation*

$$(x_1, \ldots, x_n) \longleftrightarrow (\bar{x}_1, \ldots, \bar{x}_n). \tag{2}$$

Our task is to understand the formation of prices, or 'values' from these relations of exchange or primitive joint production Theoretically, there is no difference between the two so we shall deal here only with exchange, keeping in mind that it applies equally well to joint production. The problem of exchange-value is clearly more primitive than that of assigning labour or other values in a surplus-producing economy. We assume that the system is in a self-replacing state and no net surplus is produced: namely the total input is equal to the total output as a vector of commodities. Now if the price or 'value' on the market of $c_i$ is $v_i$, the above exchange relation translates into an algebraic relation:

$$x_1 v_1 + x_2 v_2 + \cdots + x_n v_n = \bar{x}_1 v_1 + \bar{x}_2 v_2 + \cdots + \bar{x}_n v_n \tag{3}$$

Namely, the total 'values' of two bundles that exchange in the market are the same.

An *exchange table* is a set of exchange relations of bundles.

$$
\begin{aligned}
E_1 &= (x_1, \ldots, x_k) \longleftrightarrow (\bar{x}_1, \ldots, \bar{x}_k) \\
E_2 &= (z_1, \ldots, z_k) \longleftrightarrow (\bar{z}_1, \ldots, \bar{z}_k) \\
&\vdots \qquad \vdots \qquad \vdots \qquad \qquad \vdots
\end{aligned} \tag{4}
$$

With enough exchange data we can compute the 'exchange value' of each commodity. How? We seek a vector $v$ which would satisfy all the algebraic equations imposed by the exchange relations (4) between bundles. That is, we seek a *measure which is preserved in transactions.* Anyone entering an exchange with a given quantity of value must clearly leave with the same total quantity of value.

Now obviously one can write a table of exchange relations for which there is no such system of strictly positive values. For example, the following set has no non-zero values at all:

$$
\begin{aligned}
E_1 &: \quad (2,1) \longleftrightarrow (3,0) \quad (\text{i.e. } v_1 = v_2) \\
E_2 &: \quad (1,2) \longleftrightarrow (2,0) \quad (\text{i.e. } v_1 = 2v_2)
\end{aligned} \tag{5}
$$

Informally, the 'economy' to which this corresponds might be, for example,

$$2 \text{ Kg of meat} + 1 \text{ Kg of wool} \longleftrightarrow 3 \text{ Kg of meat}$$

$$1 \text{ Kg of meat} + 2 \text{ Kg of wool} \longleftrightarrow 2 \text{ Kg of meat}$$

Can such an example serve as a definite proof that exchange values for bundle-exchanging economies or subsistence joint production are meaningless? The answer is no!

The above table may look confusing, but if we write a simpler one the point emerges even more clearly:

$$E_1: \quad (1, 0) \longleftrightarrow (0, 2) \quad (\text{i.e. } v_1 = 2v_2)$$
$$E_2: \quad (1, 0) \longleftrightarrow (0, 1) \quad (\text{i.e. } v_1 = v_2)$$

(6)

Informally this would be an 'economy' in which you can either exchange 1 Kg of meat for 2 Kg of wool or for 1 Kg of wool. Thus the table contains contradictory information about exchange, as indicated in the brackets. Clearly we cannot simply compute values on the basis of this exchange table even though each relation involves only one commodity on each side. If the above data $(E_1, E_2)$ were to correspond to reality, we would have to say that on average one unit of our first commodity exchanges for x units of the second, where $1 \leqslant x \leqslant 2$, and the size of x depends on the actual volume of transactions performed in $E_1$ and $E_2$. If only very few transactions were of the $E_1$ type, then the value of $c_2$ would be very close to that of $c_1$. If we were told that the table represents final averages, then it is not consistent and must be treated as economically unrealizable. The same applies to table (5).

How can we tell if a given table is consistent? First, we notice that if the vector **x** of commodities is exchanged for **y** then for any number $\alpha$ the vector $\alpha$**x** is exchanged for $\alpha$**y**, and if $\mathbf{t} \longleftrightarrow \mathbf{u}$, then $\alpha\mathbf{t} + \beta\mathbf{x} \longleftrightarrow \alpha\mathbf{u} + \beta\mathbf{y}$. This is an assumption about linearity of exchange. Informally, it means that bundles of commodities figuring on both sides of any two possible exchanges can be added up to produce a further possible exchange. Thus, if as in table (5) 2 Kg of meat and 1 Kg of wool exchange for 3 Kg of meat, then it must be possible to exchange 4 Kg of meat and 2 Kg of wool for 6 Kg of meat; and by combining this with, say, an exchange of type $E_2$, to exchange 5 Kg of meat and 4 Kg of wool for 8 Kg of meat.

Notice that negative coefficients are perfectly acceptable since, for example, if $(-1, -2)$ exchanges for $(-3, 0)$ it could mean that a debt of $(1, 2)$ exchanges for a debt of $(3, 0)$ or, changing sides, that $(3, 0) \longleftrightarrow (1, 2)$. From thexe simple linearity assumptions we can see, subtracting $E_2$ for $E_1$ in table (6), that a strictly positive bundle can be got for nothing: the zero commodity vector. This is a sure sign that not all averages were taken, or that the table has nothing to do with the reality of linear exchange.

What is the upshot? We claim that a table has values if and only if it is economically meaningful in the sense that an exchange of the above type is not possible, i.e. if no-one can get something for nothing. To paraphrase using a well-known expression from neoclassical economics, the table has values if and only if there ain't no such thing as a free lunch. Formally: *Given any exchange table* $E_1, \ldots, E_k$, *one can assign strictly positive exchange values to each commodity if and only if no linear combination* $\sum \alpha_i E_i$ *exists in which the zero vector can be exchanged for a strictly positive vector.*

Furthermore, the joint exchange table is 'reasonable' precisely when *no merchant can come to the market with a bundle of goods and emerge with a greater bundle of the same goods.* This runs contrary to certain older theories concerning the origin of merchant profit. One would hope that such theories will not also be revived. We have seen that, under exactly the same conditions, the non-existence of wise merchants who buy cheaply and sell dearly the same goods is the foundation of labour value theory in joint production. (Note that our condition is given in terms of physical data only and that a condition for the existence of positive values is not the same thing as a determination of those values. It may turn out that the data given in the table do not uniquely determine values. This is not surprising: we need $(n - 1)$ linearly independent exchange relations to specify unique values over bundles of n commodities. The above method of analysis of exchange values applies to values in production processes where the product and the input are bundles of commodities assuming no surplus.)

## Joint Production with Surplus

The moment we drop the assumption that our primitive economy has no surplus the above method for the determination of values fails. The reason is that the total output vector $(x + z + \cdots)$ is greater than the total input for each individual commodity, and therefore their values cannot be equated as in (3). Moreover, there is no way we can in general assign equal profit rates to all industries as Sraffa does for the case of a single product.[8] The simplicity of the single product case hides the difficulty.

Defining value, as Sraffa does, by demanding a uniform rate of profit does not work as can be seen from the following: consider a table of production which includes the real wage bundle as an input,

$$2c_1 + 3c_2 \rightarrow 3c_1 + 3c_2$$
$$5c_1 + 6c_2 \rightarrow 6c_1 + 6c_2 \qquad (7)$$

$$\text{Total: } 7c_1 + 9c_2 \rightarrow 9c_1 + 9c_2$$

There is clearly a surplus of $2c_1$. But suppose we now try to calculate prices $p_1$, $p_2$ and a profit rate r. Sraffa's equations are

$$(1+r)(2p_1 + 3p_2) = 3p_1 + 3p_2$$
$$(1+r)(5p_1 + 6p_2) = 6p_1 + 6p_2$$

and have no reasonable solution. If we set $p_2 = 1$ then one set of solutions is $r = -1$, $p_1 = -1$, $p_2 = 1$ while another is $r = 0$, $p_1 = 0$, $p_2 = 1$.

The Sraffian method therefore fails. For us the very fact that total output is greater than total input indicates that notice has not been taken of all inputs. Explicit labour inputs must be taken into account whenever there is a net surplus. Thus labour accounts are essential and are forced on us in all market economies which produce a surplus. We have seen that only by explicitly taking labour into account can we give a physical criterion for the existence of positive values. Whenever there is no surplus, one may simply identify the labour input with the labour-power inputs, as Sraffa does, by including the sustenance of the workers in the inputs. Notice that even then not every production table can be regarded as consistent, even with Sraffian prices. It is so if and only if it does not allow us to get something from nothing.

Once again we see that one cannot simply take 'raw' physical data about exchange or subsistence joint production and jump directly into elementary matrix algebra. One has to look at the tables critically. And if this is the case for exchange tables, all the more is it so for tables of production, joint production, and so on.

## Steedman's Precise Assumptions

Having shown that labour values are in fact necessary in any reasonable approach, we now turn to the assumptions imposed by

Steedman in his own economic models. We find that because no reasonable conditions will guarantee Sraffa's framework of positive prices and a positive rate of profit, Steedman has to resort to a strange collection of 'precise assumptions' gathered from various mathematical game-theoretic models. He challenges the reader to reject any one of these. I will take up this challenge in this section.

I begin with a small sample which are necessary to his analysis (although not always sufficient for his conclusions because of hidden assumptions, to some of which I shall refer.) I conclude that by any reasonable economic or social standard each and every one of them must be rejected.

## 1. Uniform Rate of Profit

We have discussed above at some length this assumption which, in one form or another, is basic to all neo-Ricardians. With Steedman, however, it takes on a particular dogmatic form. He does not consider the calculated uniform rate simply as some theoretical parameter of the given input-output system but treats it as a precise measure of the actual rate of profit under conditions of perfect competition. He is forced to take this dogmatic approach by the way he refutes labour value categories, relying on simple inequalities between numerical estimates of the rate of profit in the two frameworks. Clearly at best both estimates are rough indicators of the relative size of the surplus product. There is no reason to expect two such indicators to give identical numerical results for the same input-output matrix. We say 'at best' to indicate that the value of these indicators depends on the validity of the assumptions on which they are built.

In general those indicators are preferable which use the smallest number of additional unverifiable assumptions. On this score labour indicators have a decisive advantage, since they demand no assumptions concerning a uniform profit rate, nor many others among Steedman's assumptions. Of course one should not expect these, or any other indicators to be numerically identical with whatever indicators or indices might be constructed from statistical data. The problem is to analyse and understand the relations between reality in all its forms and the behaviour of these abstract indicators.

## 2. The Indecomposability Assumption

This assumption enters invariably into most post-Sraffian discussions. It says simply that every commodity is 'basic', that is it enters directly or indirectly into the production of any other product.

Non-basic commodities cannot enter into the determination of the profit rate or prices. But there is nothing inherent about the capitalist mode of production which guarantees the existence of a single basic commodity in the Sraffian sense. Indeed the whole point about labour is that it *is* the only commodity which necessarily enters the production of every other commodity (except, of course, itself). Given a full breakdown of all commodities, there will be millions of them (for Steedman each is differentiated according to age). Probably none, or only very few accidental ones, will be 'basic' in the Sraffian sense. Are flat rolled iron sheets of specific quality of thickness 'basic'? Since the existence of basic products is not in reality a necessary feature of universal commodity production, it is unreasonable to construct a theory which collapses without them. One can easily imagine a capitalist economy without a single basic commodity: Sraffa's account will tell us nothing about it.

Furthermore, the forces which create an effective average rate over time have nothing to do with indecomposability. The free movement of money capital, the creation of average prices and profits will continue unabated even in an economy which decomposes into relatively self-contained subsectors or disconnected subeconomies. There will still be free movement of money-capital between these sections as a result of variations in the various rates of profit. But in Sraffa's and Steedman's model the very existence and uniqueness and thus the uniformity of the rate of profit stands or falls with this assumption, and therefore this uniqueness and the formation of an effective average is left essentially unexplained.[9] It imposes yet another far-fetched assumption whose implication in distorting capitalism's features is anybody's guess. In addition, non-basic products which are the most common, are shown by Sraffa himself to cause grave problems.[10]

### 3. The Zero Price Assumption

This is one of the most common, albeit least realistic assumptions in formal, game-theoretic models of the von Neumann type, used by Steedman in the second half of his book. Any product that is over-produced, no matter how slightly, (say by 0.001%) is assumed to have zero price, distributed free even though it is both produced and consumed by capital. Steedman provides absolutely no justification for this assumption but he maintains that conclusions drawn from it give a good picture of accumulation.[11] He sometimes calls such overproduced products waste products, which must be a slip since waste products are not used as inputs and his zero-priced products may very well appear as inputs.[12] Again the question is: why does this assumption give us a good picture of capitalist accumulation? Is all the gold produced actually used in production?

Here again is an assumption which is very rigid, absolutely necessary for the von Neumann analysis but of purely formal and arbitrary nature, in spite of the far fetched justification given to it in game-theoretical mathematical economics which, one must understand, is a branch of mathematics, not economics! It makes certain formulas neat and easy to prove but it does not make them any truer, nor even close to the truth. The truth is that at all times in our world many commodities with positive price are over produced. The zero-price assumption is rather like the flat earth assumption. It is mathematically simple, very obvious for people who see only their flat desks or flat floors near their noses, but still false!

To what extent one can use this zero price assumption to understand anything about the global or local structure of capitalism is a mystery. Steedman's discussion of a zero-priced commodity is misleading, self-contradictory and dogmatic. It is introduced simply by quoting von Neumann who 'imposes the (reasonable) rule that if . . . more of commodity 1 is produced each period than is used as input the following period then commodity 1 will have a zero price'.[13] The insertion 'reasonable' is the only theoretical explanation as to why this assumption can be taken up. The discussion is self-contradictory because the only examples of such products given by Steedman are precisely products which do not enter as input in the following period ('waste smoke', 'waste mud' and 'about to be scrapped machines'[14]). But waste smoke as an example of a zero-priced commodity has no relation to any definition of von Neumann's.

For von Neumann, if the consumption of crude oil, cars or butter is lower by as little as, say, 0.001 per cent than their production then their prices must drop to zero. Steedman gives no real example of a zero-priced commodity which is produced both for consumption and input. To do so would reveal the arbitrary nature of this assumption, used extensively throughout the second half of the book, including of course the negative values discussed in chapter eleven. The entire discussion of joint production collapses with the slightest dent in this crucial assumption.

## 4. Assumptions on Numbers of Processes

Yet another very strong assumption which has very little to do with reality, as freely admitted by Steedman and Sraffa, concerns the number of processes in joint production models. This assumption is extremely strong and there is no discussion of it anywhere except a very weak justification hidden behind realistic-sounding talk about waste smoke.[15]

The assumption says that the number of production processes is exactly equal to the number of different products, which include old machines of all ages. In the real world the number of products (with non-zero price) is of a greater order of magnitude than the number of processes on which anybody can claim to make any profit accounting and there is certainly no necessary logical relation between number of processes and number of products. Now as long as one works with a formal system, it is perfectly legitimate to make strong assumptions. This is exactly what Sraffa does in order to discover certain inconsistencies in marginalist theory. But this approach fails when one wants to argue against a completely different framework like the labour theory of value. The reason is simple. Suppose the number of processes in a Sraffian model was smaller by one out of a thousand than the number of commodities. So instead of dealing with matrices of the size $1000 \times 1000$ one would have to work with matrices of the size $1001 \times 1000$. It is not hard to see then that each and every one of Steedman's 'proofs' against labour value theory would collapse without any hope of resurrection.

Take for example his argument comparing the different calculations of the rate of profit. In the hypothetical model ($1001 \times 1000$), his calculations of the rate of profit would be entirely consistent with the labour approximation $S/(C + V)$ because one can simply add one equation to his system which has one degree of freedom, namely the equation which says that the uniform rate equals $S/(C + V)$. Of course this may lead to some modifications of classical labour values but not to any radical degree. Values would still have the social labour content, but maybe with a few degrees of freedom, which will provide for the incorporation of any restrictions on the rates of profit. It is not surprising that Steedman's numerical counter-examples collapse as soon as he drops for a moment the square matrix and zero-price assumptions.[16] Without these his von Neumann analysis becomes 'homogeneous growth' and leads to the old formula $S/(C + V)$ for the profit rate for any notion of 'values'. This triviality is inherent in the von Neumann free-goods rule.

## 5. The Maximum Rate of Profit Assumption

Steedman further assumes that the prevailing rate of profit is the maximum possible among all possible rates. This is a far-reaching assumption which says that various firms will always coordinate their individual choice of techniques, prices and so on so as to maximize the overall rate of profit. Such a high degree of coordination is nowhere explained and the resulting argument is weak and unconvincing.[17]. It ignores a basic feature of commodity production, namely the independence of various firms and their competition with each other. This anarchy is built into the system just like the random nature of the movement of gas particles. The task is to build parameters which depend on this very randomness and not on some arbitrary hypothesis of coordination or uniform behaviour of individual elements. If this assumption is taken seriously, then it would contradict other basic assumptions of Steedman. Also one can easily construct examples of the market behaviour of individual firms which, by trying to maximize their individual profit rate, bring about an overall reduction in the rate. This is so because it is clear that by a proper manipulation of prices, disregarding the uniform rate, one may get a higher overall rate of profit than the corresponding uniform rate. In many cases there is a high reward for breaking agreed behaviour as long as not too many firms break the rules. This is a well-known phenomenon in mathematical game theory, as well as in real-life markets.

### Inconsistencies in Sraffian Prices

I have already examined the bizarre and unrealistic conditions Steedman must impose on his system of equations in order to guarantee the existence and uniqueness of his solutions. But of course a heavy price must be paid for imposing such strange conditions, for the solutions turn out to have unrealistic properties. In this section I shall give a small sample of the erratic and evidently meaningless behaviour and properties of his solutions. Some of these faults were in fact discovered by Schefold, a careful observer of the neo-Ricardian school who seems to have concluded correctly that the whole approach is misguided. Steedman tends to avoid these problems or alternatively bury them in obscure footnotes. I will consider three major issues.

The first issue is that negative prices and rate of profit can exist in an input-output production table which is admissible from the point of view of either physical data or labour values. Thus there is no way to tell from the material flow of commodities and labour whether such a system is admissible to Steedman. Similarly real wages which look perfectly reasonable from the physical point of view, in that they are allowed by the net output of the system, are sometimes regarded as impossible from a Sraffian point of view. So the first issue is the very existence of positive solutions to Steedman's equations.

The second even more important issue is the question of stability. It will be shown that some of Steedman's tables which are reasonable from his point of view will be rendered meaningless after an arbitrarily small change in the physical data. Stability is an absolutely necessary condition for any model of such a complicated and chaotic system of social production. Unstable models must always be rejected. It is however not hard to show that labour values always produce stable solutions.

The third issue related to stability is the lack of limits on the rate of profit in joint production systems. If prices can be so chosen as to guarantee an *infinite rate of profit* without any change in the working of the production or consumption processes themselves, the model concerned cannot be regarded as reflecting the logic of the familiar notion of the rate of profit in industrial production.

## 1. Negative Prices

Consider the following table of joint production:

### Figure 5

|            | $c_2$ | $c_2$ | labour days |     | $c_1$ | $c_2$ |
|------------|-------|-------|-------------|-----|-------|-------|
| Process $P_1$ | 2     | 3     | 1           | →   | 3     | 4     |
| Process $P_2$ | 5     | 6     | 1           | →   | 6     | 7     |

The real wage is assumed to be one unit of $c_1$ per day. Total production is

$$P_1 + P_2: \quad 7c_1 + 9c_2 + 2 \text{ days} \rightarrow 9c_1 + 11c_2$$

so we have plenty of surplus product to pay workers, to restock and satisfy the capitalists. The Sraffian price-profit equations are:

$$(1+r)(2p_1+3p_2)+p_2 = 3p_1+4p_2$$
$$(1+r)(5p_1+6p_2)+p_2 = 6p_1+7p_2 \tag{9}$$

The solutions are, if $p_2 = 1$, either

$$p_1 = 0, \quad p_2 = 1, \quad r = 0$$

or

$$p_1 = -1, \quad p_2 = 1, \quad r = -1.$$

Neither solution is acceptable, of course, because profit and or prices are non-positive. The corresponding labour value equation has many possible solutions, for instance $\lambda_1 = \lambda_2 = \frac{1}{2}$.

## 2. Instability

Consider the following further example:

Figure 6

| | $c_1$ | $c_2$ | labour days | | $c_1$ | $c_2$ |
|---|---|---|---|---|---|---|
| Process $P_1$ | 2 | 0 | 1 | $\rightarrow$ | 4 | $\frac{1}{2}$ |
| Process $P_2$ | $\varepsilon$ | 1 | 1 | $\rightarrow$ | $2\varepsilon$ | 4 |

where $\varepsilon$ represents a small non-negative number.

$$P_1+P_2: \quad (2+\varepsilon)c_1+c_2+2 \text{ days} \rightarrow (4+2\varepsilon)c_1+4\tfrac{1}{2}c_2, \tag{10}$$

so we have enough to pay workers a wage of one unit of $c_2$ per day, restock and keep capitalists happy with some surplus product for their hoarding and consumption. Being reduced ($0 \leqslant \varepsilon < 2$), the table yields positive values (see Appendix), but prices are negative.

If we consider Steedman's price system,[18] we get for the above real wage, putting $p_2 = 1 = w$,

$$(1+r)(2p_1+0)+1 = 4p_1+\tfrac{1}{2}$$
$$(1+r)(\varepsilon p_1+1)+1 = 2\varepsilon p_1+4$$

or

$$(1+r)2p_1 = 4p_1 - \tfrac{1}{2}$$

$$(1+r)(\varepsilon p_1 + 1) = 2\varepsilon p_1 + 3.$$

Now if $\varepsilon \geqslant 0$, $r \geqslant 0$, we can divide and get

$$\frac{2p_1}{\varepsilon p_1 + 1} = \frac{4p_1 - \tfrac{1}{2}}{2\varepsilon p_1 + 3}$$

whence

$$p_1(2 + \tfrac{1}{2}\varepsilon) = -\tfrac{1}{2}$$

so

$$p_1 = -\frac{1}{4+\varepsilon}$$

For $\varepsilon = 0$, for example, we get $r = 2$, $p_1 = -\tfrac{1}{4}$.

Thus we get a negative solution to a perfectly reasonable table for all values of $\varepsilon$. Notice that if in the output of $P_2$ we put $3\varepsilon$ instead of $2\varepsilon$, we shall get radically different results, no matter how small $\varepsilon$ is as long as it is positive. Thus for Steedman, prices and profits are extremely unstable and he offers no explanation of such phenomena. Notice also that the zero in the first production process can be set to a small number rendering all products 'basic' without changing the result.

To conclude: For a whole interval of $\varepsilon \geqslant 0$ one has positive r and negative $p_1$, since these vary continuously with $\varepsilon$. For small $\varepsilon$ there will be no other solution with a positive rate of profit. This means that in our example the above wage is impossible from Sraffa's point of view, yet is reasonable from both a physical and a value point of view. Of course if one adopts a different view of the wage, one may repair the above situation and get positive prices. The point to remember is that price calculations are extremely sensitive to the precise assumptions on the nature of the wage, profit, time of payment, and so on, and thus the economic meaning of Steedman's positive prices is far from clear.

## 3. Infinite Rate of Profit

Finally I would like to point out that the general definition of prices as cost plus profit leads to infinitely large rates of profit as a solution to reasonable economic examples. Thus the Sraffian notion of rate of profit allows for an unlimited rate of profit in a joint production system if the slightest deviation from a uniform rate of profit is allowed. A production table of a hypothetical economy can be constructed that, while paying the labourers a fixed real wage, permits the capitalists to receive arbitrarily high rate of profit by manipulating prices. If the only motive of capital is assumed to be generating the highest possible rate, as it is often assumed, one gets a contradiction between a uniform Sraffian rate and a maximum Sraffian rate, since the system has no maximum.

The economy is assumed to have two commodities, $c_1$ and $c_2$. The commodity $c_2$ will represent consumption goods which don't enter directly into the production process, such as bread. Consider the joint production table:

Figure 7

|  | $c_1$ | $c_2$ | labour days |  | $c_1$ | $c_2$ |
|---|---|---|---|---|---|---|
| Process $P_1$ | 6 | 0 | 1 | $\rightarrow$ | 7 | 3 |
| Process $P_2$ | 5 | 0 | 3 | $\rightarrow$ | 9 | 5 |

It follows that the labour values are $L_1 = \frac{4}{7}$, $L_2 = \frac{1}{7}$, and the surplus generated allows for a real wage of $c_1 + c_2$. If we put the price of the second commodity to be $p_1 = 1$, then the money wage of $p_1 + 1$ will allow the labourer to buy the above real wage of $c_1 + c_2$ per one labour day.

The Sraffian equations for the rate of profits $r_1, r_2$, and the price $p_1$, are:

$$(1 + r_1)6p_1 + p_1 + 1 = 7p_1 + 3$$

$$(1 + r_2)5p_1 + 3p_1 + 3 = 9p_1 + 5.$$

Since we have two equations with three unknowns, $p_1$ can be freely chosen. It follows that the rates of profit both tend to infinity as $p_1$ becomes smaller, tending to zero.

The two rates of profit are related by

$$\frac{1 + r_1}{1 + r_2} = \frac{5}{6}.$$

Since both processes are needed for production and reproduction, investors could equalize the rates of profit by taking shares in both processes in the appropriate proportion. Thus on the investment portfolio we get equal and unlimited rates of profit. It is not hard to see that one can make the two rates of profit as close to each other as one wishes and still get a situation in which proper pricing will lead to infinite rates of profit. No rational economic model should allow such behaviour.

## Appendix: An Algebraic Account

I will now give a somewhat more formal presentation of the conditions for the existence of a positive solution to the labour value equations in the most general joint production case. The basic result I use is that if $A$ is any matrix, then there exists a strictly positive solution vector $x$ to $Ax = 0$ if and only if there is no solution co-vector $y$ to the inequalities $0 \neq y \cdot A > 0$.

A production table is a list of production processes $T_1, T_2, \ldots, T_k$ over commodities $c_1, c_2, \ldots, c_n$. In each process $T_i$, one needs $l_i$ units of labour-time to transform an input bundle consisting of a given specific combination of the n available commodities into an output bundle consisting of a second such combination. We represent $T_i$ by the transformation schema

$$T_i: \quad (t_{i1}, t_{i2}, \ldots, t_{in}), \quad l_i \rightarrow (s_{i1}, s_{i2}, \ldots, s_{in}), \tag{1}$$

where $t_{ij}, s_{ij}, l_i$ are all non-negative numbers.

Economically, the size of the inputs or outputs of a given process or combination of processes is less important than the net output. If a process uses a large amount of a commodity c, but that same process reproduces c intact, then from the practical economic point of view the net amount of c used is nil. It is therefore useful to consider with each process $T_i$, and for the economy as a whole, the associated net process, that is, the net output resulting from the application of $l_i$ units of labour-time in the process $T_i$. We denote this by $NT_i$ and symbolically write

$$NT_i: \quad l_i \rightarrow (s_{i1} - t_{i1}, s_{i2} - t_{i2}, \ldots, s_{in} - t_{in}) \tag{2}$$

or

$$NT_i: \quad l_i \rightarrow (N_{i1}, N_{i2}, \ldots, N_{in})$$

where $N_{ij} = s_{ij} - t_{ij}$ is the net output of $c_j$ in $T_i$. For example in the car industry $N_{ij}$ will be positive for $c_j = $ cars and $N_{in}$ will be negative for $c_n = $ electricity, while the opposite will be the case in the electric power industry.

A production table $T = (T_1, \ldots, T_k)$ comprising k processes is called productive if overall it produces no less of each commodity than it consumes, and if for at least one commodity it leaves a surplus:

$$0 \neq \sum_j NT_j \geqslant 0. \tag{3}$$

An economy with a fixed set of commodities must produce at least as much of each commodity as it consumes to keep production going. It also has to have some surplus for real wages and profit.

I now want to consider the possibility of reallocating labour from one process to another. This means reducing the level of production in the process $T_i$ by a proportion $\alpha_i$, where $0 \leqslant |\alpha_i| \leqslant 1$, while using the labour saved, namely $|\alpha_i| l_i$, to increase the level of activity in another process $T_j$ by a proportion $\beta_j \geqslant 0$. If we choose $\alpha_i, \beta_j$ such that $\alpha_i l_i + \beta_j l_j = 0$, then exactly the same amount of labour is used after the reallocation as before. Such a reallocation is denoted by $\alpha_i T_i + \alpha_j T_j$, where $\alpha_i l_i + \alpha_j l_j = 0$. More general reallocations are denoted by $\{\alpha_i T_i\}$ where $\sum \alpha_i l_i = 0$, $|\alpha_i| \leqslant 1$. In practice we may consider only small reallocations where $|\alpha_i|$ are much smaller than 1.

Let me now turn to value theory. If we have a process $T_i$, we want the total value of the inputs plus the value $l_i$ itself to be equal to the total value of the output. Thus for the net process

$$NT_i: \quad l_i \rightarrow (N_{i1}, N_{i2}, \ldots, N_{in}),$$

if the value of $c_i$ is $\lambda_i$, then one must have $l_i = \sum_{j=1}^{n} \lambda_j N_{ij}$. This is for example impossible if $l_i = 0$ while $N_{ij} > 0$. So in general one cannot assign labour values in an arbitrary situation. The good news is that the above is essentially the only exception, and a very welcome one, because one does not want non-zero labour values to be assigned to commodities that can reproduce themselves without any labour or other input. In fact it is clear that economically their value must vanish.

Now if by transferring labour from $T_i$ to $T_j$ we can get additional net output without any additional labour, it is clear again that simple algebra will not yield positive labour values. A reducible table of production processes is a table which allows us to increase total net output without any addition to the total labour and with no new processes introduced, simply by increasing the level of some processes at the expense of others. In other words, a table is reducible if some reallocation of labour $\{\alpha_i T_i\}$ with $\sum \alpha_i l_i = 0$ has the property that the associated total net product $\sum \alpha_i NT_i$ is a non-zero non-negative vector.

It is not hard to prove the following result: *a table has no positive labour values if and only if it is a reducible table.*

Hence an irreducible table, and only such a table, has strictly positive labour values. This is a crucial advantage of the concept of labour values because reducible tables cannot possibly represent a stable economy which is at an 'economic equilibrium' and which produce day after day the same product, which is the general framework of all input-output models. Thus even in this very special domain of equilibrium, labour values have a decisive advantage. In practice there is no need to restrict attention to stable equilibrium models with a fixed set of commodities being reproduced indefinitely. In a more general context the exact properties depend of course on the model used to represent the economy.

# The Transformation from Marx to Sraffa

## Anwar Shaikh

### I. Introduction

Recent history has seen a tremendous revival of Marxist economic analysis. But this process has also produced its own specific problems, because as Marxist economics gain in respectibility, the temptation to represent itself in respectable terms grows accordingly. And these terms, in the end, are almost always the wrong ones.

There is no question but that Marxism must appropriate all modern developments. But to appropriate them involves much more than merely adopting them. It involves tearing them out of the bourgeois framework in which they appear, examining their hidden premises, and re-situating them (when and if possible) on a Marxist terrain—a terrain which cannot be derived merely by algebraic variation or sociological transformation of the premises of orthodox economics. We must, and indeed we do, have our own ground to stand upon.

It is my contention that the Sraffian, neo-Ricardian, tradition is by far too respectable. Its roots in left Keynesianism are easy to establish, and its refuge in mathematical economics is quite revealing. Nonetheless, the claims made by this school must be addressed, and its real contributions must be separated out from what is merely part of its cloak of respectability.

In this paper I do not intend to reproduce previous criticisms of the neo-Ricardians, nor even to reproduce my own arguments in favour of Marx's theory of value. Instead, in the discussion that follows I would like to show that even within the algebraic framework of which the neo-Ricardians are so proud, there are a host of issues which they do not, and cannot, face. These issues depend crucially on the difference between Marx's concepts and those of the neo-Ricardians. The very same algebra that they use, when asked different questions, will generate different answers. And these answers, it turns out, favour Marx much more than they do the neo-Ricardians.

In the discussion which follows, I will therefore examine in some detail the neo-Ricardian arguments concerning the redundancies and inconsistencies in Marx's theory of value. Since their treatment of both joint production and fixed capital are embellishments on their main argument, and since they are discussed by Emmanuel Farjoun in this volume, I shall ignore them here. An adequate treatment would in any case require a separate analysis.

Throughout this discussion, the difference between value and form-of-value is crucial. Thus all prices are distinct from values because price is always money price, the monetary expression of value within the sphere of circulation. From this point of view, the transformation brought about by the tendential equalization of profit rates is a transformation in the form-of-value: from direct prices, prices proportional to values, to prices of production. All price differences are thus differences between existing prices and direct prices. Nonetheless, in deference to traditional usage, I will frequently speak of 'price-value' and 'profit-surplus-value' deviations, when what is meant is respectively the deviations between prices and direct prices, and profits and direct profits (money profit proportional to surplus-value).

Lastly, I should mention that this paper is a prelude to a more general critique of the neo-Ricardians, the first thrust of which is a direct confrontation with their major claims. Ian Steedman's book *Marx after Sraffa* provides a welcome opportunity to take issue with the neo-Ricardians, which I do in a recently published paper entitled 'The Poverty of Algebra'.[1]

## II. Production, Reproduction and Exchange

### 1. The Contradiction of Commodity Production

In all societies, the objects required to satisfy human needs imply a certain allocation of society's labour-time, its productive activities, in specific proportions and quantities. Otherwise the reproduction of society is impossible. The relationship of people to nature must be reproduced if society is to be reproduced. But in the case of commodity production, the products of labour which constitute the material basis of this reproduction process are produced without any direct connection to social needs. They are produced for exchange, as the products of private autonomous labours carried out independently of one another, but within and through the social division of labour. 'Hence, lacking any conscious assignment or distribution on the part of society, individual labour is not immediately an articulation of social labour; it acquires its character as a part . . . of aggregate labour only through the mediation of exchange relations or the market.'[2]

We know of course that commodity production is generalized only under capitalism, hence only when labour-power becomes a commodity. But the very fact that commodity production is generalized gives rise to a paradox. It rests on private autonomous labours carried out independently of one another with only exchange, generally exchange for profit, in mind. In order to be undertaken, each constituent labour must presuppose, must risk, the existence and reproduction of other such labours, along with the reproduction of their social basis. In other words, each such independent labour must be undertaken on the presupposition of the social division of labour.

In order actually to be reproduced, however, private and apparently anarchic labours must somehow end up being allocated in specific proportions and quantities consistent with the social division of labour. It is precisely through exchange that this presupposition is realized, that private independent labours are forcibly articulated into a social division of labour. Exchange is the process by which, as Marx puts it, the contradictions of commodity production are 'both exposed and resolved'.[3] And since the generalization of commodity production implies the generalization of exchange, at the same time it implies the generalization of the forcible articulation of private independent labour into a social division of labour. The necessity of this forcible articulation then appears to the individual agents as an 'inner law, . . . as a blind natural force . . .'[4] Thus the society comes to possess particular and peculiar laws of motion, which assert themselves in-and-through the collision of the producers in exchange.[5]

## 2. The Double Role of Exchange

Exchange now appears in a double role. On the one hand, because exchange is the mediating process, the outcome of exchange is the immediate regulation of reproduction. It is through the movements of wages, prices and profits that the immediate regulation of social production is accomplished. On the other hand, it is precisely because exchange functions to articulate private independent labours into the social division of labour that the necessity of the distribution of social labour asserts itself as the domination and regulation of wages, prices and profits by social labour-time. The sphere of exchange has a relative autonomy, but it is ruled, regulated and dominated by the conditions of production and reproduction. The operation of this double relation is what Marx means by the *law of value:* prices as the immediate regulators of reproduction, social labour-times as the intrinsic regulators of prices and hence of reproduction.

> 'Every child knows that a nation which ceased to work, I will not say for a year, but even for a few weeks, would perish. Every child knows, too, that the masses of products corresponding to the different needs require different and quantitatively determined masses of the total labour of society. That this necessity of the distribution of social labour in definite proportions cannot possibly be done away with by a particular form of social production but can only change the mode of its appearance, is self-evident. No natural laws can be done away with. What can change in historically different circumstances is only the form in which these laws assert themselves. And the form in which this proportional distribution of labour asserts itself, in a state of society where the interconnections of social labour are manifested in the private exchange of the individual products of labour, is precisely the exchange-value of these products.
>
> Science consists precisely in demonstrating how the law of value asserts itself.'[6]

## 3. Money and Price

The above understanding of capitalist exchange implies several things for a Marxist analysis of price phenomena. First of all, it implies that money is an absolutely necessary aspect of developed commodity production. Exchange is a process in which people must equalize different use-values, that is abstract from their differences as use-values. As the sphere of exchange grows, so too does the necessity for a universal equivalent in which this abstraction is expressed, and through which the articulation of independent labours is accomplished. Money is the medium of abstraction, and the means of forcible articulation.

Second, because money is a necessary aspect of exchange, the elementary relation of exchange is sale and purchase, not barter (C–M not C–C). This means that each commodity now has a price, a quantity of money which represents its quantitative worth. Conversely, it also implies that money itself has no price. It does not have to be sold, it is money.

Third, all price phenomena now appear in a double light. On the

one hand, as price magnitudes they are distinct from value magnitudes, and have a more complex determination. For instance, even in
the case of exchange in proportion to value, the price of a commodity
is a quantity of gold determined by the commodity's relative value,
that is, value relative to the standard of price, say one ounce of gold,
and is therefore already a form of the commodity's value. As such, the
movements of prices need not parallel those of commodity values. A
fall in a commodity's value, for example, can be manifested as a rise
in its price if the value of gold happens to fall even faster.[7]

More generally, as the price-form is developed by Marx, so too is its
relative complexity. In the first volume of *Capital*, price is generally
treated as a simple money-form of value, but wages, as time-wages
and piece-wages, are already more complex forms of the value of
labour-power. In the second volume, costs of circulation and
turnover add fresh determinations to the price-form. Lastly, in the
third volume, the development of prices of production and of the
splitting of surplus-value into profits, rents and interest further
consolidate the price-form, while the distinction between individual
value and average value consolidates the determination of value
magnitudes, and through them, those of price magnitudes (individual,
average and regulating prices of production, differential profitability,
and rent, absolute and differential). It must be noted here that the
increasing complexity of the price-value relationship is no defect. Since
price magnitudes are the immediate regulators of reproduction, the
law of value must contain within it a theory of the structure of price
phenomena, right down to their most concrete determinations.
Otherwise the law remains abstract, unable to grasp the real
movements of the system.

On the other hand, because the price magnitudes are themselves
regulated by the socially necessary distribution of labour, the various
forms of price categories must be developed in relation to the
quantities of socially necessary labour-time whose magnitude and
movements dominate and regulate these price phenomena. We must
be able to conceive not only of the relative autonomy of price
magnitudes, as expressed in their variability and complexity relative
to values, but also of limits to these variations and of the
connection of these limits to social labour-time. It is significant that in
his own development of the increasingly complex categories of price
phenomena, Marx never loses sight of the domination of these
phenomena by the law of value.

'In whatever way prices are determined, the following is the result:
    (1) The law of value governs their movement in so far as the reduction or

increase in the labour-time needed for their production makes the prices of production rise or fall . . .

(2) The average profit, which determines the prices of production, must always be approximately equal to the amount of surplus-value that accrues to a given capital as an aliquot part of the total social capital . . . Since it is the total value of the commodities that governs the total surplus-value, while this in turn governs the level of average profit and hence the general rate of profit—as a general law or as governing the fluctuations—it follows that the law of value regulates the prices of production.'[8]

In a highly modern vein, Marx goes on to note how meaningless it is—but also how very convenient it is—to treat the difference between price and value, that is the relation between the two, as a mere separation.

'The price of production includes the average profit. And what we call the price of production is in fact the same thing that Adam Smith calls "natural price", Ricardo "price of production", or "cost of production" and the Physiocrats *"prix necessaire"*, though none of these people explained the difference between price of production and value. We call it price of production because in the long term it is the condition of supply, the condition for the reproduction of commodities, in each particular sphere of production. We can also understand why those very economists who oppose the determination of commodity value by labour-time, by the quantity of labour contained in the commodity, always speak of the prices of production as the centres around which market prices fluctuate. They can allow themselves this because the price of production is already a completely externalized and *prima facia* irrational form of commodity value, a form that appears in competition and is therefore present in the consciousness of the vulgar capitalist and consequently also in that of the vulgar economist.'[9]

I remind you that Marx is speaking of the economists who claim to ground themselves in classical economics—less the embarrassment of the labour theory of value, of course!

## 4. Tendential Regulation

It follows from the above that within the moving contradiction that is capitalist commodity production, the reproduction of society is necessarily a process of trial through error, in which discrepancies of one sort are constantly followed by those of an opposite nature. It is only in and through perpetual disorder that the necessary distribution of social labour-time asserts itself.[10] This is why Marx always speaks of a process of tendential regulation and not of some static equilibrium situation. Conversely, it is precisely the concept of equilibrium which enables orthodox economics to abolish all the contradictions of the forcible articulation, thus abolishing both the necessity of money and the possibility of crises.[11]

> '[The] determination of [market] price by [the price] of production is not to be understood in the sense of the economists. The economists say that the average price of commodities is equal to the [price] of production; that is a law. The anarchical movement, in which rise is compensated by fall and fall by rise, is regarded by them as chance ... But it is solely these fluctuations, which, looked at more closely, bring with them the most fearful devastations and, like earthquakes, cause bourgeois society to tremble to its foundations—it is solely in the course of these fluctuations that [market] prices are determined by the [price] of production. The total movement of this disorder is its order.'[12]

## III. The Aggregate Effects of Price–Value Deviations

In the preceding section I have been concerned to emphasize the distinctiveness of Marx's conception of the relation between production and exchange in the process of social reproduction. But these differences between Marx's conceptions and those of orthodox economics, be they classical or marginalist, need not, indeed cannot, be restricted to this level of abstraction. Every real difference in conception inevitably implies a difference in the questions to be asked, in the empirical phenomena to be examined, and ultimately in the conclusions to be drawn. Consequently, in the sections that follow I would like to demonstrate exactly how these differences manifest themselves in a set of problems which, according to some modern Marxists, have already been definitively resolved:[13] namely, the host of issues which have their origins in the debates around the so-called transformation problem.[14] Since the transformation problem is itself a special case of the general problem of price-value deviations (differential rent and market prices are two other equally important cases), I will often deal with the general case first and only then, where necessary, restrict the analysis to the consideration of prices of production alone.

One last point. Throughout what follows I will explicitly accept the mathematical formulations which are now so widely accepted in the post-Sraffian literature on these issues. These are exactly the tools and formulations which are the cornerstone of the most recent attacks on Marx's theory of value, and it is my intention to show that even on this terrain, Marx's answers are superior because Marx's questions are superior. Only at a later point will it be possible to show how the existing formulations are themselves inadequate—precisely because their very structure already embodies many conceptions of orthodox economics.

## 1. Calculation Versus Conception; The Redundancy Argument

It has always been a popular claim among Marx's critics that value categories are unnecessary in the analysis of capitalism because they are somehow less direct than price categories. Steedman, for instance, insists that given the physical flows of inputs and outputs, of the labour requirements for these outputs, and of the real wage of this labour, one can determine prices of production and the rate of profit without 'any reference to value magnitudes'. Indeed, Steedman goes on, since the 'physical data' which is required to determine values is also an element in the determination of prices of production, it would follow that values can 'play no essential role in the determination of the rate of profit or of prices of production.'[15]

Steedman's use of words is quite revealing. To begin with, the very use of the term 'physical data' is symptomatic of the whole neo-Ricardian approach to social reproduction. In Marx's analysis, 'relations between men within the process of creating and reproducing their material life' appear as a double relation, in which the people–nature relation exists in-and-through the people–people relation.[16] These are different aspects of the same set of human activities. In the neo-Ricardian conception, however, these double-edged relations are separated and alienated into 'physical data' and 'distribution'. The labour process, a fundamental social relation which involves the performance of labour and the forcible extraction of surplus labour, disappears from view. It is replaced instead by so-called given conditions of production.[17]

It is worth considering the various senses in which the conditions of production may be said to be 'given'. We begin by noting that the overall circuit of capital can be represented as $M–C \ldots P \ldots C'–M'$. In the first phase, capitalists invest money-capital M in the purchase of commodity-capital C—means of production and labour-power. At this point, therefore, we might say that they possess given conditions of production, but only as pre-conditions of production: as the necessary objective and subjective factors of the yet-to-be-performed labour process.[18] The capitalists must still unite these factors in the labour process itself, in the form of productive capital P, and only if this is done successfully will they be in the possession of the results of production: expanded commodity-capital C'.

Once the labour process has been completed, and input translated into output through the actual performance of labour, then, and only then, can we conceptually appropriate the results of the labour process in the form of input-output measurements—the so-called physical data to which Steedman constantly refers. But now this physical data is itself a conceptual summary of the real expenditures of social labour-time. In the real economy, the results of production on which the so-called physical data are based are themselves given only through the actual materialization of social labour-time, and hence only because value has been actually created. Values are, so to speak, built into the very fabric of this physical data.

As observers of the process, we can now extract from this data estimates of the value flows that were actually involved, just as we can also extract from it estimates of the prices of production that might correspond to such data (actual prices are of course market prices). We might then fall into the simple error of confusing our estimation process with the real determination of values. We might even naively believe that since we can calculate estimates of values and prices of production with almost equal facility from the physical data,[19] they are indeed co-equal in reality—ignoring completely how this so-called physical data comes into being. We might then, in this idealist fashion, arrive at the neo-Ricardian conception of production, in which input proceeds magically to output without the toil and misery of real labour, and in which values acquire a real existence only if we deign to consider them. The production of things by means of things.

## 2. The Sum of Values and the Sum of Surplus-Values

We noted earlier that for Marx price is itself always the monetary expression of value, the form necessarily taken by value in the sphere of exchange. The social labour process results in a given mass of commodities with given values: in circulation, these commodities acquire specific monetary expression in the form of prices. But it is obvious that in exchange these money prices can do no more than bring about the distribution of the social product among the individuals involved. They cannot in themselves change the mass of use-values so distributed. As such, neither can they change the mass of value and surplus-value represented by these commodities.

It follows from the above that different possible exchange relations among producers of a given mass of commodities involve only different possible distributions of the total mass of value and surplus-value contained in these commodities. This is precisely why Marx argues that price-value deviations cannot in themselves alter the sums of values and surplus-values involved. 'It needs no further elaboration here that, if a commodity is sold above or below its value, there is simply a different distribution of the surplus-value, and that this distribution, the altered ratio in which various individuals partake of the surplus-value, in no way affects either the magnitude or the character of the surplus-value itself.'[20]

It must be said, however, that just because different patterns of distribution cannot alter the total mass of surplus-value to be distributed, it by no means follows that the monetary expression of this total surplus-value (money profit) cannot—within certain strict limits—vary in magnitude. In what follows we shall show that Marx approaches the question of how and why a given mass of surplus-value materialized in a given surplus product can nonetheless have a variable monetary expression in circulation. How and why, in other words, profits can deviate from surplus-value and still remain determined by it.

## 3. Profit and Surplus-Value

The distinction between the sphere of production and the sphere of circulation is essential in Marx's analysis of reproduction. The production of social wealth (goods and services) occurs in the former, while in the latter the objects or performances produced are transferred via exchange from their owners to their consumers. Obviously, both production and circulation are absolutely necessary for capitalist reproduction. Nonetheless, their effects are quite distinct: the former sphere results in the creation of value and surplus-value, and the latter in their transfers.[21]

The essential mechanism for the transfer of value is the deviation of prices from proportionality to values. We will follow Marx in referring to these as price-value deviations with the understanding that, as in Marx, this always means deviations of prices from direct prices. For instance, when a commodity is sold at a price below its direct price, then the seller receives in money-form a value less than the value represented by the commodity sold. Conversely, the buyer receives in commodity-form a value greater than that which he or she handed over in the form of money. The surplus-value transferred out of the hands of the seller therefore directly reappears in the hands of the buyer. Something quite important follows from this. Suppose that some sellers have prices below direct prices, and others have prices above direct prices, but that for the economy as a whole the sum of these prices is equal to the sum of direct prices. Then what some sellers lose in exchange is exactly offset by what other sellers gain, so that in their capacity as sellers the capitalist class as a whole receives money in proportion to the total value materialized in their commodity-capital. But note: the capitalist sellers who lose in value do so to their own buyers, while those who gain in value do so from their own buyers. The question then arises: who are these buyers and how do their gains and losses appear in the determination of total money profits?

To answer this, we need to look at the process of capitalist reproduction in greater detail. To keep the exposition simple, let us initially assume a system in simple reproduction in which all production takes one year, at the end of which capitalists and workers meet in the market-place to buy and to sell. Capitalists enter the market with commodities $C'$, and with money $M'$. Workers, having consumed their wages during the previous period of production, enter the market with only their labour-power LP which they hope to sell afresh so as to be able to consume once again. On the basis of their investment plans for the coming year, capitalists invest money-capital $M$ to purchase the elements for next year's production. Of this money, $M_c$ represents constant money-capital advanced for means of production MOP: it therefore buys back a portion of the overall commodity-product $C'$. The remaining portion of capitalist investment expenditures consists of variable-capital $M_v$, which is used to purchase labour-power LP for next year's production. The workers in turn spend this money on their means of subsistence MOS, thus buying back a second portion of the available commodity-product $C'$. Finally, capitalists must also buy a certain amount of goods for their own personal consumption. They therefore expend an amount of money-revenue m to buy back the remaining portion c of the total product $C'$. Figure 1 below summarizes money flows in the overall process. The flows remaining within the circuit of capital, which as we shall see shortly are crucial to the analysis, are contained within the rectangle drawn below.

It is evident from the above that the circuit of capital M–C (the rectangle in Figure 1) encompasses the purchase of the vast bulk of the social commodity-product $C'$: directly, through the exchange $M_c$–MOP, and indirectly through the circuit $M_v$–LP–MOS. It follows that any transfer of value arising from price-value deviations of means of production MOP and workers' means of subsistence

Figure 1

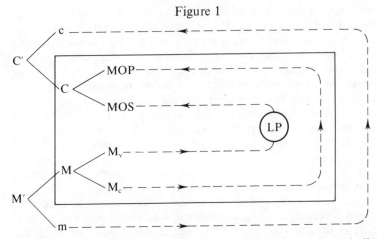

MOS remain internal to the circuit of capital: what one capitalist loses as capitalist-seller of MOP and MOS, another gains as capitalist-investor in MOP and LP.

The remaining circulation to consider is that encompassed by the capitalists' own circuit of revenue m – c. Here too, what the sellers of commodity-capital lose in value through a price below direct price is gained by the capitalists in the form of a lower price for their articles of consumption. But now a crucial difference arises. What the capitalists in this case lose as sellers will show up in business accounts as the amount by which actual profit is below direct profit (by which actual profit is below profit proportional to surplus value). But what they gain as consumers shows up only in their personal accounts, as a lower amount of money required to purchase the same articles of consumption. In other words, value is transferred out of the circuit of capital into the circuit of revenue, and in the business accounts this transfer manifests itself as profits lower than direct profits.

In most analyses of social reproduction, the circuit of capitalist revenue is not explicitly accounted for. Of course, under these circumstances it appears completely mysterious that as prices deviate from values a given surplus-product and hence a given mass of surplus-value can manifest itself as a variable mass of profit.[22] However, once the whole of social circulation is analysed, the mystery disappears. To the extent that price-value deviations give rise to transfers between the circuit of capital and the circuit of capitalist revenue, these transfers will manifest themselves as differences between actual profit and direct profits. Ironically, though this phenomenon is evidently a mystery to most Marxist discussions of this issue, it was no mystery to Marx himself.[23] 'This phenomenon of the conversion of capital into revenue should be noted, because it creates the illusion that the amount of profit grows (or in the opposite case decreases) independently of the amount of surplus value.'[24]

None of this should come as any surprise once the difference between value and form-of-value has been grasped. Value and surplus-value are created in production, and expressed as money magnitudes in circulation. Since the circulation magnitudes are more concrete, they are necessarily more complexly determined than value magnitudes, for they express not only the conditions of production of value but also the conditions of its circulation. As such, the relative autonomy of the sphere of circulation necessarily expresses itself as the relative autonomy of price magnitude from value magnitudes. Profits, in other words, depend not only on the mass of surplus-value but also on its specific mode of circulation. The concept of the relative autonomy of circulation from production implies not only that profit can vary independently of surplus-value, but also that this independence is strictly limited. It is necessary, therefore, to show how value categories themselves provide the limits to the variations in their money expressions.

Intuitively, it is evident from the preceding discussion that the overall deviation of actual profits from direct profits is the combined result of two factors. First, it depends on the extent to which the prices of capitalists' articles of consumption deviate from the values of these articles—that is, it depends on the manner in which surplus-value is distributed among capitalists, and on the resultant pattern of individual price–value deviations. And second, it depends on the extent to which this surplus-value is consumed by capitalists as revenue—that is, on the distribution of this surplus-value between capital and revenue. Even when prices deviate from values, the size of any transfer from the circuit of capital to the circuit of revenue will also depend on the relative size of the circuit of revenue. Where all surplus-value is consumed (as in simple reproduction), then the relative deviation of actual profits from direct profits will be at its maximum. When, on the other hand, all surplus-value is re-invested (as in maximum expanded reproduction), then there is no circuit of capitalist revenue and consequently no transfer at all. Total actual profits must, in this case, equal total direct profits, regardless of the size and nature of individual price–value deviations.[25]

Let $\pi° =$ direct profits (money profits proportional to surplus-value), $\pi$ = actual money profits, b = the fraction of actual profits which goes towards capitalist consumption, $\bar{g}$ = the average growth rate of the economy, and $\bar{\delta}_F$ = the average percentage price–value deviation of articles consumed by capitalists. Then, as derived in appendix A, it can be shown that the percentage deviation of profits from surplus-value (from direct profits) is a fraction $b(1/1 + \bar{g})$ of the average percentage price-value deviation of capitalist consumption goods.

$$\frac{\pi - \pi^{\circ}}{\pi} = \frac{b}{1 + \bar{g}} \, \bar{\delta}_F \tag{1}$$

where $0 \leqslant b \leqslant 1$, $(1/1 + r) \leqslant (1/1 + \bar{g}) \leqslant 1$, r = the uniform rate of profit and

$$\bar{\delta}_F \equiv \sum_{i=1}^{n} \left( \frac{p_i^{\circ} - p_i}{p_i} \right) \frac{F_i}{F}$$

in which $p_i$, $p_i^{\circ}$ refer to actual and direct prices of the i-th good, $F_i$ to the capitalist expenditures on these goods, and $F \equiv \sum_{i=1}^{n} F_i$ to the total consumption expenditure of capitalists. $\bar{\delta}_F$ is therefore a weighted average of individual negative and positive deviations.

It should be noted at this point that this result holds for arbitrary prices, the only restriction being that aggregate money-value of the social product be held constant, so that the purchasing power of money is held constant. The latter condition of course implies that the average price-value deviation for the total product is exactly zero. Insofar as capitalist consumption goods encompass a wide variety of objects produced in industries having a wide range of production conditions, then their average price-value deviation will be the weighted average of many positive and negative individual deviations. In general, therefore, the average price–value deviation $(\bar{\delta}_F)$ of capitalist consumption goods is likely to be quite small. Further discussion on this issue will have to be reserved for section IV of this paper, where the determinants of individual price–value deviations will be analysed.

To get an idea of the magnitudes actually involved, it is useful to recognize that $(1 - b)$ is the fraction of profits invested by capitalists. It follows therefore that it is also the ratio of total investment to total profits, or, what is the same thing, the ratio of the average growth rate $\bar{g}$ to the average profit rate $\bar{r}$. This means that equation (1) can also be written as

$$\frac{\Delta\pi}{\pi} \equiv \frac{\pi - \pi^\circ}{\pi} = \left(\frac{\bar{r} - \bar{g}}{\bar{r}}\right)\left(\frac{1}{1 + \bar{g}}\right)\bar{\delta}_F. \qquad (2)$$

For the US economy over the postwar period, the average rate of profits (before taxes) was roughly 12%, and the average growth rate roughly 4%.[26] For these orders of magnitude the resulting profit–surplus deviation would be roughly 64% of $\bar{\delta}_F$, the average price–value deviation of capitalist consumption goods. If the latter deviations were of the order of $-10\%$ (given the definition of $\bar{\delta}_F$, this means that capitalist consumption goods sell at prices roughly $(0.1/1.10) \cong 9\%$ lower than values), the direct profits would differ from actual profits by roughly $-6\%$.

$$\frac{\Delta\pi}{\pi} \equiv \frac{\pi - \pi^\circ}{\pi} \cong -0.064.$$

It is worth remembering, incidentally, that the above formula abstracts from fixed capital and differences in turnover time. A proper treatment of these factors is beyond the scope of the present paper, but their inclusion would imply an even lower profit–surplus-value deviation.

With only a little more effort we can extend the preceding results on the mass of profit to the case of the rate of profit. Let M, W, P stand for the money values of production used up, the total wage bill, and the aggregate sum of prices, respectively, all at arbitrarily given relative prices. Now let $M^\circ$, $W^\circ$, $P^\circ$ stand for the corresponding money aggregates when relative prices equal relative values (when prices 'equal' values). Then

$$P \equiv M + W + \pi \qquad (3)$$

$$P^\circ \equiv M^\circ + W^\circ + \pi^\circ. \qquad (3a)$$

Since we are abstracting from turnover and fixed capital, the actual average rate of profit $\bar{r}$ is simply the ratio of profit $\pi$ to cost-price (=capital advanced) M + W. Hence

$$\bar{r} = \frac{\pi}{M + W} \quad \text{whence} \quad \pi = \bar{r}(M + W)$$

whence

$$\frac{\pi}{P} = \frac{\pi}{M + W + \pi} = \frac{\bar{r}}{1 + \bar{r}} \tag{4}$$

$$\frac{\pi^{\circ}}{P^{\circ}} = \frac{r^{\circ}}{1 + r^{\circ}} \tag{4a}$$

where $\bar{r}$ = the average money rate of profit with actual prices and $r^{\circ}$ = the average money rate of profit with prices proportional to values = the average value rate of profit.

Finally, since the sum of prices is held constant, $P = P^{\circ}$. Dividing (2) by P and applying (4), we can, after a little manipulation (see appendix A), write:

$$\frac{\Delta \bar{r}}{\bar{r}} \equiv \frac{\bar{r} - r^{\circ}}{\bar{r}} = \frac{\bar{r}\left(\dfrac{\Delta \pi}{\pi}\right) + \dfrac{\Delta \pi}{\pi}}{\bar{r}\left(\dfrac{\Delta \pi}{\pi}\right) + 1}. \tag{5}$$

Intuitively, given that the sum of prices is held constant, if price-value deviations cause $\pi$ to be below $\pi^{\circ}$, they must also cause $(M + W)$ to be above $(M^{\circ} + W^{\circ})$ (see equation (3)). This means that the average rate of profit will be lower than the value rate because its numerator $(\pi)$ is lower and also because its denominator $(M + W)$ is higher, which in turn implies that profit rate deviations will tend to be a bit larger than profit mass deviations $\Delta \pi / \pi$. This is exactly what (5) tells us, and if we use the previously calculated magnitudes of $\Delta \pi / \pi \cong -0.064$ along with the previously given value of $\bar{r} \cong 0.12$, we get

$$\frac{\Delta \bar{r}}{\bar{r}} \equiv \frac{\bar{r} - r^{\circ}}{\bar{r}} \cong -0.07 > \frac{\Delta \pi}{\pi} = -0.064.$$

It is important to understand what this numerical result implies: given that $\bar{r} \cong 0.12$, (5) implies that $r^{\circ} \cong 0.13$! Such a difference, incidentally is considerably less than the probable error in any empirical measurement of $\bar{r}$, and we may as well say that for empirical purposes $\bar{r}$ and $r^{\circ}$ (as well as $\pi$ and $\pi^{\circ}$) are virtually indistinguishable— providing, of course, that our estimate of price—value deviations is of the correct order of magnitude. Before we come to that, however, we need to clarify a bit further the inner relation between value rate of profit and its monetary expression.

## 4. Prices of Production: The Profit Rate

The preceding discussion was based on more or less arbitrary prices. In order to derive more precise results, we must now restrict ourselves specifically to prices of production. In this regard, since we have already established in (5) that even in the general case there exists an intrinsic connection between profit mass deviations and profit rate deviations, it is sufficient to deal with the latter alone.

We begin by noting that for given conditions of the labour process, the value rate of profit $r^\circ$ can always be expressed as a steadily increasing function of the rate of surplus-value:

$$r^\circ = \frac{S}{C+V} \tag{6}$$

where $S$ = surplus-value, $V$ = value of labour-power. Let $L \equiv V + S$ = value added by living labour (if $N$ = the number of workers employed, and $h$ = the length of the working day in hours, $L = Nh$). Let $k \equiv C/L$ = the ratio of dead to living labour. Then

$$r^\circ = \frac{\left(\dfrac{S}{V}\right)}{\dfrac{C}{L}\left(\dfrac{L}{V}\right)+1} = \frac{\left(\dfrac{S}{V}\right)}{k\left(1+\dfrac{S}{V}\right)+1}. \tag{7}$$

Since $k$ depends only on the technology and the length of the working day $h$, when these conditions of the labour process are given $r^\circ$ will vary directly with the rate of surplus-value. Thus the value rate of profit is a monotonic increasing function of the rate of surplus-value.

In recent years, several authors have shown that when direct prices are transformed into prices of production, though the transformed money rate of profit $r$ will in general deviate from the value rate (we have explained how and why in the preceding section of this paper), nonetheless this transformed rate is also a monotonic increasing function of the rate of surplus-value.[27] But once it is recognized that the value rate of profit $r^\circ$ and the transformed rate $r$ both increase as $S/V$ increases, it follows at once that they must move together: when the value rate of profit rises (or falls) its reflection in the sphere of circulation, the transformed rate of profit, also rises (or falls).

We can be even more specific. In general, the average value rate of profit $r°$ is a weighted average of individual industry value rates of profit, the weights being all positive and summing to 1 (this is known as a convex combination of the individual industry value rates of profit). Let us suppose that the actual system is growing at a rate g, $0 \leqslant g \leqslant r$ (this includes simple reproduction). The level of this actual rate of growth g will of course depend on b, the proportion of profits consumed by the capitalist class. By way of comparison with the actual economy, let us now consider what would happen to the system if capitalists progressively consumed less and less out of profits ($b \rightarrow 0$). As this happened, the growth rate would rise, and the fraction of the social product destined for capitalist consumption would fall. In the limit, capitalists would consume nothing, all profits would be invested, and the growth rate g would equal the transformed rate of profit r. Moreover, as indicated in section III.3, when $g = r$ the average value rate of profit under these hypothetical circumstances would itself equal the transformed rate r.

The situation pictured above is one of maximum expanded reproduction (MER). Since there is no capitalist consumption under these circumstances, it follows that of the industries which exist under the actual rate of growth, a small subset—industries whose products are consumed only by capitalists (yachts?)—would not be in operation in MER. This in turn implies that the average value rate of profit in MER is a weighted average of all industry value rates of profit except those industries producing pure luxury goods, the weights being strictly positive fractions determined by the output proportions necessary for MER.

But since this average value rate in MER is exactly equal to the transformed rate of profit r, we can immediately say that the transformed rate of profit is itself a weighted average of individual value rates of profit, the weights and the industry coverage being determined by the MER output proportions. Though we arrived at these MER weights by considering what would happen as $g = r$, we can equally well consider them to be weights which define a sort of 'composite industry' in the actual system. This composite industry, which I will call the central industry, is invariant to the transformation process since its transformed rate of profit is equal to its value rate. As such, it corresponds to what Marx calls 'spheres of mean composition, whether these correspond exactly or only approximately to the social average', for it is to the rate in 'those average spheres of production where the average composition of capital prevails' that the rate of profit is adjusted among industries.[28]

The preceding result is quite powerful, for it tells us that the average value rate of profit r° and the transformed rate of profit r are merely different kinds of weighted averages of a common set of individual industry value rates of profit. The former of course corresponds to the value rate of profit for capital of what Marx calls the 'social average' composition, while the latter corresponds to the central composition (what Marx simply calls the 'average' composition), a composition which, as we have seen, he correctly perceives to be 'only approximately the same as the social average'. The sole difference between the two types of averages arises from the fact that the industry coverage differs somewhat, and from the fact that though each set of weights is composed of positive fractions which add up to one, the individual weights in the two sets will not exactly correspond to each other. As is expected, therefore, these two types of averages behave in essentially the same way, and in a real economy even their respective magnitudes are likely to be virtually the same.

Figure 2 below summarizes the results of the preceding discussion. For the sake of illustration it is assumed that r° is larger than r, though of course it could equally well be the other way around.[29] Their actual relation to each other will in general depend on the relation between the social average composition of capital (which determines r°) and the central composition (which determines r).

It is interesting to note that although Marx insists that the equalization of the rate of profit and the formation of individual

Figure 2

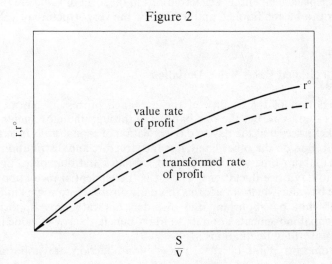

prices of production are of great importance for individual capitals or subsets of capitals, he at the same time also insists that for the system as a whole the previously derived laws are basically unaltered. In a letter to Engels, after having developed the basic phenomena arising from the transformation process, Marx goes on to summarize the remaining tasks. 'Further: the changed outward form of the law of value and surplus-value—which were previously set forth and which are still valid—after the transformation of value into price of production.'[30]

At all times and in all places, price is the outward form of value, the reflection of value in the sphere of circulation. What the transformation does, Marx argues, is to transform this outward form, to introduce into it certain fresh determinations and new sources of variation, but to do so exactly in such a way as to leave the intrinsic connections unchanged. Look again at Figure 2: it illustrates this conception perfectly. In the relatively autonomous mirror of circulation the transformed rate of profit appears as a displaced image of the value rate of profit, essentially the same in determination but somewhat different in exact magnitude. The autonomy of the sphere of circulation expresses itself in this displacement of magnitude. On the other hand, the limited nature of this autonomy manifests itself precisely through the fact that it is the structure of value categories (the pattern of organic compositions, and the proportion of surplus-value which is converted into revenue) which provides the limits to this displacement effect. The variations in the form of value are thus shown to be conditioned and limited by the very structure of value itself.

### IV. Individual Price–Value Deviations

The notion of the duality of the exchange process is central to Marx's analysis. On the one hand, it is through the movements of market prices that the day to day regulation of capitalism is brought about. But, on the other hand, it is the structure and distribution of social labour-time which in the end regulates and dominates these day-to-day price fluctuations. Thus it is the tendential regulation of price by value which transforms this daily disorder into some kind of order—not by abolishing the disorder, but rather by imposing tendential movements upon it. As Marx puts it, the law of value is a 'law governing fluctuations'.

From this point of view, prices of production are important

because they mediate the relation between values and market prices. The competition of capitals tends to equalize rates of profits across industries, and in so doing tends to reduce market prices towards prices of production. Prices of production are therefore the regulating prices of market price, 'the centre around which the daily market-prices revolve, and at which they are balanced out in definite periods.'[31] Values then in turn regulate these regulating prices of production, and thereby through them dominate the movements of market prices. It is for this reason that the relation between individual values and individual prices of production, the transformation process, plays such an important role in Marx's analysis.

As we have seen, at the level of the whole the individual price-value differences brought about by the transformation process do not substantially alter previously derived laws. But once we move to a more concrete analysis, then these differences, and the transfers of value which they give rise to, become important in their own right. When we examine the relation of one firm to another, of agriculture versus industry, of North versus South, of developed versus under-developed capitalist countries, then knowledge of individual price-value deviations is of great importance. The current debate on unequal exchange is an excellent example of this sort of problem even though I have argued elsewhere against the unequal exchange thesis itself.[32]

Once we consider these issues, then two questions immediately arise. First, what are the relative magnitudes of these deviations and how do they affect the regulation of individual prices of production by individual values? And second, what are the determinants of the directions of these deviations and how do they bring about transfers of value between capitals?

The first question can be answered by analysing the determinants of the size of the typical individual price–value deviation. Of course, if the sum of prices is held constant, the average deviation is zero, since it is the sum of positive and negative deviations. But if we look at the absolute size of these deviations, regardless of their signs, then we can get an idea of the typical deviation and its effects.

The second question is much harder, however, because it requires us to specify both the size and the direction of all individual deviations. Marx of course does just this, but the difficulty arises in generalizing Marx's results. In the traditional case of three 'depart-ments', Francis Seton has already established that completely transformed prices of production deviate from values in the same directions as do the prices of production derived by Marx—that is, according to the relation of the individual department's organic composition to the social average composition. But in the more general case of a given number of industries the problem remains unsolved. Therefore, in what follows I will focus on the first problem alone: namely, on the regulation of individual prices by individual values.

## 1. The Significance of Individual Price–Value Deviations

The notion that variations in prices are dominated by variations in values can be expressed formally through the notion that the correlation between prices and values is high. And this notion of correlation can in turn be applied to two distinct questions concerning the price–value relation. First of all, as we move across industries during any given period of time, how do the inter-industry price variations compare to the corresponding variations in values? In other words, how close is the cross-sectional correlation between prices and values? Second, how do variations in prices over time compare to the corresponding variations in values? In other words, how strong is the inter-temporal correlation between prices and values?

It is worth recalling that neither Marx nor Ricardo argue that cross-sectional variations are negligible. Indeed, they both emphasize that at any moment of time prices of production may significantly differ from values. Still, it is interesting to note that even in their own examples on the importance of this difference, the actual deviations involved are themselves quite moderate: Ricardo's numerical examples concerning this problem in fact yield relative prices which deviate by only 10% from relative values, whereas Marx's famous transformation tables yield a typical deviation on the order of only $\pm 12\%$. Even the infamous von Bortkiewicz example, around which so much debate has swirled over the years, yields a typical deviation of only about $\pm 10\%$.[33]

Granted that particular price–value deviations can be quite large (in Marx's tables, they range from a low of $+2.2\%$ to a high of $+85\%$), it is nonetheless important for two reasons to establish what determines the typical deviation. First of all, we have already seen that for the economy as a whole the percentage deviation of the transformed rate of profit from the value rate is itself a fraction of the net price–value deviations of the goods consumed by capitalists. A similar statement applies to the transformed mass of profits. If, for instance, the typical deviation is on the order of $\pm 20\%$ of values, then the net deviation of any bundle of commodities (such as those consumed by capitalists) is likely to be much smaller than this because positive and negative deviations will tend to offset each other, so that the earlier assumption that $\bar{\delta}_F \cong 0.10$ is fully justified. This in turn would imply that for the economy as a whole the corresponding profit-rate and profit-mass deviations would be very small indeed.

A second reason for examining cross-sectional correlations is that they can provide us with a clue to the inter-temporal correlation between prices and values. The closer that prices are to values at any one moment, the greater is the likelihood that their variations over time will be highly correlated. The reverse is not true, however, since it is perfectly possible to have prices differing significantly from values at any moment, and still have the two moving at roughly the same speeds. This latter outcome is the one Marx emphasizes when he argues (along with Ricardo) that notwithstanding the possibility of large price-value deviations at any moment, over time the significant variations in prices of production are brought about 'by changes in the value of commodities, that is [by] changes in the quantity of labour employed in their production (Ricardo is far from expressing this truth in these adequate terms)'.[34]

All of the preceding discussion has concerned the relation between values and prices of production. But prices of production, it will be recalled, are important primarily because they mediate the relationship between values and market prices, and it is this latter relation which a Marxist analysis ultimately seeks to grasp. Consequently, this latter connection will also be analysed in the sections which follow.

## 2. The Determinants of Individual Price–Value Deviations

By definition, price is simply the sum of wage costs, material costs, and some arbitrary amount of profit. Let us suppose that the wage rate is uniform, so that the wage cost is $wL$, where $w =$ the uniform wage per hour, and $L =$ the number of hours worked (the value added by living labour). If $M =$ materials costs and $\pi =$ (arbitrary) profits, then any arbitrary price $P$ can be written as

$$p = wL + \pi + M. \qquad (8)$$

In this expression, the term $M$ represents the price of the material inputs (including depreciation) used up in the process of production. But this price in turn can be thought of as itself being composed of wages, profits and material costs of the industries which produced these means of production. Designating these by $wL^{(1)}$, $\pi^{(1)}$ and $M^{(1)}$ (the superscript (1) tells us that they refer to a production cycle which is one conceptual stage behind the current stage), we can write $M = wL^{(1)} + \pi^{(1)} + M^{(1)}$, or

$$p = wL + \pi + wL^{(1)} + \pi^{(1)} + M^{(1)}. \tag{9}$$

Clearly, the new (residual) material cost $M^{(1)}$ is smaller than the original material cost M. What is more, if we repeat the above process we can reduce $M^{(1)}$ to its wages, profits and material costs, so that $M^{(1)} = wL^{(2)} + \pi^{(2)} + M^{(2)}$, and then in turn reduce this remaining material cost to its components, and so on, until in the limit there is no residual material cost at all. In this way, no matter how the price is actually determined, we can always express it as an infinite series of wages and profits in conceptually receding stages of production.

$$p = W^T + \pi^T \tag{10}$$

where

$$W^T = wL^T \equiv w(L + L^{(1)} + L^{(2)} + L^{(3)} + \cdots)$$

and

$$\pi = \pi + \pi^{(1)} + \pi^{(2)} + \pi^{(2)} + \cdots$$

In the above expression, the term $\pi^T$ represents the sum of the direct profits $\pi$ actually received by the sellers of this commodity, plus all the indirect profits $\pi^{(1)}$, $\pi^{(2)}$, $\pi^{(3)}$, . . ., each of which represents a prior stage of production. We will call this sum $\pi^T$ the integrated profits of this commodity.[35]

The same thing applies to $L^T$. It is the integrated labour-time of this commodity, the sum of the direct labour-time expended in the production of this commodity, and of all the indirect labour-times required to produce its means of production, and the means of production of these means of production. Thus the term $W^T = wL^T$ is the integrated wage bill. But $L^T$, the integrated labour-time, has another interpretation also: it is simply the (labour) value of the commodity, the sum of direct labour-time L (the value added by living labour), and all indirect labour-times $L^{(1)} + L^{(2)} + L^{(3)} + \cdots$ (the latter sum being C, the value transferred to the product through the means of production used up). Thus:

$$\Lambda = \text{value} = L^T = \text{integrated labour-time.} \tag{11}$$

In preparation for the next step, let us rewrite the price expression in (10) using (11)

$$p = w\Lambda(1+Z) \tag{12}$$

where

$$Z \equiv \frac{\pi^T}{W^T} \equiv \text{the integrated profit–wage ratio.}$$

Now let us use the above expression to write the relative prices of any two commodities i and j. Denote the price of i by $p_i$, its integrated labour-time by $\lambda_i$, and its integrated profit–wage ratio by $z_i$. Since the wage rate w cancels out of numerators and denominator, we get

$$p_{ij} = \lambda_{ij} z_{ij} \tag{13}$$

where

$$p_{ij} \equiv \frac{p_i}{p_j}, \quad \lambda_{ij} \equiv \frac{\lambda_i}{\lambda_j}, \quad z_{ij} \equiv \frac{(1+z_i)}{(1+z_j)}.$$

Equation (13) tells us that for any arbitrary prices, the deviations of relative prices from relative values depend on the extent to which the integrated profit–wage ratios of the two commodities differ from each other (where $z_{ij}$ differs from 1). But these immediately gives us a very powerful analytical explanation of the limits to individual price–value deviations. To see why, let us write out the expression for a given integrated profit–wage ratio:

$$Z \equiv \frac{\pi^T}{W^T} \equiv \frac{\pi + \pi^{(1)} + \pi^{(2)} + \pi^{(3)} + \cdots}{wL^T}$$
$$= \frac{\pi}{wL^T} \cdot \frac{w}{w} + \frac{\pi^{(1)}}{wL^T} \cdot \frac{w^{(1)}}{w^{(1)}} + \cdots$$

$$= \frac{\pi}{W} \frac{wL}{wL^T} + \frac{\pi^{(1)}}{W^{(1)}} \frac{wL^{(1)}}{wL^T} + \frac{\pi^{(2)}}{W^{(2)}} \frac{wL^{(2)}}{wL^T} + \cdots$$

$$Z \equiv \left(\frac{\pi}{W}\right)^T = \left(\frac{\pi}{W}\right) \frac{L}{L^T} + \left(\frac{\pi}{W}\right)^{(1)} \frac{L^{(1)}}{L^T} + \left(\frac{\pi}{W}\right)^{(2)} \frac{L^{(2)}}{L^T} + \cdots \qquad (14)$$

We see from the above that the integrated profit–wage ratio $(\pi/W)^T$ is a weighted average of the direct profit–wage ratio $(\pi/W)$ and of all the profit–wage ratios of commodities which enter either directly, via this commodity's means of production, or indirectly, via the means of production of its means of production, into its production. Moreover, since $L^T \equiv L + L^{(1)} + L^{(2)} + \cdots$, the weights themselves are strictly positive and sum to one. Thus $(\pi/W)^T$ is a convex combination of the direct and indirect profit–wage ratios of this commodity.

But it turns out that as long as the economy is connected, i.e. is composed of basic goods in the sense of Sraffa, then all industries will enter either directly or indirectly into the production of any given industry,[36] which in turn implies that the integrated profit–wage ratio of any commodity is a weighted average of all the direct profit–wage ratios in the economy. But if that is so, then it follows from equation (13) that the deviations of relative prices from relative values depend on the extent to which different weighted averages (convex combinations) of the same set of direct profit–wage ratios differ from each other. In an actual economy with its extensive network of industrial interconnections, it becomes quite clear why even large variations in direct profit–wage ratios $(\pi/W)_i$ can be reduced to relatively moderate variations in integrated profit–wage ratios $Z_i \equiv (\pi/W)_i^T$. The influence of the variations in $z_i$ is then further reduced by the fact that for price–value deviations it is the variations in $(1 + z_i)$ which are the relevant ones, these latter variations being always smaller than the former ones. For direct, and hence integrated, profit–wage ratios which are generally less than one, which is the case in all the major capitalist economies, this latter effect is important in its own right.

All of the above applies to any arbitrary prices. It therefore also applies to prices of production. But here we can specify the argument somewhat more by noting that in the case of prices of production the mass of profit equals the uniform rate of profit r times the (transformed) money value of the capital advanced K. But then integrated profits must be equal to r times the integrated capital advanced $K^T$. Thus for prices of production:

$$\pi = rK$$

$$\pi^T = rK^T$$

$$z_i = \left(\frac{\pi}{W}\right)_i^T = \frac{r}{w}\left(\frac{K^T}{L^T}\right)_i \tag{15}$$

$$p_{ij} = \lambda_{ij} \cdot z_{ij} \tag{16}$$

where now

$$z_{ij} \equiv \frac{1 + \dfrac{r}{w} k_i^T}{1 + \dfrac{r}{w} k_j^T}$$

and

$$k_i^T \equiv \left(\frac{K^T}{L^T}\right)_i = \text{the integrated capital–labour ratio.}$$

In this case we see that the variations in integrated profit–wage ratios are proportional to the variations in the integrated capital–labour ratios. The previous analysis for profit–wage ratios then applies also to capital–labour ratios: namely, even large variations in direct capital–labour ratios $(K/L)_i$ can be reduced to relatively small variations in integrated ratios $k_i^T \equiv (K/L)_i^T$, and these in turn are further reduced in their influence on price–value deviations because it is the variations in $[1 + (r/w)k_i^T]$ which matter. In the end, the resulting deviations of prices of production from direct prices can be quite moderate even though the variations in direct capital–labour ratios are quite large.

Equation (16) applies to cross-sectional variations in price–value deviations. If we now consider observations at two different periods t and $t_0$, then we can write an expression for the determinants in inter-temporal variations in relative prices and relative values.

$$(p_{ij})_{\Delta t} = (\lambda_{ij})_{\Delta t} \cdot (z_{ij})_{\Delta t} \tag{17}$$

where

$$(p_{ij})_{\Delta t} \equiv \frac{(p_{ij})_t}{(p_{ij})_{t_0}}, \qquad (\lambda_{ij})_{\Delta t} \equiv \frac{(\lambda_{ij})_t}{(\lambda_{ij})_{t_0}}$$

and

$$(z_{ij})_{\Delta t} \equiv \frac{(z_{ij})_t}{(z_{ij})_{t_0}}.$$

Equation (17) tells us that the change over time in relative prices will differ from changes over time in relative values to the extent that the relative integrated capital–labour ratios of the two commodities themselves change over time. What this means is that if over some period of time the different elements in the constellation of integrated capital–labour ratios all rise at roughly the same rate, so that their relative positions are not altered terribly much, then the changes in relative prices over time will correspond fairly closely to changes in relative values. As Ricardo and Marx foresaw, this is clearly possible even when the individual integrated capital–labour ratios differ quite a bit at any one moment of time.

Lastly, the nature of the expressions for cross-sectional and inter-temporal correlations of relative prices and relative values (equations (16) and (17) respectively) suggests that we can rewrite them in the following useful forms:

$$\ln p_{ij} = \ln \lambda_{ij} + \ln z_{ij} \tag{18}$$

$$\ln (p_{ij})_{\Delta t} = \ln (\lambda_{ij})_{\Delta t} + \ln (z_{ij})_{\Delta t}. \tag{19}$$

When written in the above form, we can see that the relation between relative prices and relative values is a log-linear one, in which the terms $\ln z_{ij}$ and $\ln (z_{ij})_{\Delta t}$ play the parts of a 'disturbance' term. This in turn suggests that we can picture the extent of price–value deviations by drawing up a scatter diagram of the log of relative prices versus the log of relative values. Moreover, it also suggests that a natural form for cross-sectional and inter-temporal hypotheses is that empirical correlation between relative prices and relative values is log-linear.

*Cross-Sectional* Hypothesis $H_0$:

$$\ln p_{ij} = \alpha + \beta \ln \lambda_{ij} + u_{ij} \tag{20}$$

*Inter-Temporal* Hypothesis $H_0$:

$$\ln (p_{ij})_{\Delta t} = \alpha + \beta \ln (\lambda_{ij})_{\Delta t} + u_{ij}. \tag{21}$$

It is evident that we cannot develop this argument much further without resort to some evidence on actual dispersions of integrated capital–labour ratios, and, where possible, on the dispersions of price–value deviations themselves. We turn to that next.

## 3. Empirical Evidence

The line of reasoning I have adopted in the preceding sections is no accident. On the contrary, the very nature of Marx's conception of the relation between production and exchange forces us to pose not only the question of the differences between prices and values, but also the question of their inter-connections, their correlations. On this latter issue, it is interesting to note that most of the empirical evidence which I will draw upon in the discussion that follows has been available for quite some time. In a sense, the answers have been there all along. It is the questions, however, which have been missing.

### A. Marzi and Varri Data

Let me begin with the evidence on prices of production. Suppose we ask the following question: given an actual economy, what would the prices of production for this economy look like, and how would they compare to direct prices? We could answer this question by using an actual input–output table to calculate prices of production corresponding to different possible rates of profit, and then comparing these hypothetical prices of production to estimates of direct prices. Such experimental data, it turns out, already exists in the form of a study published in 1977 by Graziella Marzi and Paolo Varri (see appendix B). These authors take the 1959 and 1967 25-order input–output tables for the Italian economy, and for each year they calculate prices of production relative to the money wage, for profit rates ranging from $r = 0$ to $r = 0.80$, the maximum rate of profit. The basis of their calculations in Sraffa's circulating capital model which Steedman, for example, also uses in his numerical examples. I should point out, incidentally, that because this model abstracts from fixed capital the rates of profit it generates are higher than they would be otherwise. Since price–value deviations increase as profit rates increase, this means that such a model actually tends to exaggerate the extent of these deviations.

At $r = 0$, capitalists are assumed to make no profits, the calculated prices are proportional to values, and their ratios therefore equal relative values. At the other extreme, at $r = 0.80$, workers are assumed to receive no wages, so that labour does not enter at all into the costs of production, and the calculated prices in turn therefore bear no relation to labour-times. Clearly, neither extreme can be meaningfully said to represent prices of production. The relevant range has to be somewhere in between, and for the sake of illustration I will utilize the Marzi–Varri data for $r = 0.40$, the midpoint between the two extremes (see appendix B for the actual data). In figure 3 below, the vertical axis represents the natural logarithm of the ratios of individual prices of production to the average price of production, at $r = 0.40$. The

Figure 3

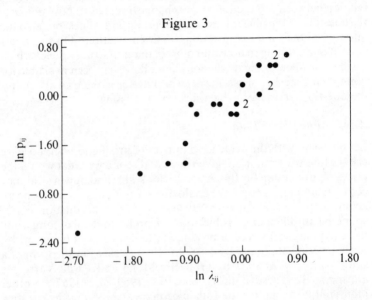

horizontal axis, on the other hand, represents the natural log of the ratios of individual values to the average value, which as I explained above can be calculated from the prices of production at $r = 0$. Lastly, this particular data refers to 1967. The corresponding data for 1959 gives virtually the same picture, though, with only a slightly lower correlation (see equation (22) below).

Since this sort of data is cross-sectional we can test the correlation between relative prices of production and relative values using the log-linear hypothesis of equation (20). The results of both the 1967 and 1959 tests are summarized in equation (22) below (t-ratios are given in parentheses below each coefficient).

For this data, we find that the typical percentage deviation (the absolute value of the average deviation as a percentage of the average price) is about 17% for 1967 and 19% for 1959.

*Cross-Sectional* (r = 0.40)

$$1967: \quad \ln p_{ij} = 0.0095 + 0.8470 \ln \lambda_{ij} \qquad (22)$$
$$(0.23) \quad (16.60)$$

$R^2 = 0.920$ (adjusted for degrees of freedom)

$$1959: \quad \ln p_{ij} = -0.0096 + 0.8717 \ln \lambda_{ij}$$
$$(-0.20) \quad (12.48)$$

$R^2 = 0.866$ (adjusted for degrees of freedom).

The above graph and regression results are unambiguous. The cross-sectional variations in the calculated prices of production are entirely dominated by the corresponding variations in relative values, with between 87% and 92% of the former being explained by the latter.

Because the data covers two different time periods, we can also use it to test the inter-temporal correlation between changes in relative prices and changes in relative values. Figure 4 below pictures $\ln(p_{ij})_{\Delta t}$ and $\ln(\lambda_{ij})_{\Delta t}$ on the vertical and horizontal axes, respectively, where both are in terms of 1959 prices relative to 1967 prices.

Figure 4

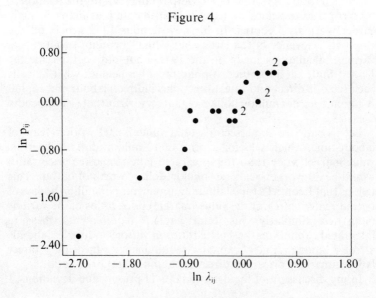

Using the log-linear inter-temporal hypothesis of equation (21) above, we get:

$$Inter\text{-}Temporal \ (r = 0.40)$$

$$1959/1967: \quad \ln (p_{ij})_{\Delta t} = \begin{array}{l} -0.0298 + 1.008 \ln (\lambda_{ij})_{\Delta t} \\ (-1.90) \quad\quad (16.08) \end{array} \quad (23)$$

$$R^2 = 0.915 \text{ (adjusted for degrees of freedom)}$$

In the light of the closeness of the cross-sectional correlation in each period, the closeness of the inter-temporal correlation is not surprising. Nonetheless, the above result tells us that almost 92% of the changes in calculated prices of production are explained by changes in calculated values. This is Ricardo with a vengeance—the very Ricardo scorned for over a century for having a so-called '93% theory' of prices of production! Of course, this particular aspect of Ricardo's analysis is carefully avoided by the neo-Ricardians.

## B. The Leontief Data

The Marzi-Varri data pertains to prices of production and values calculated from a 25-order input–output table. But for the relation of market prices to values, even more detailed data is available in some earlier work by Leontief. In his now famous 1953 article on the empirical relevance of the Heckscher-Ohlin Theorem, Leontief lists various calculations made on the 1947 input–output table for the United States at 190-order. Among these he includes what he calls each sector's direct and total (direct plus indirect) labour and capital requirements, per million dollars of that sector's output (see appendix C).

Let us suppose some sector's total value is 200 worker-years of labour-time, which sells for a price of 10 million dollars. Then its value/market price ratio (its integrated labour/market price ratio) would be 20 worker-years per million dollars worth of output. This tells us that Leontief's total labour requirements per million dollars of output really represent the value/(market) price ratios of the various industries. Similarly, his total capital requirements measure integrated capital/(market) price ratios in various industries, and his direct labour and capital requirements measure direct labour/(market) price and direct capital/(market) price ratios.[37]

In my discussion of the determinants of price–value deviations, I had argued on theoretical grounds that the integration process by which one moves from direct capital–labour (and profit–wage) ratios to the corresponding integrated ratios will greatly reduce the variations involved. Leontief's data enables us to test this proposition, since has direct and total labour and capital requirements data enable us to compute direct and integrated capital–labour ratios. We then find that although the coefficient of variation (the ratio of the standard deviation to the mean) of the direct ratios $(K/L)_i$ is 1.14, that of the integrated ratios $(K/L)_i^T$ is only 0.60. The integration process, in other words, cuts the degree of variation by almost 50%.

Leontief's data does not provide us with data on integrated profit–wage ratios. Nonetheless, we can approximate these by assuming that the integration process more or less averages out whatever variations exist in market profit rates and wage rates, so the ratio of the integrated profit rate to the integrated wage rate tends to be equal across industries.[38] Let $\bar{r}$ = the average profit rate in the economy as a whole, and $\bar{w}$ = the average money wage per worker-year. Then $(\pi/W)_i^T \cong (\bar{r}/\bar{w})(K/L)_i^T$. Since the coefficient of variation is unchanged when the variable is multiplied by a constant, this means that the coefficient of variation of $(\pi/W)_i^T$ is roughly 0.60 also.

Lastly, we saw earlier that it is the variations in $\left[1 + (\pi/W)_i^T\right]$ that are crucial for the deviations of market prices from values. For the US in 1947, $\bar{r} \cong 0.14$, and $\bar{w}$ = \$2612 per worker-year.[39] Using this data to estimate the term in brackets above, we get a coefficient of variation of about 0.20. We see therefore that in the end the disturbance term has only about 18% of the variability of direct capital–labour ratios. This is exactly the kind of result anticipated by the theoretical analysis in section IV.2.

Leontief's data enables us to do even more than this, however. Because his total labour requirements represent the ratios of total values to total sales for each of 190 sectors, we can use industry sales data to derive total values for each industry, and by using the average value–price ratio as the value of the dollar, we can derive direct prices from the values. These in turn can then be compared directly with market prices (sales). Figure 5 below is a graph of the natural log of relative market prices versus that of relative direct prices, for 190 sectors (the real estate and rental sector is excluded on theoretical grounds, since differential rent, though determined by surplus-value, is not expected to be proportional either to prices or to values).

The closeness of the correlation between market prices and direct prices is obvious. For this data, the typical deviation is about ±20%, and, as indicated below, a log-linear regression yields excellent results

Figure 5

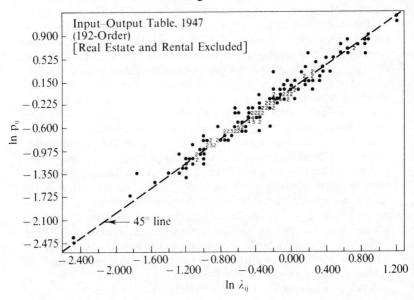

(standard errors are in parentheses below the coefficients. A parametric test indicates no significant heteroskedasticity in the data):[40]

*Cross-Sectional: 1947*

$$\ln (p_{ij}) = -0.00095 + 0.96809 \ln (\lambda_{ij}) \qquad (24)$$
$$\quad\quad\quad (0.0106) \quad\quad (0.01498)$$

$$R^2 = 0.95814$$

On the basis of data made available by Edward Wolff of New York University, I was able to repeat the preceding experiment for the 1967 input–output table, on 83-order data. The results are virtually identical to those for Leontief's data:

*Cross-Sectional: 1963*

$$\ln (p_{ij}) = 0.01380 + 0.99078 \ln (\lambda_{ij}) \qquad (25)$$
$$\quad\quad\quad (0.01457) \quad (0.02602)$$

$$R^2 = 0.94894$$

Both the preceding results attempt to test the relation between market prices and values directly. But we also have on hand indirect evidence on this very same issue, in the form of a very clever statistical test performed on business-cycle data by the US mathematician Jacob Schwartz. To understand the rationale of this test, let us look again at equation (13):

$$p_{ij} = \lambda_{ij} \cdot z_{ij}$$

where

$$z_{ij} \equiv \frac{1 + z_i}{1 + z_j}, \qquad z_i \equiv \left( \frac{\pi}{W} \right)^T_i$$

This quite general relation tells us that relative prices equal relative values times a disturbance term $z_{ij}$, a term whose elements are dependent on the integrated profit–wage ratios of the two commodities involved.

In the course of a business cycle, the movement from peak to trough can be very rapid, usually taking less than a year. Both because of the phase of the cycle and the short length of time involved, there is little change in the structure of production under these circumstances but there are large fluctuations in outputs and profits. Since $\lambda_{ij}$ reflects the (input–output) structure of production and $z_{ij}$ the conditions of profitability, the relative prices in this phase of a business cycle are bound to primarily reflect the variations in the disturbance term $z_{ij}$: variations which are themselves likely to be abnormally high because of the very turbulent conditions under which they are examined.

Reasoning in a similar way, Schwartz proceeds to examine relative price movements for the average of four business cycles from 1919–1938 (one of these 'business cycles' is the Great Depression!). His results, summarized below, once again reveal that even under these extreme circumstances the average relative price variation is about 7%.

It is interesting that a brilliant mathematician like Jacob Schwartz should so strikingly parallel Ricardo's famous argument while the many grey eminences who populate mathematical economics should so confidently dismiss it as being unrigorous. But then, no doubt this is in good part because much of the so-called mathematics in mathematical economics is merely bourgeois economics in thin disguise.

Figure 6

Peak to Trough Average Prices, Relative to the
Wholesale Price Level, For 4 Cycles 1919–1938

| | % Variation |
|---|---|
| Wholesale Prices of Semi-Manufactured Goods | 0.07 |
| Raw Materials | 0.09 |
| Wholesale Foods | 0.02 |
| Retail Foods | 0.04 |
| Pig Iron | 0.12 |
| Farm Prices | 0.10 |
| (Simple) Average | 0.07 |

## 4. Summary of the Empirical Evidence

The results of the previous section can now be briefly summarized. In general, for both prices of production and for market prices, the typical percentage deviation (the sum of the absolute values of deviations divided by the sum of prices) is moderate: for the price of production data it is of the order of $\pm 17$–$19\%$; and for the market price data of the order of $\pm 20$–$25\%$. The fact that for an individual commodity a typical deviation is on the order of $\pm 20\%$ means that when we consider a bundle of commodities such as those consumed by capitalists, then the net deviation $\bar{\delta}_F$ of this bundle is likely to be much smaller than $\pm 20\%$ because negative and positive deviations will tend to offset each other. This justifies the assumption that $\bar{\delta}_F \cong 10\%$, which I used earlier (see p. 65) to estimate aggregate profit and profit-rate deviations from their corresponding value categories.

A typical deviation of $\pm 20\%$ of course implies that the typical non-deviation is on the order of $\pm 80\%$. In other words, it implies that the variations in prices are likely to be highly correlated with corresponding variations in values. And we find that this is just the case. For price of production data, the cross-sectional regression yields an $R^2 = 0.92$ for 1967 and $R^2 = 0.87$ for 1959, while the inter-temporal regression yields an $R^2 = 0.92$. For market price data, we get a cross-sectional $R^2 = 0.96$ for 1947 and $R^2 = 0.95$ for 1963. Finally, on the basis of the data utilized by Jacob Schwartz, we find that even under the turbulent conditions of business cycle downturns, relative price variations are small enough (about 7%) for us to conclude that by far the major source of variations in relative prices over a period of several years will be the variations in the corresponding relative values. Ricardo, it seems, had a vastly superior grasp of these issues than the neo-Ricardians.

## V. Summary and Conclusions

Throughout this paper, I have tried to emphasize that Marx's conception of capitalist production and reproduction is quite distinct from that underlying the work of many modern Marxists (such as Steedman). I have particularly stressed Marx's concept of the relative autonomy of the sphere of circulation, because it is only thus that it becomes possible to understand why and how prices can differ systematically from values and yet at the same time be regulated by them. Moreover, the preceding conceptions enable us to examine the status of arguments concerning so-called redundancies and inconsistencies between values and prices. Even accepting the conventional mathematical formulations on these subjects, it becomes possible to show that these formulations exhibit a set of properties which remain hidden to the neo-Ricardians because they lack (or refuse) the conceptions necessary to uncover them. These properties are, moreover, by and large exactly those anticipated by Marx.

To take an example, it is a well-known mathematical result that the transformation from direct prices (prices proportional to values) to prices of production will in general cause the transformed rate of profit to deviate from the overall value rate of profit. To the critics of Marx, this difference implies a break, a complete divorce of any inner connection. But the notion of relative autonomy requires us to show not only how and why such a difference can exist, but also how and why its effects are strictly limited. This approach then enables us to show that the value rate of profit and its transformed rate necessarily move together: in the mirror of circulation, the value rate of profit appears as a displaced image, somewhat different in magnitude but essentially the same in determination. Further consideration enables us to argue that even the displacement effect is likely to be quite small, with typical differences in magnitude of the order of 8–10%.

These results for the economy as a whole are then extended to individual price-value deviations, which are important in their own right because they mediate the transfer of value between capitals, between regions and even between nations. Here too, it becomes possible to argue on both theoretical and empirical grounds that these deviations are strictly limited in magnitude ($\pm 20\%$ for the absolute value of the typical deviation) and even more limited in scope since deviations of this magnitude necessarily imply a high co-variation of prices and values. This latter concept of co-variation is very important because Marx's argument (and Ricardo's also) that the variations in prices are dominated by variations in values can be expressed in terms of the correlation between the two. Theoretical considerations developed in this paper provide strong support for Marx's argument, and what is more, a variety of empirical tests of the relations involved fully bear out the theoretical expectations. As a typical result, for both prices of production and market prices, roughly 93% of both cross-sectional and inter-temporal variations in these prices can be explained by the corresponding variations in values.

As I noted earlier, these are results which can be derived from the very same framework that the neo-Ricardians themselves use to criticize Marx. It is a great irony that this so-called Ricardo–Marx tradition is so adamant in its opposition to these fundamental theses of Ricardo and Marx, while at the same time its own ties to orthodox economics are seldom explicitly acknowledged.[42]

In ending, I might note that the issues I have analysed here are only a small part of those that could be treated in a similar manner. I have not treated fixed capital or joint production, for example, nor indeed the striking absence of money in an algebraic framework which claims to represent the formation of prices. Each of these issues can and must be addressed, and when they are, even the algebra behind which the neo-Ricardians hide will become increasingly transparent.

### Appendix A

In the case of a circulating capital model, prices reflecting arbitrary positive profits can be written as:

$$p = p(A + bl) + \pi \tag{1}$$

where $p$ = row vector of unit prices
$\quad A$ = input–output coefficients matrix
$\quad b$ = column vector of wage-goods per worker
$\quad l$ = row vector of labour coefficients
$\quad \pi$ = row vector of profits per unit output.

By definition, direct prices are prices proportional to value. These can be expressed as:

$$\mathbf{p}^0 \;=\; \mathbf{p}^0(\mathbf{A}+\mathbf{bl})+\pi^0 \tag{2}$$

where $\mathbf{p}^0$ = row vector of unit direct prices

$\mathbf{p}^0(\mathbf{A}+\mathbf{bl})$ = row vector of unit direct cost-prices

$\pi^0$ = row vector of unit direct profits.

Lastly, outputs in reproduction can be written as:

$$\mathbf{x} \;=\; (\mathbf{A}+\mathbf{bl})\mathbf{x} \cdot (1+g)+\mathbf{f} \tag{3}$$

where $\mathbf{x}$ = column vector of industry outputs

$\mathbf{f}$ = column vector of commodities consumed by the capitalist class

$g$ = the rate of growth.

In simple reproduction, $\mathbf{f}$ absorbs the whole surplus product (i.e. $\mathbf{f}=\mathbf{x}-(\mathbf{A}+\mathbf{bl})\mathbf{x}$), whereas at the other extreme of maximum expanded reproduction, $\mathbf{f}=\mathbf{\Phi}$ (where $\mathbf{\Phi}$ is a null vector).

If we hold the sum of prices (the purchasing power of money) as constant, then:

$$\mathbf{p}^0\mathbf{x} \;=\; \mathbf{px} \tag{4}$$

Multiplying (3) by $\mathbf{p}$ and $\mathbf{p}^0$, respectively, subtracting the latter from the former, and recalling (4), we get:

$$(\mathbf{p}-\mathbf{p}^0)(\mathbf{A}+\mathbf{bl})\mathbf{x} \;=\; \left[\frac{1}{1+g}\right](\mathbf{p}-\mathbf{p}^0)\mathbf{f} \tag{5}$$

On the other hand, multiplying (1) and (2) by x, subtracting, and recalling (4), we get:

$$(\mathbf{p}-\mathbf{p}^0)(\mathbf{A}+\mathbf{bl})\mathbf{x} \;=\; \pi^0\mathbf{x}-\pi\mathbf{x} \tag{6}$$

The first term on the right-hand side of (6) is the mass of direct profits and the second is the mass of actual profits. Designating these scalars by $\Pi^0$ and $\Pi$, respectively, and combining (5) and (6):

$$\Pi^0-\Pi=\frac{1}{1+g}(\mathbf{p}-\mathbf{p}^0)\mathbf{f} \tag{7}$$

Let $p_i$, $p_i^0$, and $f_i$ represent the i-th components of $\mathbf{p}$, $\mathbf{p}^0$, and $\mathbf{f}$, respectively, for $i=1,\ldots,n$. Then:

$$\Pi - \Pi^0 = \frac{1}{1+g} \sum_{i=1}^{n} (p_i^0 - p_i) f_i$$

Let $\mathbf{pf} = F =$ the money value of the goods consumed by the capitalist class, and $p_i f_i = F_i =$ their expenditure on the i-th good. Then:

$$\frac{\Pi^0 - \Pi}{\Pi} = \frac{1}{1+g} \frac{F}{\Pi} \sum_{i=1}^{N} \frac{(p_i^0 - p_i)}{p_i} \frac{F_i^0}{F}$$

The term in the summation sign is a weighted average of the individual price/direct price percentage deviations, the weights being determined by the pattern of capitalist expenditures on various commodities. Since $F_i = 0$ for all goods which are not consumed by the capitalist class, the term in the summation sign clearly represents the average price-value deviation of capitalist consumption goods. This deviation, it should be noted, is likely to be much smaller than a typical individual deviation because negative and positive deviations will tend to offset each other.

**Appendix B**

(Graziella Marzi and Paolo Varri, *Variazioni de Produttivita Nell' Economia Italiana: 1959–1967*, Bologna 1977)

In Marzi-Varri's notation, $_iw_t$ represents the reciprocal of the i-th price of production relative to the money wage (the wage-price), for the year t (t = 1959, 1967). These are listed for rates of profit from $r = 0$ to $r = 0.85$. The actual maximum rate of profit is $r = 0.80$, however. For reasons explained in the text I select the midpoint, $r = 0.40$.

Cross-sectional relative prices of production are formed for year t, $r = 0.40$, by expressing the i-th wage-price relative to the average wage-price, the latter calculated as a simple average of the individual wage-prices. Cross-sectional relative values are formed in the same way, by using the $r = 0$ data.

Inter-temporal data is formed by dividing 1959 relative prices of production by the corresponding 1967 data, and by dividing 1959 relative values by the 1967 ones.

*Techniques of Calculation*

1. In theory, an input–output matrix $\mathbf{A}$ and the corresponding row vector of direct labour-coefficients $\mathbf{L}$ are:

$$\mathbf{A} \equiv [a_{ij}] \equiv [x_{ij}/x_j]$$
$$\mathbf{L} \equiv [l_j] \equiv [l_j/x_j]$$

where $x_j$ = amount of commodity j, produced in a given year

$x_{ij}$ = amount of commodity i used in the production of commodity j, in a given year

$l_j$ = worker-years of direct labour employed in the production of commodity j in a given year.

From this we may derive the vector of total labour coefficients:

$$\lambda = \mathbf{L} \cdot [\mathbf{I} - \mathbf{A}]^{-1}$$

2. In practice, however, input–output coefficients are measured in terms of the dollar cost of the i-th input per dollar of the j-th output. If we let $\mathbf{A}^*$ be the matrix whose coefficients are costs per dollar of output, and $\mathbf{L}^*$, the vector of direct labour requirements per dollar of output in each sector, then:

$$\mathbf{A}^* \equiv [a_{ij}^*] \equiv [(p_i x_{ij})/(p_j x_j)]$$

$$\mathbf{L}^* \equiv [\mathbf{L}_j^*] \equiv [l_j/(p_j x_j)]$$

where $p_j$ = the money price of the commodity. From this, we may define the vector $\lambda^*$ as:

$$\lambda^* \equiv \mathbf{L}^* [\mathbf{I} - \mathbf{A}^*]^{-1}.$$

The question is, what does $\lambda^*$ represent and what is its relation to $\lambda$?

3. We begin by noting that we can relate $(\mathbf{A}, \mathbf{L})$ to $(\mathbf{A}^*, \mathbf{L}^*)$ through a diagonal matrix $\langle \mathbf{P}_i \rangle$ whose elements are the unit prices $p_i$:

$$\mathbf{A}^* = \langle \mathbf{P}_i \rangle \mathbf{A} \langle \mathbf{P}_i \rangle^{-1}$$

$$\mathbf{L}^* = \mathbf{l} \langle \mathbf{P}_i \rangle^{-1}$$

It follows, therefore, that:

$$\lambda^* = \mathbf{L}^* [\mathbf{I} - \mathbf{A}^*]^{-1} = \mathbf{L} \langle \mathbf{P} \rangle^{-1} [\mathbf{I} - \langle \mathbf{P}_i \rangle \mathbf{A} \langle \mathbf{P} \rangle^{-1}]^{-1}$$

Since, $\mathbf{I} = \langle \mathbf{P}_i \rangle \langle \mathbf{P}_i \rangle^{-1}$, we may write:

$$\lambda^* = \mathbf{L} \langle \mathbf{P}_i \rangle^{-1} [\langle \mathbf{P}_i \rangle \langle \mathbf{P}_i \rangle^{-1} - \langle \mathbf{P}_i \rangle \mathbf{A} \langle \mathbf{P}_i \rangle^{-1}]^{-1}$$

$$\lambda^* = \mathbf{L} \langle \mathbf{P}_i \rangle^{-1} [\langle \mathbf{P}_i \rangle (\mathbf{I} - \mathbf{A}) \langle \mathbf{P}_i \rangle^{-1}]^{-1}$$

The term in square brackets is the product of three matrices; its inverse is therefore the product of their inverses, in reverse order: $(\mathbf{ABC})^{-1} = \mathbf{C}^{-1} \mathbf{B}^{-1} \mathbf{A}^{-1}$:

$$\lambda^* = L\langle P_i\rangle^{-1}\langle P_i\rangle(I-A)^{-1}\langle P_i\rangle^{-1}$$
$$\lambda^* = \{L(I-A)^{-1}\}\langle P_i\rangle^{-1}$$
$$\lambda^* = \lambda\langle P_i\rangle^{-1}$$

Thus, the j-th element $\lambda_j^* = \lambda_j/p_j$. That is, each element of the row vector $\lambda^*$ is in fact the ratio of total labour requirements per unit output. Clearly, this ratio is independent of any choice of the unit of output (lbs., tons, etc.)

4. The preceding results point to a simple way of deriving the data necessary for our calculations. Beginning with the empirical input–output matrix $A^*$ and the corresponding vector $L^*$ direct labour requirements per dollar of output, we can immediately calculate $\lambda^*$, total labour requirements per dollar of each sector's output. These correspond to the data we used from Leontief. The elements of $\lambda^*$ are $\lambda_j/p_j$. Hence if we know the gross sales $p_j/x_j$ for each sector, we can immediately derive the total labour requirements $\lambda_j x_j$ which correspond to these sales (even though we do not at any time actually define any units of output $x_j$).

$$\lambda_j x_j = \frac{\lambda_j}{p_j}p_j x_j = \lambda_j^*(p_j x_j)$$

The last operation gives us total labour requirements $\lambda_j x_j$ in worker-years and total prices (gross sales) $p_j x_j$ in dollars.

5. Two data sets were used, in which $\Lambda_j = \lambda_j x_j$ and $p_j = p_j x_j$ are derived in manner indicated in 4 above. Defining the average value of the dollar as $\alpha \equiv (\sum \Lambda_j)/(\sum P_j)$, we can then use this to define total direct prices $P_j^0 = (1/\alpha)\Lambda_j$. Finally, both $P_i^0$ and $P_j$ are expressed as prices relative to their respective average prices $\bar{P}^0 = (\sum P_j^0/N)$ and $\bar{P} = (\sum P_j/N)$. Note that by construction, $\bar{P}^0 = \bar{P}$.

The first data set is based on Leontief's 1947 data, from W. Leontief, *Input–Output Economics*, Oxford, New York, 1966, appendix III, pp. 129–133. Total Sales $P_j$ were taken from US 1947 input–output table, 192-order.

The second set was provided by Edward Wolff of New York University. In this data, the direct labour requirements vector was computed in two ways: first, in worker-years of undifferentiated labour requirements; and second, in a skill-weighted index of worker-years where relative wages were used as weights (for lack of better indexes). The latter data are the ones actually shown, but the regression results are substantially the same with either set.

Lastly, both the graphs and regressions leave out the real estate and rental sector, since on theoretical grounds within both the Ricardian and Marxist theories of rent, though the magnitude of rent can be derived from value relations it is not related to any labour-time expended in the collection of rent (in the real estate and rental sector). Once again, however, this makes little difference to the log-regression results.

# Marx, Sraffa and the Neo-Classicals in Context

## Hector Guillén Romero

### I. Introduction

Although the terms 'neo-Ricardian school' or 'Cambridge school' are sometimes applied to the contribution on growth theory of Joan Robinson, Nicholas Kaldor, Luigi Pasinetti and others, in this work I deal almost exclusively with the theory of prices elaborated by Piero Sraffa.[1] The school's methodological foundations can be found in the works of Dmitriev and von Bortkiewicz, who wrote at the turn of the century.[2] These authors' importance has grown recently following the publication of Sraffa's work.

The neo-Ricardian school can be assessed either in relation to Marxist value theory or in relation to neo-classical theory, whether in its vulgar form (Jevons, Menger, Marshall) or its general equilibrium form (Arrow, Hahn, Malinvaud, Walras).

### 1. Neo-classicals and Neo-Ricardians

The neo-Ricardian school rejects subjective individualism and the role of supply and demand in the determination of income distribution. A recognition of the class division of society is central to its analysis.[3] It makes an internal critique of vulgar economics, showing that many of its propositions are inconsistent with its own assumptions. In particular Sraffa shows that neo-classical capital theory is incoherent and indeterminate in its vulgar version. This critical wing, fully developed since Sraffa's book appeared, seemed to have culminated in the works of the Cambridge school on macro economic production functions and problems related to the choice of techniques.[4]

While these attacks are fundamentally internal, the neo-Ricardians make a basically external critique of general equilibrium theory.

Indeed, as A. Medio recognizes,[5] general equilibrium theory is unaffected by the attacks levelled at the vulgar economists on the logical plane. His argument is that concepts such as capital, profit, or interest play no essential role in this theory, which is unable to confront socially important problems because it lacks the necessary conceptual tools. For Medio, its weakest methodological points are the individualism used in the study of the behaviour of economic agents, the technologism used in studying the production process, and the concept of an economic system as an exchange economy. The concepts of class and social production relations naturally do not enter equilibrium theory. It is, furthermore, essentially static, in the sense that it has no means of studying processes—the laws of motion which lead the system from one state to another.

## 2. Marxists and neo-Ricardians

Many economists have dealt with neo-Ricardian theory as if it were in continuity with the Marxist tradition, a view decreasingly acceptable to the Sraffians themselves and which this paper sets out to refute. Ronald Meek and Maurice Dobb have hailed Sraffa for 'rehabilitating' Marx. Meek, in his introduction to the second edition of his *Studies in the Labour Theory of Value*[6] presents Sraffa's system so as to show how some of its basic elements can be adapted and used by modern Marxists. Meek presents a sequence of five models of the Sraffa type linked by a kind of 'logical-historical' analysis similar to Marx's. From the outset he claims to show that a modern Marxist can reformulate and develop Marx's original theory with commodities themselves, rather than their values, taken as 'concrete prior magnitudes'. For Meek the transformation problem can be properly resolved only by postulating, in one form or another, specific interrelations between inputs and production. Finally, he concludes that Sraffa's procedure reflects Marx's basic idea, that prices and incomes are in the last instance determined by production relations, more clearly and effectively than Marx's.[7]

Maurice Dobb holds a similar view.[8] He affirms that what is particularly striking (some would say revolutionary) about the Sraffian system is its rehabilitation of the Ricardo-Marx approach to problems of distribution from the production side, so that relative prices are independent of the pattern of consumption and demand.

From Sraffa onward there have been many mathematical models in which relative prices are derived directly from the conditions of production without being affected by the pattern of demand. If we accept, with Dobb, that Marxist value theory is essentially a theory about 'conditions of production' in which relations of exchange have a subsidiary or almost superfluous function, we can easily derive the similarity between Marx and Sraffa.

A very similar line has been followed by other Italian authors. For Alessandro Roncaglia,[9] Marxist theory offers an underlying interpretation of capitalist society through which Sraffian concepts such as commodity, price, wage and profit can be understood. The problem of relative prices, which Sraffa confronts, is for this reason described as 'internal' to the study of the capitalist system, presupposing the institutional framework studied by Marx.[10] Thus for Roncaglia, many of Sraffa's concepts only find their fullest explanation in Marx's more general analysis. Sraffa, he says, is writing after Marx, and can thus presuppose the Marxist analysis of capitalist society without having to restate it. Roncaglia even claims that thanks to Sraffa Marxism now has a more scientific foundation.

## 3. The Importance of Studying Neo-Ricardianism

Bourgeois economic thought is divided into two camps, neo-classical and neo-Ricardian. The neo-Ricardians have rejected marginalist positions *en bloc* after an internal critique, and have returned to the earliest formulations of bourgeois economics, particularly to those of the physiocrats, of Smith and of Ricardo. We are dealing here with what Sergio Latouche calls the reswitching of dominant ideologies.[11]

The neo-Ricardian position is not yet hegemonic within dominant economic thinking, but is making progress—although in recent years the neo-classical school has been in the ascendant under the pressure of conservative policies and monetarism. The critical presentation of neo-Ricardian theory is very important, not just because this theory plays a role in dominant economic thinking but because it has begun to win some influence within the workers' movement. Sraffa's emulators, for instance, are advisors to the FLM, the most important industrial trade-union federation in Italy. Moreover the 'Cambridge School' has its defenders in the heart of the Italian Communist Party and among many on the far left.[12]

Just as alarming were views expressed by participants in a value theory seminar at Modena University in 1978. Most accepted that Marxist value theory was invalid, and the entire discussion turned on whether this jeopardized the whole of Marx's theoretical edifice or only part of it. The commonest positions were those of Garegnani and Coletti. For Garegnani, essentially, the labour theory of value does not apply. The concept of surplus can supplant that of value and can be used, as by Sraffa, to determine prices and the profit rate.[13] In Garegnani's view this does not prevent us referring back to *Capital* for an explanation of phenomena such as accumulation and capitalist crisis. Coletti agrees that Marxist value theory is invalid but argues, more coherently than Garegnani, that this calls into question the greater part of Marx's analysis, since one can neither define the concept of commodity nor that of competition without the concept of value in Marx's system.[14] Another position worth considering for its implications is Napoleoni's. He holds that the autonomy of the value category in Marx is such that, even if it cannot be used to derive the rate of profit or prices, it can and must be discussed at a philosophical level.[15]

Although neo-Ricardian theory can be assessed either in relation to Marxist value theory or to neo-classical theory, in this essay I concentrate almost exclusively on its relation to Marxist theory. The essay is divided into two parts. In the first part I give a summary of Sraffa's scheme, and in the second I assess its relation to Marxist analysis.

## II. Piero Sraffa's System of Prices of Production

Piero Sraffa's work is essentially a study of prices of production and the influence on them of distributional variables such as the wage rate and the profit rate. He does not take into account problems concerning production and employment levels, income distribution, growth and such like.[16] This is because he wants to concentrate on an economic system whose properties do not depend on variations in the scale of production or in the proportion of its 'factors'. This precise limitation on the object of study renders it susceptible to an 'exact' treatment, in the same sense as in the mathematical sciences.

Sraffa's analysis is developed in four stages. He first presents us with a perfectly closed productive process, that is to say a process in which the same commodities appear both as means of production and as products. Furthermore, the quantities produced of each good (which are taken as given) are exactly equal to the quantities used as means of production. In this 'subsistence' economy, there is no surplus, but simply the minimum necessary for the economy to reproduce itself in the same form and with the same dimensions. Labour (and its wage) are represented as any other commodity, that is to say they form part of the means of production.[17] The problem thus reduces to that of finding the relative prices of the various commodities. These prices should be such that, respecting the law of equality between the 'values' of production (prices of physical quantities of products) and the 'values' of costs (prices of physical quantities of means of production), the initial position of the system can be restored. The system of prices of production can be formalized as follows:

Let us denote by A, B, ..., K the quantities of commodities a, b, ..., k produced annually. Let us denote by $A_a$, $B_b$, ..., $K_a$ the quantities of these commodities needed for the production, of A, and similarly for B, ..., K. The amounts produced and the technological requirements of production are given as data. The unknowns to be determined are the prices of the k commodities $P_a$, $P_b$, ..., $P_k$. As we can see these prices result from the technology and they play no role in the assignment of resources. The only thing they do is signal those 'values' of units of the commodities, a, b, ..., k which, if adopted, will allow the initial position of the system to be re-established. This subsistence system can be written as follows:

$$A_a P_a + B_a P_b + \cdots + K_a P_k = A P_a$$
$$A_b P_a + B_b P_b + \cdots + K_b P_k = B P_b$$
$$\cdots \cdots \cdots \cdots \cdots \cdots \cdots \cdots \cdots$$
$$A_k P_a + B_k P_b + \cdots + K_k P_k = K P_k$$

Since by the definition of subsistence economy $A = A_a + A_b + \cdots + A_k$, and the same for **B** $\cdots$ **K**, any one of the equations can be deduced from the sum of the others. Therefore this system contains $k - 1$ independent equations which determine $k - 1$ relative prices. The prices are expressed in terms of a commodity chosen as unit of measurement, whose price is set equal to 1.

One of the effects of the appearance of a surplus is the introduction of the notion of luxury, or non-basic goods. Luxury products are those used neither as means of production nor as means of subsistence in the production of others. Obviously, this category of product could not exist in a subsistence model, since the surplus being by definition zero, every commodity played the role of product and instrument of production at one and the same time.

Luxury products do not figure in the determination of the system. Their role is purely passive. If, for example, says Sraffa, we were to eliminate one equation corresponding to the production of a luxury good, we would eliminate an unknown (the price of this good) which would appear only in this equation and the remaining equations would continue to form a determinate system which would admit of the same solutions as the previous one. This would not happen if we were to eliminate a non-luxury good, which Sraffa designates a basic product (a good which enters into the production of every good, either directly or indirectly).

In the *second* stage Sraffa introduces a surplus. He maintains the hypothesis that inputs and outputs are made up of the same commodities. The difference is that the technological structure is such that the quantity of each good produced can be equal to or greater than that used as means of production. The 'value' of production (price of the physical quantity produced) will be greater than that of the costs (price of the physical quantity consumed) because there is a surplus. The equation system which expresses this schema simultaneously determines the set of relative prices and the general rate of profit. This general rate of profit manifests the fact that the surplus (or profit) is distributed to each productive activity in proportion to the 'value' of means of production used up. As in the preceding stage, labour is not present in its direct form, but only through the commodities consumed by workers. The workers, and these commodities, appear as part of the means of production.

In this case we denote the rate of profit by r, and the system of prices of production can be written as follows:

$$(A_a P_a + B_a P_b + \cdots + K_a P_k)(1+r) = AP_a$$
$$(A_b P_a + B_b P_b + \cdots + K_b P_k)(1+r) = BP_b$$
$$\vdots \qquad \vdots \qquad \qquad \vdots \quad \vdots \qquad \vdots$$
$$(A_k P_a + B_k P_b + \cdots + K_k P_k)(1+r) = KP_k$$

$$\tag{1}$$

Since $A \geqslant A_a + A_b + \cdots + A_k$; $B \geqslant B_a + B_b + \cdots + B_k, \ldots$, with at least one strict inequality, we have k independent equations which simultaneously determine the $k-1$ relative prices and the rate of profit.

In the *third* stage, Straffa changes the assumptions concerning wages which he made in the two previous stages. Previously it was assumed that wages were represented by the means of subsistence needed by the workers, so that they appeared in the system on the same level as vehicles or fuel consumption. But in reality wages can contain not just the ever-present element of subsistence (which is constant) but also a share of the surplus (which is variable).

In this situation, the most correct procedure would be to divide the wage into its two component parts, that is to say, to continue to treat those goods needed for the workers' subsistence as means of production, like fuel, and deal with the variable element as part of the surplus of the system. We then have a net or surplus product which divides up into wages and profits. The wage rate and the profit rate are not simultaneously determined by this equation system, so that one of the magnitudes has to be externally determined and the other will be determined as a function of it. In this case, as Sraffa indicates 'the system can move with one degree of freedom; and if one of the variables is fixed the others will be fixed too.'[18]

If we call the given quantities of labour of uniform quality $L_a$, $L_b, \ldots, L_k$ (not labour power as Altvater, Hoffman and Semmler erroneously do!)[19] and if we denote by w the wage per unit of labour, the system of production prices appears in the following form:

$$
\begin{aligned}
(A_a P_a + B_a P_b + \cdots + K_a P_k)(1+r) + L_a w &= AP_a \\
(A_b P_a + B_b P_b + \cdots + K_b P_k)(1+r) + L_b w &= BP_b \\
&\vdots \\
(A_k P_a + B_k P_b + \cdots + K_k P_k)(1+r) + L_k w &= KP_k
\end{aligned}
\tag{2}
$$

If we set the price of the net total product equal to 1, we will have the following additional equation:

$$
[A - (A_a + A_b + \cdots + A_k)]P_a + [B - (B_a + B_b + \cdots + B_k)]P_b + \cdots \\
+ [K - (K_a + K_b + \cdots + K_k)]P_k = 1 \tag{3}
$$

The system will now consist of $k+1$ equations and $k+2$ variables (k prices, the wage w and the rate of profit r). The system has *one degree of freedom*: if we now fix the level of one of the distributional variables (wage or profit rate) as an independent variable, we can determine prices and the other distributional variables.

### The Search for the Standard Commodity

One of the important aspects of Sraffa's work is that it introduces a very special unit of measurement of value. In order to understand this measure we must refer to Ricardo's aims in explaining the general rate of profit beginning from the rate of profit in agriculture.

If we assume as Ricardo did in his famous essay of 1815[20] that in agriculture only one good is produced—corn—and that the subsistence of agricultural workers consists only of corn, then the rate of profit in agriculture, that is to say the relation between the surplus agricultural product and what was set aside for the agricultural labourers' means of subsistence can be calculated directly as such, without recourse to the price of goods, provided that the terms of the relation are physically homogeneous. Thus, in the agricultural sector, the rate of profit does not vary as a result of changes in real wages. But since the rate of profit has to be the same in all productive activities, the price system must be such as to allow equality of rates of profit in other sectors with that which holds in agriculture.

Malthus exposed an important defect in this reasoning. There is no economic sector, not even agriculture, where both capital advanced and all the results of production consists of a single product. Wages are not made up of corn alone. Workers consume manufactured goods. This means that the calculation of the rate of profit involves a comparison of aggregate of heterogenous goods, with the product, wages and total investment. But in order to compare these heterogenous goods they must be converted into common units.

To overcome this objection, Ricardo sought a unit of value capable of measuring, as if dealing with a single quantity, the heterogeneous mass of produced goods. His theory required a *measure of value* which would make it possible to convert into a homogeneous unit of measurement, analogous to the unit of corn in his simple model, the heterogeneous groups of goods divided up in the form of rent, profit and wages. Now, the heterogeneous goods could be converted into a homogeneous measurement as a function of their relations of exchange on the market, that is to say, as a function of their relative prices. But from this a complication arises, since these prices depend on the rate of profit.

In confronting this same problem, Adam Smith had previously tried to formulate a theory of labour value.[21] In order to explain exchange-value, he begins from a hypothetical society in which everyone works and exchanges the products of their labour. In such a society, according to Smith, products would be exchanged in proportion to the quantity of labour needed for their production. If this did not happen, some members of society would lose out and the exchange system could not function. In constructing this model, Smith tried to refer to a primitive type of society. But contemporary sociologists have shown that primitive exchange differs greatly from Smith's conception. In reality, we have had to wait until capitalist economies came into being to find a way of life in which labour expended in production determined exchange relations. Smith, on the other hand, thought that his explanation of value was not valid for a capitalist economy. In fact for him, if the natural price of a commodity were equal to the amount of wages paid in order to obtain it, everything would be very simple. An object for which twice as much had to be paid would necessarily be an object into which twice as much labour had gone. But the price includes capital's profit.

Can we say that the profit on capital is the remuneration of a kind of work, that of the firm's management? No, because for Smith profits and wages are determined by completely different principles. Profits depend solely on the amount of capital employed and are greater or small depending on the size of this capital. Smith did not think it possible to maintain that the exchange value of products would be determined by labour costs in the economy he contemplated. But intending to maintain a relation between exchange value and labour, he finally declared that the normal price of each object corresponded to the amount of labour which could be 'commanded', that is, bought with the object—a solution which failed to overcome the problem of the dependence of prices and profit rates.

To avoid this complication of the interdependence of relative prices and the rate of profit, Ricardo tried to find an 'invariable measure of values'. He scouted a number of possibilities, one of which was the elaboration of a theory of labour-values, but he realized that labour-values did not precisely reflect relative prices. He also attempted to take an 'average' good as a standard, but realized that only limited progress could be made in this direction. In fact, as he recorded in his *Principles*, 'when commodities varied in relative value it would be desirable to have the means of ascertaining which of them fell and which rose in real value, and this can be effected only by comparing them one after another with some invariable standard of measure of value, which should itself be subject to none of the fluctuations to which other commodities are exposed'. Unfortunately, he adds 'Of such a measure it is impossible to be possessed, because there is no commodity which is not itself exposed to the same variations as the things the value of which is to be ascertained; that is, there is none which is not subject to require more or less labour for its production.'[22] This idea was maintained in his final written work, shortly before his death, in which he confessed that 'there is no perfect measure of value in nature'.[23]

Ricardo's idea of using an 'average good' as a standard of value has resurfaced with Sraffa. Sraffa shows how such a good can be conceived as a composite good and used in the analysis of income distribution over a given period in an economy which produces reproducible goods.[24] He analyses the effects of a variation in wages on prices and on the rate of profit, taking into account the fact that the rate of profit is the same in all branches—the hypothesis of the equalization of profit rates.

He supposes furthermore that production methods do not change and that quantities produced remain given. Under these conditions Sraffa seeks a commodity which, although it will be no less susceptible than any other to rises or falls in price with respect to individual commodities,[25] as a result of movements in the wage rate, will be such that we would know with certainty that 'any such fluctuations would originate exclusively in the peculiarities of production of the commodity which was being compared with it, and not in its own.'[26]

'It is not likely that an individual commodity could be found which possessed even approximately the necessary requisites', he notes.[27] But a 'composite commodity' could be produced, that is, an aggregate of commodities such that the commodities which compose it also figure, in the same proportions, in the means of production of the aggregate. Sraffa calls this aggregate the *standard commodity* and uses the term *standard system* to refer to the set of industries concerned, taken in the proportions needed to produce the standard commodity.

### The Standard System

The formal method of construction of the standard commodity is equivalent to taking a set of K appropriate multipliers which can be designated $q_a, q_b, \ldots, q_k$ and applying them respectively to the equations of production of the commodities A, B, ..., K. 'The multipliers', says Sraffa, 'must be such that the resulting quantities of the various commodities will bear the same proportions to one another on the right-hand sides of the equations (as products) as they do on the aggregate of the left hand sides (as means of production).'[28] This implies that the percentage by which the production of a commodity exceeds the quantity entering as means of production will be equal for all commodities. This percentage Sraffa calls the standard relation, and denotes it by R.

Under these conditions the system q can be written down as follows:

$$(A_aq_a + A_bq_b + \cdots + A_kq_k)(1+R) = Aq_a$$

$$(B_aq_a + B_bq_b + \cdots + B_kq_k)(1+R) = Bq_b$$

$$\vdots \qquad \vdots \qquad\qquad \vdots \qquad \vdots \qquad\qquad \vdots \qquad (4)$$

$$(K_aq_a + K_bq_b + \cdots + K_kq_k)(1+R) = Kq_k$$

We can define the units in which the multipliers must be expressed thanks to an additional equation which incorporates the condition that the quantity of labour embodied in the standard system is the same as in the actual system being studied:

$$L_aq_a + L_bq_b + \cdots + L_kq_k = 1 \qquad (5)$$

Here we have a system of $k+1$ equations which determine the k multipliers and R.

Solving this equation system, we obtain a set of numbers for the muliipliers $(q'_a, q'_b, \ldots, q'_k)$ which Sraffa applies to the equations of the production system,[29] converting them into a standard system in the following manner:

$$q'_a[(A_aP_a + B_aD_b + \cdots + K_aP_k)(1+r) + L_aw] = q'_aAP_a$$

$$q'_b[(A_bP_a + B_bP_b + \cdots + K_bP_k)(1+r) + L_bw] = q'_bBP_b$$

$$\vdots \quad \vdots \quad \vdots \qquad\qquad \vdots \quad \vdots \qquad \vdots \qquad\qquad \vdots \qquad (6)$$

$$q'_k[(A_kP_a + B_kP_b + \cdots + K_kP_k)(1+r) + L_kw] = q'_kK_pk$$

From here Sraffa derives the standard national income, which he adopts as a unit of measure of wages and prices for the original production system.

The equation which tells us that the price of the net product is equal to 1 is replaced by the following, in which the $q'$ represent known numbers, whilst the p are variables:

$$[q'_aA - (q'_aA_a + q'_bA_b + \cdots + q'_kA_k)]P_a +$$

$$[q'_bB - (q'_aB_a + q'_bB_b + \cdots + q'_kB_k)]P_b + \cdots +$$

$$[q'_kK - (q'_aK_a + q'_bK_b + \cdots q'_kK_k)]P_k = 1 \qquad (7)$$

This 'composite' commodity is the standard of wages and prices. The introduction of the normalization conditions into the standard system means that there are now $k+1$ equations (K price equations and 1 normalization equation) and $k+2$ unknowns (k prices and two distributional variables). The system still has one degree of freedom.

In the standard system, the relation between net product and means of production can be calculated in physical terms, given that we are dealing with two aggregates in which the commodities making them up are the same. In this framework, the standard commodity plays the role of Ricardo's 'corn'. With the help of the standard commodity, Sraffa only resolves part of the problem which Ricardo fails to solve in passing from corn to embodied labour. In effect, Ricardo was looking for a standard which would be invariable, both in relation to changes in the conditions of production of commodities, and in relation to changes in the distribution of incomes under fixed production conditions. Sraffa abandons the search for an invariable commodity with respect to variations in the conditions of production, and his analysis leads him to the search only for a standard of prices which would be 'invariable' when income distribution changes, taking production conditions as given.

Thus, as the rate of profit obtaining in corn cultivation was, for Ricardo, the rate of profit which would impose itself as a general rate of profit, Sraffa shows in the same manner that if the wage is expressed in terms of the standard commodity then the rate of profit which, in the standard system, is obtained as a ratio between quantities of commodities, will give rise in the actual system to a relation between aggregate values. More specifically, if we recall that R is the relation established in the standard system between the net product and the means of production, and that it is therefore the maximum rate of profit for the real system, and that w, the wage, is expressed in terms of the standard commodity (remember that, as with Sraffa, the total quantity of labour is set equal to one, wage and wage rate coinciding), the prevailing rate of profit in the real system is given by $r = R(1 - w)$.

After showing that the standard system is unique, Sraffa makes abundant use of the relation between wage rate and profit rate to deal with many theoretical problems. Thus, for example, he analyses the case in which commodities are produced with means of production which have been produced at different points in the past (and thus in succession) so as to show that the profit element in the prices of these means of production is different, and he asks how relative prices of commodities will change with changes in the rate of profit.

In the second part of his book, Sraffa studies new problems which arise out of looking at the existence of branches of industry with multiple outputs (joint production) and fixed capital. Sraffa further introduces land into his analysis and constructs a more complex system of equations which, with given wages, determines the price of all products, the rate of profit, and the rent on land of different quality.

## III. Problems of Interpretation

### 1. Sraffa's Theory of Prices of Production in Relation to Marginalist Theory

Attempts have been made to characterize Sraffa's theory using marginalist categories. In doing this some authors have committed many errors. For example, H. G. Johnson has indicated that Sraffa's theory represents a system of 'incomplete' general equilibrium, in the sense that he downplays consumption (demand) by speaking only of production (supply).[30] The same idea is expressed by R. F. Harrod when he asserts that 'the most notable features of Sraffa's book is that he makes no reference to the scale or elasticity of demand for final products, when one of the central themes that he takes up is the determination of prices . . . It is surprising', he adds 'that a price system can be determined without reference to final demand.'[31] Joan Robinson reflects along the same lines, when she asserts that 'he has only given us half an equilibrium system.'[32]

However, the reference to general economic equilibrium is incorrect. Sraffa looks at prices of production, determined on the basis of a hypothesis that profit rates equalize. He is interested in a different problem from the marginalist problem of 'equilibrium prices' which would guarantee the equality of supply and demand.[33] Just as it is wrong to speak of an 'equilibrium system' in the traditional, that is 'marginalist' sense of the term, it is also incorrect to speak of a 'general system'. Sraffa takes into consideration in his analysis only those factors necessary for the resolution of his problem. For this reason he separates out all elements which by definition exercise no influence upon prices of production, or whose influence is exercised via distribution, technology and the scale of production, elements which are given in Sraffa's system. It is thus not possible to speak of a partial analysis in the neo-classical sense, since Sraffa does not concentrate on one part of an economic system with the aim of producing an approximate solution to a problem whose true solution can only be ascertained within the framework of a more general analysis. Rather, he considers all those elements necessary for the solution of the problem as it is posed.

What we have just said is valid for the distinction which neo-classical economists frequently make between static analysis and dynamic analysis. According to the neo-classicals, dynamic analysis is characterized, essentially, by the inclusion of variables relating to different times. More specifically, Harrod asserts that dynamic analysis includes 'propositions in which the rate of growth appears as an unknown quantity.'[34] This idea is reiterated by Hicks, who asserts that in order to make a dynamic analysis every magnitude must be dated.[35] From this point of view, we can define a static analysis as an economic analysis which is not dynamic. By this definition Sraffa's analysis of prices of production would be static. However, if we attempt a positive definition, looking at the 'static theories' of the neo-classicals, we can see that what typifies them is their atemporal context. They try to interpret the values of the variables under consideration as *equilibrium* solutions to the economic system under consideration.

From this point of view it is more correct to say that Sraffa does not make a static analysis but 'photographs' a moment of growth, which is very different. He makes no abstraction from time, since the moment under consideration is determined by past history and is limited to generating the following moment in time. Thus previous errors of interpretation of Sraffa's work have their origin in an insufficient comprehension of the difference between neo-Ricardian economics and neo-classical economics.

Neo-Ricardian economics is that which, on the basis of the existence of a *physical surplus*, studies its distribution thanks to a price system with the restriction that the economy concerned must reproduce itself. In all this, the hypothesis of equalization of profit rates plays a decisive role. Neo-classical economics, using the concept of *factor of production*, leads towards the determination of prices of goods and services of the factors of production, and therefore the rate of profit, since capital is conceived as a factor of production, corresponding to an equilibrium amongst all economic agents.

The neo-Ricardian school rests on the notions of surplus and reproduction, whilst the neo-classical school rests on the notions of factor of production and equilibrium. The logical structures of both schools, like the categories they use, are very different. Thus, for example, the concept of profit, for the neo-Ricardians, is not the reward due to a factor of production but a part of the surplus. Equally, the notions of capital and wage do not have the same meaning for the neo-classicals and the neo-Ricardians.[36]

The existence of a physical surplus implies prior knowledge of the quantities produced and used in production, so that prices do not depend on the forces of supply and demand. On the other hand, these forces play a central role in the neo-classical system, since they simultaneously determine quantities and prices, in order to finalize the equilibrium process. This calls for a hypothesis about returns, and about the form of the demand functions, before prices are known. For the neo-Ricardians, the hypothesis about returns is only important for the theory of accumulation, but is logically independent of price theory. Therefore, the neo-classicals insist on consumers' preferences, on utility and more generally on the problems of individual choice. These quantities are of little interest to the neo-Ricardians who construct an analysis in terms of social classes (even though their concept of social class is far removed from that of the Marxists), and are not interested in the logic of individual behaviour.

Everything that we have just said makes Harrod's aims in respect of Sraffa illusory, in the sense that they attempt to establish inter-connections between the Sraffian system and the neo-classical system instead of dealing with the Sraffian system as a·'prelude to the critique of economic theory'.[37] From our point of view, the two systems can only coexist with the greatest of difficulty.

## 2. Sraffa's Theory of Prices of Production in Relation to Marxist Analysis

### A. The Standard Commodity and the Status of Labour in the Neo-Ricardian Economy

The standard commodity is the central element in the analysis of prices of production. We know that the standard system is built from the initial production system by taking as data the quantities produced and the conditions of production. To each production system there corresponds a unique standard system. It is necessary to ascertain, Benetti asserts,[38] whether Sraffa's standard commodity lets us study the process through which prices reach the levels defined by the system of prices of production. This calls for a price standard defined when the profit rate is not equalized, since the system is in motion towards a final state not yet attained. In spite of what has been achieved in this respect, such a construction is far from having been demonstrated.

Even if it were possible, we would have to compare the system at two distinct points in time to make sense of the process of price formation (or profit equalization). This is necessary in order to determine the tendencies of prices and profit rates in different branches of production to rise or fall. But at least one of the data of the system—quantities produced—varies during this process. Thus, we obtain different standards corresponding to different moments in the process. 'The comparison of prices determined at different points in time is therefore impossible. That is, Sraffa's standard commodity does not let us take into account a fundamental aspect of capitalist practice—competition.'[39]

Further, even accepting the uniformity of profit rates, it is necessary to examine the suppositions on which the construction of the standard commodity is based. The function of this commodity is to compare prices corresponding to a single production system in different distributional states. It is built under the hypothesis that labour does not form part of advanced capital. For some authors this hypothesis is of no great importance. Thus Maurice Dobb asserts that 'this is done merely for convenience in order to define the maximum profit of a standard commodity and demonstrate the effect of changes in the wage–profit couple on relative prices.' 'In Principle', adds Dobb, 'nothing is implied by this change.'[40]

F. van de Velde argues that labour is omitted from advanced capital only because 'the relation between profit rate and wage rate appears simpler and clearer.'[41] Henri Denis indicates that 'for reasons that are not explicit (which are, I think, of a mathematical character) Sraffa eliminates variable capital, saying: we shall suppose that wages are paid after the produce has been sold—consequently out of the income from the period under consideration, for example out of the income for the year.'[42]

We shall study the consequences of suppressing this hypothesis, by treating the wage as part of advanced capital. There are two possibilities: to treat it in the Ricardian manner as a bundle of goods or a good, or consider it only as a price with a completely different status from that of a commodity price. In the first case, it is obvious that any change in the wage will involve a change in the technical coefficients representing the quantities of wage-good. Thus, a datum in the system must be changed. Since there is a one-to-one relation between standard systems and production systems there cannot be a single standard system. It is impossible to compare prices corresponding to different wage levels. In this case, Sraffa's wage-standard does not exist and the movement of relative price is unintelligible.

We get into the same difficulties in the second case, expressing the wage in the form of a price. Whether the commodity whose price is the unit of measure of the wage is consumed or not consumed by the workers, changes in the wage will necessarily be translated into changes in the quantities of commodities consumed by the workers and, therefore, into changes in the production system. The problem that we indicated previously simply reappears.[43]

An intermediate possibility is to resort to the artifice suggested by Pasinetti, although previously suggested by Sraffa of considering the wage rate as divided into two parts: one portion necessary for subsistence which is comparable with those commodities constituting means of production (their composition being rigidly determined by biological necessities), and the other part forming part of the surplus. But, if this distinction is accepted, the subsistence portion of the wage rate will acquire the same status as a technical datum and will be included in the matrix of technical coefficients. This leads to a reinterpretation of Sraffa's system, making w refer only to that part of the wage which forms part of the surplus. In this case when w varies, no technical datum will change and prices corresponding to different wage levels can be compared.[44] Sraffa's standard commodity will exist and the movement of relative prices will be intelligible. However, it should be noted that the construction of Sraffa's standard commodity suggests that at least part of the wage forms part of the net product.

In order to avoid ambiguities it should be made clear that the problem is not that the wage is paid *post factum* in Sraffa, as several of his critics have suggested,[45] but the fact that the wage does not form part of advanced capital. These are two different things and therefore should not be confused.[46] For Marx wages are paid *post factum* and can still form part of advanced capital.[47] Thus, in the majority of branches of economic activity the wage is paid *post factum* but time must still pass until the capitalist can realize his merchandise, that is to say, recuperate advanced capital (including variable capital) and obtain his surplus value.

The idea that at least part of the wage must be a fraction of the net product is an indispensible condition for the existence of a standard commodity in Sraffa's sense. That is to say, Sraffa's system is only acceptable if at least part of the wage is solely considered as a distributional category. But, this is impossible, since the wage is only a distributional category because it forms part of advanced capital, and is hence a production category.

When the essential link between production and distribution is broken, as is the case with Sraffa, the 'wage' variable can no longer designate the wage in its proper specificity. It could be interpreted as some kind of deduction from the net product: for example a tax on the net product of each branch, fixed at a uniform rate (the wage rate) on the basis of a different amount (the quantity of labour used) in each branch.

Furthermore, profit no longer appears as the means to an ulterior accumulation, but is reduced to simple purchasing power. For this reason, it appears as identical in nature to the wage, from which it is distinguished only by its specific mode of distribution between branches. Profit is no longer defined by its origin (exploitation of the labour force) nor by its destiny (accumulation): it is present, but it is not known from where it comes or where it goes. Wage and profit are neither distinguished by their origin nor by their destiny, but appear as a pure purchasing power, as two masses of the same formless substance, distinguished from each other only because they are distributed between branches in two different ways. From this we can deduce that Sraffa's system is unable to reproduce capitalism's essential characteristic—the wage relation. The relation between production and distribution is broken, and Marx's analysis of this relation bypassed.

For Marx, 'The structure of distribution is completely determined by the structure of production. Distribution is itself a product of production, not only in its object, in that only the results of production can be distributed, but also in its form, in that the specific kind of participation in production determines the specific forms of distribution.'[48] But production is also determined by distribution. For example, 'A conquering people divides the land among the conquerors, thus imposes a certain distribution and forms of property in land, and thus determines production. Or it enslaves the conquered, and so makes slave-labour the foundation of production. Or a people rises in revolution and smashes the great landed estates into small parcels, and hence, by this new distribution, gives production a new character.'[49]

## B. The Closure of Sraffa's System

The system established by Piero Sraffa is formally closed when, given production levels, production methods and one of the distributional variables, prices of production are determined. However, this closure is obtained by fixing one of the distributional variables (the rate of profit or the wage rate) at an arbitrary level. A logical closure of the system demands either a theory which determines the wage rate, or one which determines the profit rate. The main efforts in this direction have comprised, essentially, an explanatory theory of profit rates. There are in existence several attempts to explain wage rate, but all they do is make a vague allusion to the class struggle, avoiding the problem under study. Moreover they encounter the awkward problem that wage bargaining by trade unions can have no meaning before the price system is known.

Attempts to fix the profit rate have followed four principal courses.

The *first* possibility is to close the model following Sraffa's suggestions in his work. He points out that the 'rate of profit, as a ratio, has a significance which is independent of any prices and can well be "given" before the prices are fixed.' To that extent, he adds, it is 'susceptible of being determined from outside of the production system, in particular by the level of the money rates of interest.'[50] However this solution does not stand up to a careful study of the facts. Explaining the profit rate by means of the rate of interest only displaces the problem. What determines the rate of interest?

Moreover this solution assumes that the profit rate is regulated by the monetary rate of interest. This last hypothesis can clearly be defended. Competition between capitalists guarantees that the profit rate is uniform and cannot permanently exceed the rate of interest. But the correspondence between interest rates and profit rates is far from close since the interest rate depends on many other factors. The creation of a causal chain between interest rate and profit rate presupposes that the interest rate can be fixed independently of the profit rate, for example by the policy of a central bank, and that then the central bank takes such control over the firms that their rate of profit is tightly linked to the rate of interest. As we shall see, the causal chain is too subject to over-restrictive conditions to be really acceptable.

A *second* solution, more commonly accepted, is to close the system with the Cambridge relation $r = g/Sc$, in which $r$ is the rate of profit, $g$ the rate of growth and $Sc$ the capitalist propensity to save.[51] This solution leads to many difficulties. In the first place we have to accept a movement of causality from the rate of growth to the rate of profit, which is not at all evident and indeed seems without foundation, involving as it does a simple dynamic equilibrium equation. Second this solution rests on various assumptions: the rate of growth is independent of the real wage, investment is financed by a fixed part of profits and returns to scale are constant. Finally, it leaves unsolved the problem of what determines the rate of growth.

A *third* solution assumes that the entrepreneurs make use of what is known as a 'normal' rate of profit. This is the rate used by the entrepreneurs in their provisional economic calculations, which fixes the level of the profit rate. This idea is also not free from serious difficulties. Nothing justifies the *a priori* assertion that the entrepreneurs' understanding is so advanced that they all have the same idea of what constitutes a normal profit. This profoundly subjective element is being introduced into a price theory which is supposed to be 'objective'. We must not make the determination of prices depend on such a 'volatile' element as the entrepreneurs' 'animal spirits'.

A *fourth* solution makes the profit rate depend on the relation of forces between social classes, that is to say, on the class struggle. With this, according to some authors,[52] we can reintroduce political considerations into economics. Furthermore, it is thought that the authors who are turning to this solution are revitalizing the Marxist approach to distribution.[53] This solution has the defect that it cannot explain exactly what role is played by the class struggle in the determination of the rate of profit, nor can it be precise as to what level, as a function of this struggle, the rate of profit must be established.

After reading the neo-Ricardians analyses one gets the feeling that once the means of production have been deployed, the produce of the economy can be distributed in any way between capitalists and workers without affecting the mode of production as such. In summary, the attempt to return to the class struggle is more of an alibi than the outline of a real solution.

## C. Sraffa and the Transformation Problem

Sraffa's system of price of production is the logical result of a certain understanding of the problem of transforming values into prices of production. More specifically, it constitutes the logical and only result of the 'corrections' brought by Claudio Napoleoni into Marx's scheme of prices of production, based on the work of von Bortkiewicz.

The Marxist procedure for transformation is presented by Marx's 'correctors' in the following manner. Designating constant capital by C and variable capital by V, surplus value by S and value by W and dividing the economy into three sectors, sector I producing means of production, sector II producing wage goods and sector III producing luxury goods, we get the following system in value terms:

$$
\begin{array}{ll}
\text{I:} & C_1 + V_1 + S_1 = W_1 \\
\text{II:} & C_2 + V_2 + S_2 = W_2 \\
\text{III:} & C_3 + V_3 + S_3 = W_3 \\
\hline
& C + V + S = W
\end{array}
\qquad (8)
$$

This initial scheme in value terms is expressed in hours of labour and not in monetary terms.[54]

Calculating the general rate of profit r as the relation of total surplus value S to the total capital advanced $(C + V)$ we can specify the system of prices of production:

$$\text{I: } C_1 + V_1 + r(C_1 + V_1) = G_1$$
$$\text{II: } C_2 + V_2 + r(C_2 + V_2) = G_2 \qquad (9)$$
$$\text{III: } C_3 + V_3 + r(C_3 + V_3) = G_3$$

---

$$C + V + r(C + V) = G$$

We can verify that $r(C + V) = S$, that is that the total profits equal total surplus value, and furthermore the $W = r$, that is to say, total value is equal to total price of production.

According to his 'correctors' Marx's equations for prices of production are logically incorrect since what enters into the price of production of a commodity, its cost of production, must also be calculated in price of production terms. Inputs should not be measured in terms of values but prices of production. In Marx's proposed solution, the same commodity is evaluated in two different ways: as an input, that is to say as an element of the prices of production, it is evaluated in value terms; as a product, that is to say, as a result of the production process, it is evaluated in terms of prices of production.

The solution proposed by many of the 'correctors' such as von Bortkiewicz, Sweezy and Sraffa, though not Steedman, begins from a value system in which the conditions of simple reproduction hold.

$$\text{I: } C_1 + V_1 + S_1 = C_1 + C_2 + C_3$$
$$\text{II: } C_2 + V_2 + S_2 = V_1 + V_2 + V_3 \qquad (10)$$
$$\text{III: } C_3 + V_3 + S_3 = S_1 + S_2 + S_3$$

In this system, as we have already said, according to Marx's 'correctors', values are measured in quantities of labour.[55] In effect, the value substance, abstract human labour, is replaced by its magnitude, units of labour time, and capital is simply reduced to inputs of labour time.

Let us suppose that the price of production of a unit of constant capital is x times its value, the price of production of a unit of variable capital is y times its value, and the price of production of a unit of luxury articles is z times its value. Furthermore, if we represent the general rate of profit as r which is not defined from the value system but from the price of production system, we can write down the following system for prices of production:

$$\text{I:} \quad C_1x + V_1y + r(C_1x + V_1y) = (C_1 + C_2 + C_3)x$$

$$\text{II:} \quad C_2x + V_2y + r(C_2x + V_2y) = (V_1 + V_2 + V_3)y \quad (11)$$

$$\text{III:} \quad C_3x + V_3y + r(C_3x + V_3y) = (S_1 + S_2 + S_3)z$$

We have three equations and four unknowns to determine (the three coefficients of transformation and the rate of profit, that is x, y, z, r). Setting $z = 1$, the system can easily be solved.

But Marx's 'correctors' correct not only Marx but von Bortkiewicz. Suppose constant capital comprises two commodities, a tractor and a thresher, whose values are $C_1$ and $C_2$, where $C_1$ and $C_2$ add up to C. The ratio of prices of production, resulting from von Bortkiewicz's schema is $C_1x/C_2x$, equal to the relation between the values $C_1/C_2$. In the words of one of von Bortkiewicz's 'correctors': 'I assume that the commodities which make up this constant capital exchange, amongst themselves, according to values and not according to prices, because I apply a single coefficient of transformation of values into prices to the whole aggregate: which means that, in the interior of this aggregate, I assume that the relations of exchange between commodities are those which correspond to relations between values.'[56] To obviate the difficulty it is enough to rewrite the system 'but in such a way that the equations refer always not to aggregates of commodities, but only to individual commodities.'[57] To produce this effect we shall denote by $L_{ij}$ the value of commodity j which is used as input in the production of commodity i. Put another way, let us use $L_{ij}$ to denote the quantity of labour contained in commodity j which is needed as input to produce that quantity of commodity i which incorporates an amount $L_i$ of labour. On the other side let us denote by $P_a, P_b, \ldots, P_k$ the coefficients of transformation of values into prices. These coefficients of transformation can be interpreted as prices of a unit of value.

With these specifications we can write down the following transformation schema:

$$(L_{aa}P_a + L_{ab}P_b + \cdots + L_{ak}P_k)(1+3) = L_aP_a$$
$$(L_{ba}P_a + L_{bb}P_b + \cdots + L_{bk}P_k)(1+r) = L_bP_b \qquad (12)$$
$$\vdots \qquad\qquad\qquad \vdots \qquad \vdots$$
$$(L_{ka}P_a + L_{kb}P_b + \cdots + L_{kk}P_k)(1+r) = L_kP_k$$

The system consists of k equations and $k+1$ unknowns to be determined (k coefficients of transformation and the rate of profit). But since we have to make one coefficient of transformation equal to 1 the system can be determined without difficulty.

Since the $L_{ih}$ and the $L_i$ are the only data of the problem, one might think that a knowledge of values is the logically prior condition to a knowledge of prices and the rate of profit. However, if we look at things more closely—say Marx's 'correctors'—we can see that values can be replaced by physical quantities of commodities without the logic of the system being altered.

In effect, the matrix of values which can be written as:

$$\begin{bmatrix} L_{aa}L_{ab} \cdots L_{ak} \\ L_{ba}L_{bb} \cdots L_{bk} \\ \vdots\; \vdots \qquad \vdots \\ L_{ka}L_{kb} \cdots L_{kk} \end{bmatrix}$$

can be replaced by the matrix of physical requirements of commodities, that is to say by:

$$\begin{bmatrix} A_aB_a \cdots K_a \\ A_bB_b \cdots K_b \\ \vdots\; \vdots \qquad \vdots \\ A_kB_k \cdots K_k \end{bmatrix}$$

For its part the vector $[L_1, L_2, \ldots, L_k]$ can be substituted for by the vector $[A, B, \ldots, K]$. Further still, if we define the units of physical quantites of commodities properly, that is, if we define a physical unit as the quantity of commodity which incorporates a unit of value, we obtain the same numerical values for the two matrices and the two vectors.

This brings us, without difficulty to the system of prices of production presented by Sraffa at the beginning of the second chapter of his book:

$$(A_a P_a + B_a P_b + \cdots + K_a P_k)(1 + r) = A P_a$$
$$(A_b P_a + B_b P_b + \cdots + K_b P_k)(1 + r) = B P_b$$
$$\vdots \qquad \vdots \qquad \quad \vdots \quad \vdots \qquad \vdots$$
$$(A_k P_a + B_k P_b + \cdots + K_k P_k)(1 + r) = K P_k$$

With this, the neo-Ricardians think that Sraffa has resolved the debate over transformation. Thus Napoleoni, who now proclaims the Marxist theory of labour to have a purely philosophical validity, says 'I have mentioned Sraffa's results as a confirmation of the possibility of determining prices and the share of profits in this way, *independently of value*. Furthermore, what Sraffa says may justifiably be taken as a full stop in the history of the transformation problem.'[58] That is to say, for the neo-Ricardians Marx's transformation is superfluous because prices of production and profits can be obtained without reference to value or surplus value. For the neo-Ricardians it is an irrelevant detour to begin with values and transform them into prices of production. However, with Sraffa we situate ourselves within the system of prices of production and get a satisfactory theory, on the logical plane, of relations of exchange of commodities on the basis of the uniformity of the rate of profit, but we lose any comprehension of the nature of commodity, the origin of profit or the social relations of production. Accepting Sraffa's theory as a solution to the transformation problem is to fail to understand Marx's particular problem and, instead to pick up directly where Ricardo left off.

The positions defended by participants at the Modena 1978 University seminar, far from solving the problem, represent an evasion of it because they suppress one of its terms. The correct determination, on the logical plane, of prices of production by Sraffa is carried out without any reference to Marx's theory of labour value. The initial data are physical quantities of reproducible commodities which figure in inputs and products, and a law of distribution (we give ourselves a variable which states distribution between wages and profits, and a norm for distributing the global profit between various branches of production). The simple definition of prices of production is enough to determine them: the arrangement of prices is therefore, in fact, totally independent of the world of Marx's values, and the relation between the two spheres, so essential for the explanation of profit, is broken. Sraffa's posture, precisely by suppressing a specific and essential term of Marx's analysis—value—the only term which captures and unifies the social complexity of capitalist economic reality, is orthogonal to Marx's and can in no way be considered as complementary to it.[59] Because of everything that has been said, those who think that the history of the transformation problem has ended with Sraffa should be considered as being more in continuity with the Ricardian problematic than the Marxist.

Napoleoni, like all the neo-Ricardians, has not captured the nature of abstract labour as social labour and the magnitude of value as socially necessary labour time. He does not understand that money is the materialization of abstract universal labour time and that capitalist society necessarily creates its own measure of value. As Altvater, Hoffman and Semmler correctly argue: 'Sraffa abandons the *analysis of form* which constitutes Marx's special contribution in relation to Ricardo . . . From the moment value ceases to be directly social, the value of commodities can no longer be reflected in a directly comprehensible manner, since the value of each merchandise must be expressed in terms of use values of other commodities. The universal equivalent is converted, in this exchange, into commodity-money, so that "labour value" disappears as a measurable expression of human labour time . . . .'[60]

In commodity-producing societies it is a thing, for example gold as a money commodity, which takes on the task of representing value, so that Marx considered an understanding of the category of money a prerequisite to understanding the essence of value. Those who have not understood this and continue believing in the old utopia of 'labour-money' will benefit greatly from reapplying themselves to the *Grundrisse* where Marx criticized such proposals forthrightly.

For the neo-Ricardians the transformation of values into prices is an irrelevant detour, because prices of production can be calculated directly without reference to value. For the neo-Ricardian current, the important object is a theory of prices and since they see their concept of value as unnecessary for the calculation of prices, they conclude by rejecting the relevance of Marxist method.

The neo-Ricardians claim to situate themselves immediately at a shallow level of abstraction by dealing with prices of production, that is to say, making competition between capitals intervene immediately. They forget that Marx began from a sufficiently deep level of abstraction (studying capital and its forms of existence in general) in order to approximate progressively to the concrete reality which for the vulgar conception constitutes its point of departure.[61]

If we jettison the concept of value we also have to abandon the concept of surplus value, and therefore, the concept of rate of exploitation, since it is a relation expressed in value terms. However, Garegnani thinks, as did Bernstein long ago,[62] that dropping the concept of value does not mean dropping the notion of exploitation. For Garegnani, 'the proposition which refers to the existence of the exploitation of labour in a capitalist society does not at all depend on the validity of the labour theory of value, but on the validity of the whole theoretical proposition founded on the notion of surplus.'[63] Thus for him a serf is exploited by the feudal lord only because he cannot appropriate the whole of what he produces, and this is independent of any concept of value.

But what Garegnani does not understand is that Marx was fully aware that surplus labour is as old as the history of human civilization,[64] even though the product of this labour assumes the form of surplus value only when the owner of the means of production encounters a free labourer as the object of exploitation and exploits her or him with the object of producing commodities, that is to say, when the means of production take on the specific form of capital. Because of this it is clear that the particular, capitalist form of exploitation can only be understood through the Marxist categories of value and surplus value. Garegnani limits himself to the general and, therefore, totally diffuse idea of explotation as such, without dealing with the analysis of the specifically capitalist mode of exploitation. He forgets the specific economic form in which surplus labour is extracted from the direct producer, and he forgets that under capitalism social relations between persons appear as detached from social relations between things, between the products of labour.

To the extent that I base myself on orthodox Marxism in Lukacs's sense. I have the 'scientific conviction that in dialectical Marxism the correct method of investigation has been discovered, that this method can only be extended, amplified or deepened in the spirit of its founders'.[65] For this reason I think that all the attempts made by the neo-Ricardians to transcend or correct Marxism have only led to superficial deformations, to triviality and to coarse eclecticism in the style of Garegnani, when he proclaims that the explanation of profit and prices can be obtained from Sraffa but that in order to explain accumulation or crisis one must return to Marx's *Capital*.[66] From my point of view the Marxist and neo-Ricardian frameworks can only be reconciled with the greatest difficulty.

## 3. Some Final Considerations in Relation to Piero Sraffa's Theory

Sraffa defines production in isolation, in terms of technical relations, but he makes no reference to social relations in the process of production. Apart from pointing out how commodities are actually used to produce commodities in a capitalist society, Sraffa has constructed an imaginary world in which things (use values) produce things (use values).

One of the most important differences between Marx and the neo-Ricardian is that the neo-Ricardians use the term surplus in place of the category of surplus value used by Marxists. This is more than a semantic difference, since their practice of referring to the surplus is a reflection of the fundamental difference between their approach and Marx's. This conception of surplus is clearly presented in Sraffa's work. In the first phrase of the second chapter of his work he asserts that 'the economy produces more than the minimum necessary for replacement and there is a surplus to be distributed.'[67] This comes as a surprise, since the book's first chapter deals with 'an extremely simple society which produces just enough to maintain itself'[68] and nowhere does Sraffa tell us how the surplus repeatedly emerges. Since Sraffa does not see social relations in the production process, there is nothing in his discussion of the surplus comparable to the Marxist concept of capital as a coercive relation, thanks to which the working class is obliged to work more than is prescribed by the narrow limits of its vital needs.

When Sraffa elaborates his understanding of the surplus, the difference between his approach and Marx's becomes clearer. Consider, for example, the definition of surplus which Sraffa offers us using national income terminology: 'The national income of a system in a self-reproducing state consists of the set of commodities which are left over when from the national product we have removed item by item the articles which go to replace the means of production used up in all the industries.'[69]

According to Frank Roosevelt, three senses in which the Sraffian concept of surplus differs from the Marxist concept of surplus value can be discerned in this definition.[70] In the first place, Sraffa's surplus is a physical, rather than a value, phenomenon. It is the set of 'commodities' (read: use values) that remain after subtracting from the total produce of the economy those 'articles' which are necessary in order to replace those which have been used in production. In the second place, both its existence and its precise magnitude are technologically determined. In Sraffa's system, the replacement requirements of an economy are fixed by technical relations which exist in each branch. These tell us how much of each input is required to produce given amounts of each product. Once we know the technological characteristics of a society we can say whether a surplus exists or not and how big it is.

Third, Sraffa's surplus, in contrast with Marx's concept of surplus value, includes that part of the product of the economy which is consumed by workers. As we saw in the definition given above, only those products needed to replace the means of production are subtracted from the total product. The remaining products of the economy are included in the surplus and in workers' consumption, just as the part of the total product collected by the capitalists forms part of the surplus.[71]

From the Marxist point of view, Sraffa's treatment of the surplus mystifies the actual relations of capitalist production. In effect, its presentation of the surplus as a physical phenomenon obscures the significance of the fact that all the products of a capitalist economy appear as values. After reading Sraffa, one can have the impression that there is really no difference between the surplus produced by a capitalist society and that produced by any other type of society. Furthermore, one of the most serious defects of Sraffa's treatment is that by including the workers' consumption in with the surplus, he obscures the Marxist distinction between necessary and suplus labour. Marx did not include the workers' consumption in with surplus value because he wanted to bring out on the one hand the relation between surplus value and the value received by workers, and on the other, the two parts of the labour time of the workers. Marx treats the value received by the workers as the product of necessary labour and connects surplus value to surplus labour.

Sraffa never distinguishes between necessary labour and surplus labour. For him, there is no difference between the labour which produces a surplus and that which only replaces the used up means of production. His failure to distinguish between surplus labour and necessary labour and his treatment of the surplus as a physical phenomenon, leads him to say that the produced surplus is a surplus of things more than of labour. Put another way, the surplus in Sraffa's system is not a relation between people but a relation between two sets of products, one comprising the total product of the economy and the other comprising used up means of production. As Frank Roosevelt points out, the Sraffian concept of the surplus can be considered as an example of commodity fetishism.

Since the neo-Ricardians consider the surplus as a relation between things, they are incapable of understanding that its existence reflects a real struggle between social classes at the level of production. They refer to the class struggle only in relation to the distribution of the surplus once it has been produced. The neo-Ricardian and Marxist schools have a very different understanding of the nature of exploitation. For Marx, exploitation is the extraction of surplus labour in the production process. For the neo-Ricardians, it only has to do with the mode in which the social product is distributed. The tendency of the neo-Ricardians to focus solely on the distribution of the product can be seen as another manifestation of commodity fetishism. Instead of concerning themselves with the elimination of waged labour, they confine their attention to things like increasing the bargaining power of the workers. This leads to an emphasis on changing the distribution of income in favour of the workers more than changing the mode of production as such.

As Marx pointed out: 'Trade Unions work well as centres of resistance against the encroachments of capital. They fail partially from an injudicious use of their power. They fail generally from limiting themselves to a guerrilla war against the effects of the existing system, instead of simultaneously trying to change it, instead of using their organized forces as a lever for the final emancipation of the working class, that is to say, the ultimate abolition of the wages system'.[72]

Thanks to neo-Ricardianism, therefore neo-classical economics has been subjected to a series of withering critiques, while traditional reformism of the Fabian variety has acquired a more 'scientific' foundation. But in resuming the Ricardian tradition as if it stood in diametrical opposition to Marxism, rather than being the highest stage of classical economics antecedent to Marx's 'critique of political economy', latter-day neo-Ricardians have suppressed the actual, historical dialectic of classical economics' transcendence. In effect, they have turned back the theoretical and political clock. Imagining themselves to be the pioneers of a 'post-Marxist' era in political economy they have only succeeded in returning to a pre-Marxist past.

# Labour-Power: The Missing Commodity

## Paulo Giussani

### 1. Preface

Although it is now clear that Sraffa's theory is incompatible with Marx's analysis of commodity production and capital, many still view an agreement or integration between the two as possible and desirable. This is perhaps surprising, particularly since Marx himself, in *Theories of Surplus-Value*, Volume 3, extensively criticized economists such as R. Torrens who can be considered precursors of modern neo-Ricardian theory, and made an extensive critique of Ricardo in volume 2 of the same work, where he analysed in detail all Ricardo's examples relating to prices of production and the average profit rate.[1]

This is relevant to the way the neo-Ricardians present the transformation of values into prices. Input–output equation systems are widely accepted, not only as an accurate reconstruction of Marx's own transformation procedure but indeed of his analysis of the reproduction of total social capital and the distribution of total social labour. In this piece I show that equation systems of this type cannot in fact encompass the role played by labour in reproduction of aggregate social capital, and therefore offer an inadequate framework for the discussion of the real process of price formation.

### 2. Exchange and Commodity Production

In *Production of Commodities by Means of Commodities*, Piero Sraffa describes commodity production using a linear equation system. He begins from a simple self-reproducing system with no surplus:

$$280A + 12B = 400A \qquad (1)$$

$$120A + 8B = 20B$$

It is trivial to show that the relations of exchange between the producers of A and B must be $120A = 12B$. Obviously, this system works by simple bilateral exchange of A against B.

The situation changes qualitatively when we add another commodity vendor, as in Sraffa's next example:

$$240A + 12B + 18C = 450A$$
$$90A + 6B + 12C = 21B \qquad (2)$$
$$120A + 3B + 30C = 60C$$

Self-reproduction demands these exchange in the proportion $450A = 21B = 60C$.

This result is not as trivial as it may seem. If we try to restore bilateral exchange between the two producers $(A \leftrightarrow B; A \leftrightarrow C; B \leftrightarrow C)$, we encounter insurmountable obstacles and have to drop the idea of direct exchange. Each producer must temporarily become a pure merchant, acquiring something she or he does not need in order to deal with the third producer. But is is clearly absurd to introduce commerce at this point. It would not be genuine commerce, serving solely to restore the means of production to their former state. Generalizing, we can see what would have to lie behind an economic system represented by such a linear equation system: *multilateral* exchange. In the preceding example, reproduction can happen if and only if the three producers simultaneously exchange their own products via a triangular distribution. N producers would need n-lateral exchange. Such an economic system can be conceptualized, but it doesn't exist, and has no relation to production and circulation. It is governed by an absolute identity between private and social labour.

By definition exchanges of commodities and, in general, of commodities against money are purely individual and bilateral acts. If exchange were to lose this character and become multilateral, use values would cease to be commodities and labours would cease being executed independently of each other.

'Objects of utility become commodities only because they are the products of the labour of private individuals who work independently of each other. The sum total of the labour of all these private individuals forms the aggregate labour of society. Since the producers do not come into social contact until they exchange the products of their labour, the specific social characteristics of their private labours appear only within this exchange. In other words, the labour of the private individual manifests itself as an element of the total labour of society only through the relations which the act of exchange establishes between the products and, through their mediation, between the producers.'[2]

The idea that commodity-producing labour is private is not a hypothesis to be selected or rejected at will. It is the only assumption with the remotest hope of respecting reality. Further hypotheses, obviously, can lie behind different theories. But they do not have the same necessary character. Without this hypothesis one simply loses sight of what a commodity *is*, what distinguishes it from a product distributed in any other way in any other mode of production.

In Sraffa's system, prices only express the distribution of use values, for productive use or otherwise, to agents of production regulated by the demands of a completely socialized system. Moreover, this contradicts one of the essential elements of equilibrium prices in a linear system—the equilization of profit rates—since in a socialized economy this is a completely arbitrary and irrational hypothesis.[3]

## 3. Simple Commodity Production

The simple neo-Ricardian system involves n linear equations for n produced use values with $n^2$ inputs and n prices. This is a homogeneous system in which certain conditions are necessary to guarantee against null solutions and hence zero prices. The general form of the system is the following:

$$\mathbf{Ap} = \mathbf{Qp} \qquad (3)$$

that is

$$(\mathbf{A} - \mathbf{Q})\mathbf{p} = \mathbf{\Phi} \qquad (4)$$

where $\mathbf{A}$ is the matrix of inputs, $\mathbf{Q}$ the diagonal matrix of outputs, and $\mathbf{p}$ is the column vector of prices. $\mathbf{p} \geqslant 0$ implies that the determinant of the matrix $(\mathbf{A} - \mathbf{Q})$ must be equal to 0, that is, the rows and/or columns of the matrix must be linearly dependent. The only guarantee for such a condition comes either from the hypothesis of a self-reproductive state or from that of a uniform profit rate. To illustrate this, consider the following system in a self-reproducing state, with a null determinant:

$$3a + 4b + 5c = 9a$$
$$2a + b + 2c = 10b \qquad (5)$$
$$4a + 5b + c = 8c$$

If we just augment the production of a by one unit from 9 to 10, assuming a's producers consume the excess independently of the rest of the system, we get a new matrix with a determinant of 53, leading to zero prices. From a practical viewpoint, the system would continue reproducing itself with the extra unit of a being consumed unproductively by its own producers, but the relations of exchange would be indeterminate.

To make sense of prices after production has risen, a rate of profit must be assumed. But this is absurd if the producers of a are using it to augment their own consumption rather than as a commodity. This already suggests that equation systems are by their nature unsuited to represent an economic system—commodity production—based on reciprocal independence of the producers and their labours.

### 4. The Money-Commodity and the Numéraire

Sraffa assigns an arbitrary use-value a price of 1, so that each product can be measured against the same use-value. This need not be a single commodity price; there are various other possibilities. Indeed, there is an extensive literature on the 'normalization' problem.[4] The need to convert one price or a sum of prices into a given number is not economic but mathematical. The various commodities of this system could, as such, exchange perfectly well without a *numéraire* commodity since they do not have to exchange against it in order to be realized as objects for use. The function of *numéraire* can therefore be assigned indifferently to any commodity or group of commodities, which excludes the existence and functioning of a money-commodity, and makes it very hard to explain money's obvious properties.

The commodity–money exchange is notably different from its inverse, the money–commodity exchange, since money is universally and directly exchangeable for every other kind of commodity, but commodities are not universally exchangeable for money. This asymmetry is the logical result of the distinction between private and social labour, and if this distinction goes, so must the asymmetry. It then becomes completely vain to try and insert some simulation of money into the system. Because money is needed for the concrete development of exchange but is neither a means of production nor consumption, a special equation for the money-commodity cannot be inserted.

Renouncing the money-commodity and trying to resolve the problem with other kinds of money leads to even more serious problems. Credit money is based on a money–commodity, not only because it presupposes the discounting of bills and hence institutions equipped to do this, with adequate reserves, but above all because the circuit of credit is completely chance-ridden and subject to sudden interruptions by its very nature, and for this reason calls for the presence of a money-commodity in the last instance.[5] Token money is even more incompatible with a system of the neo-Ricardian type because without the mediation of a money-commodity, it is impossible to relate token money to the system itself. It becomes something metaphysical to which no price can obviously be attached.

In Sraffa's system prices are definitively not the monetary expression of various commodities, but coefficients which allocate produced resources given certain a priori principles. Marx's criticism of S. Bailey should be recalled:

'But what is this unity of objects exchanged against each other? This exchange is not a relation which exists between them as natural things. It is likewise not a relation which they bear as natural things to human needs, for it is not the degree of their utility that determines the quantities in which they exchange. What is therefore their identity, which enables them to be exchanged in certain proportions for one another? As what do they become *exchangeable*?'[6]

This question could have been addressed directly to Sraffa's system. What renders commodities exchangeable in given quantities? Predetermined productive and unproductive consumption needs. Commodities do not and cannot need a unitary homogeneous expression—money.

## 5. Circuit of Capital and Values

In the simple system (3) there was no labour. Products, it is assumed, are obtained from other products without consuming human labour-power. Suppose we introduce the consumption of labour-power explicitly, trying to mirror the labour process. We get:

$$\mathbf{Tp} + \mathbf{L} = \mathbf{p} \qquad (6)$$

where **T** is the matrix of input–output coefficients and **L** the column vector of unit labour inputs.

Equation (6), while reflecting the production process more faithfully than the preceding system, has no real content. From it we can obtain

$$\mathbf{p} = (\mathbf{I} - \mathbf{T})^{-1}\mathbf{L} \qquad (7)$$

showing that if we try to introduce the physical consumption of labour-power explicitly, the resulting prices are equal to the integrated coefficients of labour, that is to the quantity of labour directly and indirectly necessary for the production of unit quantities of various commodities. System (7) contains neither the wage nor the profit rate. Nevertheless it conforms to the succession of phases of the *circuit* of capital. The circuit of money-capital develops as follows:

$$M\text{---------}C\overset{\displaystyle MP}{\underset{\displaystyle L}{\diagdown}}\ \cdots P \cdots (C + \Delta C)$$

where MP = means of production and L = labour-power.

Given that Sraffa's system treats the analysis of the many capitals of which social capital is made up, it should correspond to the circuit of commodity–capital as does the *Tableau Économique* and the reproduction schemata of *Capital* Volume 2.[7] Abstracting from circulation, the content of this circuit is

$$\overset{\displaystyle MP}{\underset{\displaystyle L}{\diagdown\diagup}}\ \cdots P \cdots (C + \Delta C)$$

It is fairly obvious that profit will appear on the right of the equation, while the left is reserved for the elements of production. Profit, if and when it arises, is a final result of the productive process and not one of its points of departure. Rewriting our system:

$$\mathbf{Ap} + \mathbf{L} = \mathbf{Ap}(1 + r) \qquad (8)$$

$$(MP + L) \rightarrow (C + \Delta C)$$

where r is the rate of profit. We can clearly see that if we stay faithful to the circuit of capital we cannot determine prices in a system of linear equations independently of the 'quantity of labour', that is, values:

$$p = \frac{1}{r} \cdot (A^{-1}L) \qquad (9)$$

Because there is no paid wage in this rather strange system, we can contrast it with Sraffa's system when the wage is equal to zero and the profit rate is a maximum ($r = R =$ maximum profit rate).

$$Tp(1+R) = p \qquad (10)$$

which leads to

$$(\eta^*I - T)p = \pi \qquad (11)$$

where $\eta^*$ is the maximum eigenvalue of the technical matrix T. From this $R = (1/\eta^*) - 1$. While in (11) the rate of profit is a function only of the elements of the input–output matrix, in (9) it is also a function of labour inputs L. Even if workers work without costing the capitalists anything, according to Sraffa's system profits and the rate of profit would not change, provided T remains constant, if the intensity or length of the working day changed. According to system (8) or (9) it would vary directly as a function of the circuit of capital and the process of production.

## 6. Labour-Power and Wage

Despite the title of Sraffa's book, one commodity is missing from those needed for production: labour-power, whose existence as a commodity distinguishes capitalism as a distinctive mode of production in history. Neo-Ricardian theories try to escape this by asserting that labour is one of the non-produced inputs like land. But in their systems, not only is labour not produced; it is not even *sold* in the true sense of the word. It is purely a natural condition for the production of objects.

Let us write out Sraffa's system in its complete form:

$$Tp(1+r) + Lw = p \qquad (12)$$

where w is the wage per unit of labour employed. We should now ask exactly what the magnitude of w represents. If we want to use equations such as (12) to determine the rate of profit, then w can only be the price of the complex group of commodities which in given proportions enter the workers' consumption. System (12) is in fact completed by the equation

$$w = \sum_{i=1}^{i=n} p_i m_{il} \tag{13}$$

where $p_i$ are the unit prices and $m_{il}$ are the components of the real wage.

It can be completed in a different way:

$$w = 1 \tag{14}$$

The two equations (13) and (14) represent a dilemma: the choice between real wage and nominal wage. To get the solution vector of relative prices and the rate of profit, both are needed, however, because it is necessary both to know the distribution of the net product and to have a price or group of prices as *numéraire*. Hence nothing prevents equation (14) being chosen. Thus the completion of system (12) calls for the following equation:

$$\sum_{i=1}^{i=n} p_i m_{il} = 1 \tag{15}$$

Introducing equation (15) into the system (12) tacitly but necessarily presupposes two things: (a) that the quantitative and qualitative level of the real wage is known; (b) that the prices of the commodities entering the consumption of the average worker are known.

The second point is not obvious at first sight, but the matter is clear. In principle, all commodities can enter equation (13), and if equation (15) were used to resolve system (12), each commodity would express its own price as a fraction of the sum of all prices. Relative prices obviously would not vary but would be obtained through an artifice which could not have any rational basis.

The remaining choice is that of equation (14) without equation (13); but from (14) alone we cannot get started. Since in the neo-Ricardian scheme labour-power is not a produced or sold commodity, it cannot have a unit price like other commodities. Setting $w = 1$, the need to fix some other price $p_i = 1$ as *numéraire* remains, and we are driven to the unjustified step of equating the wage to an arbitrary price.

Point (b) above is equivalent to transforming the production process into something else. If we insert the vector $(m_{1l}, \ldots, m_{nl})$ of elements of the real wage into the price equation, we effectively

replace the consumption of labour-power in the production process
with the consumption of subsistence goods on the part of the worker
outside the labour process. Productive consumption would literally
be cancelled and individual consumption would be the only
consumption involved in the exchange between capitalists and
workers. Though in a certain sense this removes the labour process
from the scene, it does not eliminate the process of production of
labour-power, which consists precisely of the consumption of the
elements of the vector $(m_{1l},\ldots,m_{nl})$. At this point it becomes
necessary to include the production of labour (labour-power) in with
the other production processes, which in turn requires that a uniform
rate of profit be calculated on the price of labour (labour-power) as for
every other produced commodity.

Does anything in neo-Ricardian theory stop us doing this? In fact
nothing. On the contrary, a coherent development of their
assumptions demands that the price of 'labour' be divided into costs
and profits. The proportion of the wage represented by profits is easily
interpretable, and Sraffa himself suggests it, as the surplus wage,
while the proportion constituted by the cost of production of labour is
interpretable as a subsistence wage, that strictly needed to reproduce
labour. Adding an equation for the price of production of labour into
the system (12) would somewhat change its nature. The equation
would take the following form:

$$\mathbf{m} \cdot \mathbf{p}(1+r) = p_l \qquad (15)$$

where m is the row vector of elements of the real unit subsistence
wage, p is the column vector of prices and $p_l$ is the unit price of
'labour'.

We can study the difference between this and system (12) by means
of a simple two-sector system with two products: $l$, labour and a,
means of production and subsistence.

$$(p_a a_a + p_l l_a)(1+r) = p_a \qquad (16)$$
$$(p_a a_l + p_l l_l)(1+r)\ p_l$$

In this system the size of $l_l$, the quantity of labour needed to produce a
unit of labour, can be interpreted, for example, as the quantity of
domestic labour.

Fixing the *numéraire* with $p_a = 1$, we can study the variations of r as
a function of those of the total wage $(p_l)$.

124

$$\left(\frac{p_l}{(a_l + l_l p_l)}\right) - 1 = r(p_l) \tag{17}$$

As $p_l \to \infty$, r will tend to the limit $1/l_l - 1$ and the relation between rate of profit and unit wage will apply in the following form:

Figure 1

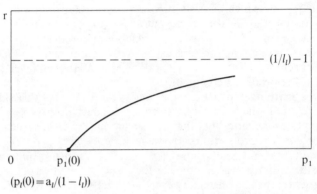

$(p_l(0) = a_l/(1 - l_l))$

In the normal neo-Ricardian 'wage-profit frontier' wages and profits are inversely related. Here they are directly correlated. In system (16) the real wage is no longer, as in the neo-Ricardian treatment, a proportion of the net product resulting, as in Khrishna Bharawaj recognizes, from an 'exogenously given distribution', that is in the absence of a theory of distribution. It is the net product to be determined, along with everything else, from the technical conditions under which labour (labour-power) is produced independent of distribution which is uniquely regulated in (16) by the assumption of a uniform rate of profit. This explains why neo-Ricardian theory cannot be internally coherent and make labour-power, on the basis of its own assumptions, a 100% commodity. In it labour-power remains, as in neo-classical theory, a natural factor of production which has to be remunerated in one form or another.[8]

We have already noted that system (12) assumes knowledge of the real wage, that is the determination a priori of which part and how much of the net product will go to the workers. In theory the real wage can vary from 0 to 100% of the net product, which is clearly absurd. Nevertheless some neo-Ricardians defend it (for example Steedman) by saying that they are only applying Marx's own method—wherein the real wage was a given quantity. But this is imprecise. For Marx the real wage is given at any point in time, but not over the timespan of the accumulation process, during which it is a variable quantity subject to definite laws.

In Marx's value theory, the level of the real wage depends on the production of surplus-value, since the possibility of securing surplus-labour and thereby labour-power is a prerequisite for lengthening the necessary part of the working day. The wage level, being the result of an exchange of commodities, is settled before, and not while, the product, net or gross, is produced. Otherwise the production system would no longer be based on the purchase and sale of labour-power but on co-operation between different types of producers. Not by chance, Marx rejected the formula $V/(V+S)$ (value of labour-power as a fraction of net product) in place of $S/V$ (rate of surplus-value) though no quantitative error would have resulted, judging that the former gave the false impression of a relation of cooperation between capitalists and workers.

The range of variation of the real and value wage as a percentage of the net product is infinitely smaller than 0 to 100%. It is a function of several variables, in particular of the productivity of sectors producing consumer goods and means of production.[9] Given these magnitudes, the theoretical range of oscillation is given, within which both the relation between supply and demand for labour-power, and the economic struggle, have their impact. If instead we leave this range of oscillation indeterminate, the class struggle becomes a demiurge which replaces a theory of national income distribution. In the theory summarized by equation (12), the determination of prices depends on the real wage, on the 'wage-bundle', and this in its turn does not depend on the prices of the various consumption goods.

This indicates that the real wage is entirely independent of the average and sectoral levels of productivity. How is this possible? Consider a tremendous crop failure which diminishes the production of grain by 100 times. To what level will the real wage readjust? If we tend to the view that the real wage will diminish, by this very fact we institute a clear link between productivity and real wage, that is between the real wage level and the *value* of consumer goods. The illusion of being able to deal with the real wage independent of commodity prices vanishes.

Worsening conditions of production would change commodity prices, and the nominal wage would have to change greatly to adjust to the new, lower productivity. Yet, given that in the neo-Ricardian system commodity prices cannot be expressed independently of the real wage, the new price vector would be the result of a highly arbitrary choice, despite the objective nature of the phenomenon (the crop failure) lying behind the entire change. As we shall later see, Marx's theory is secure from this sort of defect.

Since the system (12) does not deal with the actual production process but only the apparent costs which the individual capitalists have to sustain, labour time loses any role in it. Steedman claims that neo-Ricardian theory is in a position to determine equilibrium prices and the profit rate from the technical conditions of production and the real wage,[10] but this is manifestly false. Direct labour inputs are part of the technical conditions of production but in Sraffa's and von Neumann's systems they serve only as a wage multiplier, and can be replaced in this function by whatever else might be equally adapted to it. For example, if in place of time wages we use piecework rates, the vector of labour inputs simply vanishes. System (12) appears in the following form:

$$\mathbf{Tp}(1 + r) + \mathbf{W}_q = \mathbf{p} \tag{18}$$

where $\mathbf{W}_q$ is a column vector in which the elements $W_{iq}$ $(i = 1, \ldots, n)$ make up the wage per unit of output in the corresponding sector. Labour inputs are simply not present. Neo-Ricardian theory therefore determines relative prices and the profit rate by scrapping part of the technical conditions of production and replacing them with predetermined conditions of distribution; that is the long and the short of it.

As we have seen, in system (12) two magnitudes must be chosen a priori (the system has two degrees of freedom) in order to calculate all the others. Neo-Ricardian theoreticians limit the choice to one of the two 'distributive' variables (r, w) and the price of a commodity or basket of commodities (*numéraire*).

However, this does not in general make it possible to determine relative prices invariant with respect to the unit of measure and a uniform profit rate, with w fixed a priori. The general case in fact includes the production of non-basic articles, that is, goods which do not enter the production of other commodities (for a fuller discussion see section 9). Once the production of non-basics is admitted, the uniform profit rate becomes the particular profit rate of one part—the basic part—of the system, since only in this part is there interdependence between the price of inputs and the price of outputs. For the producers of non-basic goods there is no need to calculate the same rate of profit in the basic system, so that a solution involving positive prices can be derived for any arbitrary positive profit rate in the non-basic industries. If therefore there was a higher profit rate in the non-basic industries and a flow of capital from the basic industries into these, a new uniform rate would be attained, higher than that previously pertaining in the basic sector and lower than that in the non-basic sector.

## 7. Value and Price

We have already seen that by inserting the consumption of labour-power or labour as a real input, a solution price vector is obtained which is related in one way or another to commodity values. However in the resulting solution prices and values are always identical, which deprives it of any utility and obstructs the study of intersectoral and intertemporal deviations.

As for the uniform profit rate, in system (9) it appears as an increasing function of the coefficient of direct labour

$$r = \frac{\mathbf{y'L}}{\mathbf{y'T(I-T)^{-1}L}} \tag{19}$$

where $\mathbf{y'}$ is the row vector of gross output.

But though system (9) is useless for determining prices of production, equation (19), derived from it and from equation (7), does facilitate a rather awkward criticism of the neo-Ricardian system. Imagine a situation in which workers live on air and the wage can hence exercise no influence on the rate or mass of profit. It would still be absurd to think that the intensity or duration of labour would have no influence on the rate of profit.

Why is it absurd? One could reply that from the moment wages cease to form part of the costs of production, only the technical coefficients matter, so that if a change in $\mathbf{L}$ influences these then r will be affected, but otherwise as far as r is concerned nothing will change.

However, this is a scholastic objection. The system $\mathbf{Tp}(1+r)=\mathbf{p}$ does not just correspond to a situation in which work costs nothing, but also to that of a society of independent producers in competition with each other. If the latter find it worth diminishing their unit labour inputs, that is raising productivity, in order to secure an advantage over their competitors and become capitalists in the full sense, so will capitalists who don't have to pay their workers. Not calculating a wage among the costs of production is as if they worked on their own means of production! This is already enough to show why systems of the neo-Ricardian type are incompatible with an analysis in terms of socially necessary labour time, and for this reason it is illegitimate to use them for a critique of the transformation procedure in chapter 9 of volume 3 of *Capital*.

One thing which is not often noticed, but is nevertheless essential, is the fact that Marx's transformation depends on the analysis of the phases of the circuit of capital explained in *Capital* Volume 2, while Sraffa's system of prices of production makes abstraction from these different phases. In the circuits of industrial capital, whichever of the three is chosen, each phase presupposes the preceding, so that if any particular phase is fixed in prices of production all the others, before and after, are also fixed in prices of production.

If, on the other hand, it is fixed in value terms, then so are all the others. There is no other possibility. Transforming values of commodities into the corresponding prices of production implies the *transfer from one chain of the circuit to another*. If it is claimed to effect the transformation of values into prices in the ambit of the self-same succession of circuits, there will necessarily be a quantitative incongruence between the sum of prices and the sum of values, and/or between the sum of profits and the sum of surplus-values, except in particular circumstances. Anything else would be a source of wonderment. The problem rather is: can this circuit, or succession of circuits in prices, be self-sustaining in its own right? Or is it dominated and conditioned by the circuit of values, as Marx maintained?

Outside of all the arguments so far advanced against this possibility, one other is worth adding: the differentiation of profit rates. If instead of a single uniform rate we put a vector of sectoral rates into a neo-Ricardian system, then the average rate cannot be obtained purely as a function of all the sectoral rates, that is, taking all their levels as known. This limitation does not apply to Marx's calculation of the average profit rate which is uniquely a function of commodity values and has nothing to do with the individual or sectoral division of profits. It is therefore possible to carry out the following calculation:

$$\text{values} \rightarrow r \rightarrow r_i \, (i = 1, \ldots, n) \rightarrow p_i$$

While it is not arbitrary to pass in this way from the average to the sectoral rates, conceived as gravitating around the average rate, it *is* arbitrary to do the opposite: that is, to determine the particular rates in and of themselves and then calculate the average which results. Moreover, although without knowing particular rates it is even possible in a neo-Ricardian system to determine the hypothetical rate of equilibrium profit, this would nevertheless differ qualitatively from the average rate,[11] and hence could not serve as a reference point for the magnitudes of the sectoral rates. The average rate actually regulates the life of an economic system; the equilibrium rate does not.

The following diagram illustrates Marx's transformation procedure.

Figure 2

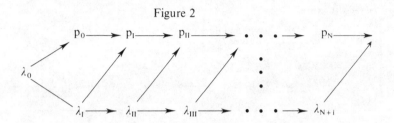

Here indices I, II, and III represent successive circuits, while $\lambda_i$ and $p_i$ are individual prices and values in any given circuit. In addition, let $s_i$, $\pi_i$ stand for surplus values and profits.

It is obvious that in general one cannot simultaneously have

$$\sum \lambda_i = \sum p_i \qquad \text{and} \qquad \sum s_i = \sum \pi_i$$

since $p_0$ of itself has no other point of departure; but by the same token it is clear that

$$\lambda_I + \lambda_{II} + \cdots + \lambda_{N+1} = p_0 + p_I + \cdots + p_N \text{ [12]}$$

The two chains of circuits have a common point of departure: the first capitalist circuit, that is the first circuit in which means of production come onto the scene as simple absorbers of other people's surplus-value.

In this first circuit the various inputs enter at their values and not at their price of production, a form that they cannot yet assume since—as Marx clarifies in *Capital* Volume 2—the initial circuit cannot be that of commodity-capital. The simultaneous equalization between total value and total price and between total surplus-value and total profit concerns the totality of circuits and not a single one.

From all this it flows that values determine and dominate prices of production, and also that within each single circuit there must be a high level of correlation between values and prices, which will show up also when input–output models are used. The difference between the way Marx determines prices of production and the typical neo-Ricardian method is illustrated below.

Figure 3

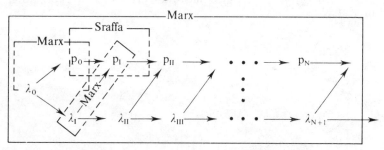

The transformation of any particular $\lambda_T$ to $p_T$ simply recapitulates the complete transformation from $\lambda_0$ to $p_T$, computed through $\lambda_I, \lambda_{II}, \ldots,$ $\lambda_{T+1}$.

The high correlation between values and prices can be verified empirically as well as theoretically. As regards the data, Anwar Shaikh shows in his piece in this collection, using input–output data relating to the US economy in successive periods, that the intertemporal and intersectoral correlation between values and market prices is very high (0.9). In and of itself this points to the conclusion that, calculating prices of production on the basis of the same data, the correlation would be even closer to one. Ian Steedman could surely object that this is an arbitrary conclusion, since both values and equilibrium prices are determined by the data, and one cannot assert that values determine prices or vice versa. This objection would however be illogical. Values are directly and unequivocally determined by conditions of production $(\mathbf{T}, \mathbf{L})$, whereas prices require in addition the conditions of distribution, which as we have seen renders superfluous the action of the direct labour coefficients. Figure 4 illustrates this process.

If we can show that distribution only acts as a small disturbance term in the variation of elements of the vector of relative prices, the conclusion flows automatically: variations in prices are dominated by variations in the technical conditions of production, which in their turn are no more than—synthesized—variations in the labour-values of the commodities.

Figure 4

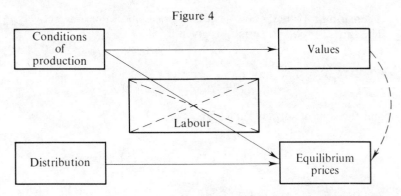

If what Steedman proclaims so categorically were true—that values play no role in determining equilibrium prices but are secondary and superfluous magnitudes, how can the high correlation between values and prices be explained? This is a result which the neo-Ricardian systems cannot anticipate theoretically. The only rational explanation is to admit that the substance of values and prices is one and the same thing—socially necessary labour-time.

This conclusion can be derived otherwise. When linear input–output systems are used to deal with the transformation of values into prices, Marx's two simultaneous equivalences hold under certain definite conditions. Among these is the case of maximum expanded reproduction in which all surplus-value is reconverted into additional capital and there is no place for the production of luxury goods. Expanded reproduction is characterized by the following equation:

$$\mathbf{y}_{t+1} = \mathbf{y}_t(1 + r) \tag{20}$$

(where $\mathbf{y}_t$ is the output from one productive period), that is, each producer expands production, and hence input, in the same proportion $(1 + r)$ during each turnover of the aggregate social capital. Moreover by definition of $\mathbf{T}$

$$\mathbf{T}\mathbf{y}_{t+1} = \mathbf{y}_t \tag{21}$$

And it can easily be shown, given (21) that if the sum of prices is set equal to the sum of values, the equality of profits and surplus-values results automatically. Equality between values and prices is given by

$$\mathbf{p}'\mathbf{y} = \mathbf{\Lambda}'\mathbf{y} \tag{22}$$

where $\mathbf{p}'$ and $\mathbf{\Lambda}'$ are the row vectors of prices and values respectively. The sum of profits in period t is given by

$$\mathbf{p}'\mathbf{y}_t - \mathbf{p}'\mathbf{T}\mathbf{y}_t = \mathbf{p}'\mathbf{T}\mathbf{y}_{t+1}\left(1 - \frac{1}{1+r}\right) \qquad (23)$$

and the sum of surplus-values by

$$\mathbf{y}_t - \mathbf{T}\mathbf{y}_t = \mathbf{\Lambda}'\mathbf{T}\mathbf{y}_{t+1}\left(1 - \frac{1}{1+r}\right) \qquad (24)$$

and since from (21) and (22) we get

$$\mathbf{p}'\mathbf{T}\mathbf{y}_{t+1} = \mathbf{p}'\mathbf{y}_t = \mathbf{\Lambda}\mathbf{y}_t \qquad (25)$$

the equality of (23) and (24) follows directly.

Where did this result come from? Was it an accident? Not in the least. Expanded reproduction has the exact property of correcting the optical distortion of incongruence between total surplus-value and total profit, and of their reciprocal independence within the framework of a single circuit or finite group of circuits of capital. In the neo-Ricardian system one begins from prices to get to prices; that is, the prices of inputs and outputs are determined simultaneously. This implies that the profits spent by the capitalists in the preceding circuit on the acquisition of luxury goods are missing from the prices of 'departure' (the inputs). In the passage from one circuit to the next, one part of the use values and hence of profit is destroyed, as if the capitalist class as a whole had suffered a total net loss. Only a fraction of this class (producers of luxury goods) get back a portion of the profits which the capitalists as a whole have spent on frivolities. In expanded reproduction this is obviously not possible, insofar as all profits are employed for productive purposes, and therefore in the passage from one circuit to another nothing is destroyed.

It is particularly interesting to note that if, little by little, we reduce the rate of growth involved in expanded reproduction until we reach simple reproduction, we find created a quantitative difference between sums of surplus-value and sums of profit which grows step by step until we reach a maximum under simple reproduction: when, that is, no part of profit or surplus-value is invested. This effect confirms the existence of the optical illusion we have just described.

## 8. Physical Surplus and Profit

Many Marxists criticize Sraffa's theory above all for its lack of an explanation for capitalist profit. Neo-Ricardian theoreticians have replied on three fronts: with the theory of the residuum, with the theory of deductions, and the theory of the physical surplus. They tend to fall back on the latter in particular, since the other two are fairly trivial, even though it turns out that rather than explaining the phenomenon of profit they try to eliminate the problem itself. Moreover, even if one manages to show that material surplus is the basis of profit, and that the level of surplus regulates the level of 'monetary' profit, this doesn't do away with the problem of explaining how in a particular economy the surplus presents itself in the form of price while in others (feudalism, slavery, communal) it doesn't. But we'll pass over this. Objections of a more fundamental and logical character can be brought to bear on the theory of the physical surplus.

A directly measurable surplus exists under rather particular circumstances. The composition of outputs must be kept homogeneous in relation to that of inputs in successive periods of production. If in each period new products and processes are invented, this homogeneity is destroyed and no direct means can be devised to find out if a surplus exists.

In fact if one is completely rigorous, even the existence of something that corresponds physically to the category of surplus is in doubt. Even the physiocrats all understood that a surplus does not exist in industry. But their reasoning can also be applied to agriculture and extractive industry: both crops in the ground and raw iron exist well before being converted into consumable products. They are distinguished from industrial raw materials by not having a price, that is, they do not constitute part of the costs of production: but this has nothing to do with a rigorous concept of *physical* surplus.

What, however, is more demonstrative, is the fact that concrete examples can be presented of systems of production in which there is a material surplus without profit, and vice versa. The case concerned is that of a joint production, the most general case of production.

Suppose there are two producers, both of whom make commodity A and commodity B, the first using only A and the second only B. A and B are both consumed by the workers. In Sraffa's notation the system is as follows:

$$ap_a(1+r) + a_1p_a + b_1p_b = A_1p_a + B_1p_b$$
$$bp_b(1+r) + a_1p_a + b_1p_b = A_2p_a + B_2p_b \tag{26}$$
$$p_a = 1$$

In this system it is obviously assumed that $l_1 = l_2 = 1$; that the real wage is given $(a_1, b_1)$; that a and b are the quantities of A and B used as inputs by producers 1 and 2 respectively; and that $A_i$ and $B_i (i = 1, 2)$ are the quantities of A and B produced by the two producers respectively.

The conditions for a physical surplus with negative profits are given respectively by

$$A_1 + A_2 - a - 2a_1 + B_1 + B_2 - b - 2b_1 > 0 \qquad (27)$$

and

$$A_1 + A_2 - a - 2a_1 < -(B_1 + B_2 + b + 2b_1)p_b \qquad (28)$$

Writing A* and B* for the surplus of A and B respectively, condition (28) can be rewritten as

$$p_b > -(A^*/B^*) \qquad (29)$$

Writing $A_i^*$ and $B_i^*$ for the surplus of A and B in 1 and 2 respectively, condition (29) can be written

$$A_1^* < -B^*p_b + A_2^* \qquad (30)$$

Both conditions (29) and (30) are perfectly admissible.

From the system (26) it can be seen directly that since $p_a = 1$, $p_b$ is the root of a second degree equation which will admit negative solutions under certain conditions. If $p_b$ is negative, there are hence values of A* and B* which render the total profit of the system negative even though the physical surplus is positive. Equation (30) shows that $p_b$ does not even have to be negative for the paradox of negative profits with a positive surplus. Many numerical examples can be constructed.[13]

## 9. Basic and Non-Basic Commodities

The distinction between basic and non-basic commodities is drawn out by Sraffa in relation to their use as productive inputs. A commodity is basic if, directly or indirectly, it is used to produce all other commodities. Otherwise it is non-basic. There can therefore exist non-basic commodities which are inputs, if these are used only in the production of other non-basics.

This seems to be quite an important distinction because only basics enter the determination of the rate of profit. As we have already seen in our discussion on the transformation problem, this is a direct consequence of the identification of production and circulation. To be precise, it happens because the circuit of capital has been eliminated. If production and circulation are identical—something implicit in making the profit rate a category of production—then non-basics have nothing to do with redistributing social profit to single capitals and/or sectors; each capitalist would receive simply a profit proportional to costs, and therefore the equations which correspond to the production of non-basic commodities can be cancelled without changing the magnitudes which determine the system. The production of non-basics does not affect the rate of profit, which is no longer the result of the 'communal' distribution of the social profit to single capitalists because a real social profit does not exist any more.

There are various objections that can be made to the category of basic commodity. The first, spontaneous question is: is the money-commodity basic or non-basic? If it is a pure *numéraire* it must be a basic commodity, or when we eliminate the non-basic equations we will also eliminate the *numéraire* equation. If, on the other hand we conceive of money as it really is, that is also as a means of realization and circulation, it must necessarily be a non-basic commodity since by its nature it cannot enter as input into the production of anything, being condemned to live forever in the sphere of circulation.

It is a non-basic commodity, yet turns out to be more important than a basic commodity for effecting exchange and hence for the continued reproduction of the economic system. For simple reproduction, Sraffa shows that non-basic commodities can arise with the production of a physical surplus, in the shape of luxury goods. But if the newly-produced non-basic commodity is the money-commodity, it cannot lead to the distribution of any surplus to the various producers, since the commodity which serves as money cannot be individually consumed by anyone. This also rules out the prospect of obtaining a rate of profit.

There are however other objections to the subdivision into basic/non-basic. First of all, there are perfectly feasible systems with no basic commodities but with a positive profit rate and prices. In the second place, it can be shown that two of Sraffa's assertions which tend to confirm the 'predominance' of the basic sector are not exact.

The first concerns the so-called 'standard' commodity, which is a composite with the same composition as the inputs required in its production at all levels of output, and which makes the wage/profit relation linear if used as *numéraire* for the wage. Sraffa maintains that this contains no non-basic commodities. This is not exact, but we won't go into it here.

More relevant is his second assertion, that there are cases in which the profit rate cannot be equalized. Such circumstances arise, for example, if non-basic commodities are used to produce other non-basic commodities.[14] It doesn't happen if the rate of material reproduction of basic commodities is higher than the rate of material reproduction of non-basic commodities. But in the contrary case a uniform rate of profit can be associated with positive prices, yet its range of variation would be determined by the conditions of production of non-basic commodities, gravely undermining the presumed supremacy of the basic sector.

If the non-basic sector determines the range of variation of the profit rate, then it must also define the range of variation of relative prices. The numerical example which follows clarifies the point.

Suppose the system has three industries. The first produces a basic commodity, a. The other two produce two non-basic inputs, each of which enters only into the production of the other (b and c). We assume that prices are divided by the wage w, and that all inputs of labour are equal to 1

$$(0.3p_a)(1 + r_1) = p_a$$
$$(0.2p_a + 0.4p_c)(1 + r_2) = p_b \qquad (31)$$
$$(0.4p_a + 0.6p_b)(1 + r_2) = p_c$$

From the first equation we can quickly deduce that $p_a$ is positive if $r_1 < 7/3$. From the second and third it can be calculated that $p_a$ and $p_b$ are positive if $r_2$ is less than the maximum eigenvalue of the matrix

$$\begin{bmatrix} 0 & 0.6 \\ 0.4 & 0 \end{bmatrix}$$

which is equal to about 0.4899. Therefore, if $r_1 = r_2 = r$, the rate of profit must vary between limits (0, 0.4899) since $0.4899 < 7/3$.

## 10. Uniform Profit Rate and Competition

In systems of the neo-Ricardian type and their precursors from Torrens to von Bortkiewicz, each sector of production and each individual capital secures an identical profit rate on advanced capital. Capitals which vary widely both in structure and in what they produce are nevertheless valorized at exactly the same rate. Where does this principle come from? Are we dealing with an absolute magnitude like the velocity of light in physics, invariant with respect to the frame of reference? In and of itself the issue relates only to the conduct of individual capitalists, who fix their prices on the basis of the whole of their invested capital and not just a particular part of it. But this does not call for a uniform profit rate at each point in time, nor for a long term tendency to the convergence of sectoral profit rates.

A treatment of the mechanism of equalization is to be found in Adam Smith's works. He argues that if there were a difference in profit rates, all capitals would tend to be transferred to those sectors where the rate of profit is highest, raising the level of production and the supply of those commodities which gave a superior rate of profit, so that excess supply would arise and market prices would fall. The reverse would simultaneously take place where the rate of profit was low, giving rise to a general tendency for the rate to become uniform in all sectors.

This mechanism is generally retained with some reservations. Nonetheless, things are not quite so simple. In Smith's explanation the uniform profit rate is in reality presupposed, since he tries to imagine what would happen if one moved from the uniform rate to the differentiated ones. If, on the other hand, one begins from a situation where rates are differentiated, then the uniform rate would arise from a *disequilibrium* between demand and supply in the various sectors and not from a pre-existing equilibrium.

Equilibrium between supply and demand would in fact leave the situation unaltered. Higher rates of profit would tend to fall because of an excess supply arising from the numbers of capitals employed in the sector, and vice versa for the lower rate of profit. Now, suppose the movement of capital from one sector to another continued as long as there were differences between demand and supply. In the most profitable sector prices would begin to fall, with the effect of tending to increase demand. If this rise in demand is sufficiently rapid, prices will cease falling. They will continue falling only if a definite limit to the increase is assumed, that is, a determinate limit to the rise in demand.

Under the opposite hypothesis, the conclusions are no different. If demand is in every case fixed, the movement of capital from one sector to another would have to slow down in a precise relation to the fall in prices, if the final result is to be a uniform rate. In both cases the assumption of a definite functional relation between supply and demand is indispensable if one wants to derive the convergence of sectoral rates towards the uniform rate. In the most general case, which Marx outlined, there is no convergence but an oscillation in particular sectors around an average constituted by the average profit rate, so that at any given time the true situation is given by a vector of differentiated profit rates and not a uniform one.[15]

Neo-Ricardian theory can still not admit that the uniform profit rate depends on a particular relation between demand and supply since this would amount to an open confession of a close family relationship between their theories and general economic equilibrium. In consequence, neo-Ricardian theory makes no attempt to justify the existence of a uniform profit rate, and Luigi Pasinetti, for example, interprets it as an 'institutional principle of economics', a phrase which certainly does not constitute an explanation.

All this has certain consequences, for example in relation to the famous question of choice of technique in the Okishio theorem. Okishio treats the uniform rate as an institutional principle and eliminates the links between the rate obtaining in a single sector and/or for a single capital, and the rates in others. This is the only way to show that the new methods of production which permit those capitalists who adopt them to obtain a rate of profit higher than the preceding one will raise the general rate of profit when they spread. The profit–rate criterion becomes identical with the cost criterion and one ends up showing that the profit rate can never fall as a result of technical progress. If, however, one clears away the false autonomy of the individual rates of profit, this whole demonstration vanishes. However, the concordance between neo-Ricardian and neo-classical approaches to the problem of choice of technique is not casual, because of a fundamental fact: both the neo-Ricardians' linear systems and general equilibrium systems make complete abstraction from the commodity character of social production and cannot therefore in any way encompass the analysis of the interaction of multiple individual capitals and sectors—that is, competition.[16]

## 11. Standard Commodity and Exploitation

The standard commodity makes it possible to construct a linear relation between wage and profit rate, eliminating the influence of prices on this relation. At the same time it has the property of constituting an 'invariable standard of prices' since these latter do not vary when distribution varies, if measured with the standard commodity. This role of invariable measure of prices is quite limited. It doesn't work when the technical conditions of production change, which has not stopped several neo-Ricardian theoreticians trying to apply the standard commodity to the analysis of capitalist exploitation, in order to establish that exploitation can also be illustrated using Sraffian theories. Other economists think the standard commodity is adapted to the construction of a theory of national income distribution, which would make it possible to overcome the limitation of a purely arbitrary determination of the real wage.

John Eatwell's demonstration of the first proposition uses the linearity of relations between wages and profits to show that the worker is deprived of a quota of her or his labour,[17] that is, a portion of the net product. But this is obvious without Eatwell's demonstration, and will be so in every economy except those in which the workers consume the entire net product—including, for example, socialism, where as Marx explained in the *Critique of the Gotha Programme*, all manner of social expenses must be met before the individual consumption of the workers, and precisely out of the net product. But it has nothing to with *capitalist* exploitation, which is the result of an *exchange of equivalents*, of which there is no trace in the neo-Ricardian system where labour-power is not a commodity.

The possibility that the standard commodity might be used to demonstrate exploitation is also limited by other, decisive factors. First, the standard commodity can serve to express wages only if wages themselves form part of national income and not of advanced capital. Second, the standard commodity can only be constructed on the assumption of a uniform profit rate, and it is clear that exploitation can neither depend on how wages are treated nor on the fact that there is by chance a single uniform profit rate.

The second proposition, due mainly to Luigi Pasinetti,[18] is based on taking for granted that the wage can be expressed in terms of the standard commodity. In order to use the standard commodity as a measure it must already have been constructed, and in turn such a construction demands that the real system be converted into the standard system, that is, that the vector of coefficients which transforms the actual system into such a system is known.

At this point we have the standard system, and no longer the real system, so that everything can be done only if it can be done in the standard system. The linear relation between the wage rate and the profit rate, in particular, is

$$r = R(1 - w) \tag{32}$$

where r is the profit rate, w the real wage expressed in terms of the standard commodity, and R is the standard relation, equal to the maximum rate of profit.

It is evident that the relation between r and w is not, however, independent of the quantity of the standard commodity which goes to the workers. Yet if the 'disturbing' influence of prices on the relation between r and w is eliminated, one is still obliged to fix the real wage a priori.

# Gold, Money and the Transformation Problem

## Ernest Mandel

The role of gold and gold production have been repeatedly invoked by different critics of Marx's solution of the so-called transformation problem. Von Bortkiewicz used gold as the production of department III, postulating its production price as invariant relative to transformation (i.e., postulating a fixed value of gold). His whole solution of the mathematical problem hinges on this postulate as it enables him to reduce a system of three equations with four unknowns to a system of three equations with three unknowns. Sweezy imitates the method and arrives at the same conclusions. Sraffa and Steedman do away with the monetary problem altogether and treat gold as a commodity identical to others.[1]

We will try to prove that the way in which gold production is treated by these critics is inadequate and introduces additional contradictions into their argument. Furthermore, we will show how the haphazard and accidental way these critics deal with gold and gold production reflects a fundamental lack of understanding of the very nature of commodity production and the capitalist mode of production. Finally, we will locate in this inadequate treatment of gold and money the reflection of all the contradictions and inadequacies of the neo-Ricardians; which is but a reproduction of the very same contradictions and inadequacies of Ricardo's theory itself, culminating in the dualism between a labour theory of value explaining commodity production in general, and a quantity theory of money explaining the value of a special commodity, gold.

### Commodity Production and Gold Production

Commodity production presupposes the separation of commodity and money. This separation is rooted in the contradictory character of commodity-producing labour: the contradiction between private labour and social labour. Commodity production presupposes a minimum degree of division of labour and a socialization of labour. Commodity producers produce for exchange instead of for direct consumption. This implies that their own consumption, be it individual consumption, family consumption or that of the primitive communities into which these producers are still integrated, occurs through exchange and not through direct appropriation of use-values. Their consumption is covered by products of other producers. Commodity production is based upon social labour mediated through exchange.

But exchange presupposes in turn private ownership in the economic sense of the word: the total labour potential of a given society, of a community of producers and consumers, has been fragmented into separate units each of which can and does dispose of the products of its labour and alienate these products only through exchange. Thereby, their labour has become private labour. Different private labours, as use-value-producing labours, as concrete labours or as labour of a specific profession or craft are incommensurable. They can only lead to exchange on a more or less equal basis, on the basis of all specific crafts being treated as as more or less equal, if abstraction is made of their professional specificity, and if they are treated as just a fragment of the society's total disposable labour-power. In other words, if they are treated as abstract labour. Commodity-producing labour is therefore simultaneously social labour and private labour, private labour being treated as a part of social labour.

However, the produced commodity cannot directly be treated as social labour, precisely because it is a product of private labour and it is private property. Its production thus presupposes private and not social control over conditions of production, appropriation and realization. Only after the realization of the exchange value of the commodity is the social character of the private labour which it contains recognized as social labour by society. Only after the measurement of the exchange value which the producer (proprietor) of the commodity receives for a product can it be determined whether all of their private labour spent upon its production has or has not been recognized as socially necessary labour. Private property, and the private character of labour in which it is rooted, imply, therefore, that producers and owners of commodities relate to each other as parts of a given society; not directly as human beings, but only through the exchange of the commodities they produce and own. The social fabric is maintained through exchange and through production for exchange.

But once it is understood that commodity-producing labour cannot immediately be recognized as social labour, it follows that only through the existence of a special commodity, money—the general equivalent—can exchange itself become regular and continuous. Since each commodity is private property, an instrument of private interests, generalized exchange requires a unique commodity which embodies social labour directly and serves as a measurement of all other commodities. This is the function of the money commodity.[2]

The social nature of labour, rooted in the social division of labour, does not lead automatically to commodity production, a market economy and a money economy. It does so only under specific social conditions. Commodity production and the division of the commodity into commodity and money do not flow automatically from the division of labour and the growing productivity of labour, through technical progress or progress in labour organisation for example. They are indissolubly linked to these specific forms of economic organization only under conditions of private property and appropriation, that is under conditions of private labour. Under different social relations of production, the social nature of the producer's labour can be, has been and will be directly and immediately recognized as such by society. It did not nor will not need any deviation or mediation through exchange before it can be recognized as social labour.

But if commodity-producing labour needs a general equivalent, a 'thing' in which the social character of its labour can be immediately recognized, money can play that role only because it is itself a commodity.[3] Money is itself the product of abstract human labour, of a fragment of the total labour potential at the disposal of a given society. Otherwise, money and all commodities would in turn remain incommensurable. The money-commodity gold is therefore the one commodity which enters the circulation process with its value and not with a price.[4] When Marx states that all commodities can enter the circulation process only price-determined (*preisbestimmt*),[5] this implies that their price is the expression of their value in the value of the money-commodity.

Any other conclusion would be based upon circular reasoning. One cannot presuppose the existence of a price determination of commodities without explaining what determines their prices. One cannot suppose that these prices depend upon the money-commodity without determining what determines the value of gold. One cannot establish the value of gold without determining the nature of all value, or upon the tacit assumption of incommensurability of commodities on the one hand—prices not determined by value—and of gold on the other hand. Eiether gold has value, ot it has a 'price' determined by 'something' else than value, different and apart from the price of all other commodities. Hence it would be incommensurable with all other commodities.

Only because gold has value can all other commodities have prices.[6] But only because the prices of all other commodities are based upon value, can the value of gold determine the prices of commodities.[7] Under commodity production, be it capitalist production or simple commodity production, changes in the general price level are always basically the result of a double movement: changes in the value, in the productivity of labour, of industrial and agricultural production on the one hand, and on the other hand changes in the value of gold.[8] (Here we do not consider price fluctuations due to competition, i.e. we consider 'capital in general'.) If the productivity of labour in industry and agriculture increases more than the productivity of labour in gold mining, the general price level will tend to decline. If the productivity of labour in agriculture and industry increases less than in gold mining, the general price level will tend to rise.

In the first case, we shift from one ounce of gold = one week of labour = ten tons of steel towards one ounce of gold = one week of labour = twnety tons of steel. Thus the price of one ton of steel falls from one ounce of gold to half an ounce of gold. In the second case, we shift from one ounce of gold = one week of labour = one ton of steel, towards three ounces of gold = one week of labour = 2 tons of steel. The price of ten tons of steel rises from one ounce of gold to one and a half ounces of gold.

Since gold production is mining, it is a part of department I and not of a putative department III.[9] Mining, depending more than other branches of production on natural conditions and the presence and relative richness of mineral deposits, generally does not have the same rhythm of increase of labour productivity as industry or agriculture. The general trend under commodity production with a gold-money standard and constantly rising labour productivity (since the beginning of the capitalist mode of production) will be one of declining prices expressed in gold. This trend will be interrupted only by the discovery of new gold fields rich enough to reverse the natural trend to a stagnating, declining or only slowly rising productivity of labour in already exploited gold mines, or by a radical revolution of mining techniques. Such a revolution in the value of gold happened three times in the history of capitalism, each time followed by a steep increase of the general price level: in the sixteenth century, as a result of the exploitation of the gold and silver mines of the Western hemisphere by the Spanish conquistadores; after 1848, with the discovery of the Californian gold field; and in the 1890s through the exploitation of the South African Rand, and, to a lesser extent, the Australian gold fields.[10]

## Capitalist Commodity Production and Capitalist Gold Production

Commodity production viewed as the production of 'capital in general' is only an analytical device, a stepping-stone in Marx's successive approximation approach from the 'essence' to the phenomena apparent in real economic day-to-day life. Real capitalist commodity production is production by many capitals and is mediated through competition. This is implicit in private property itself. It is only because of the existence of 'many capitals', with different organic compositions, different production costs, different profits and different rates of profit, that the transformation problem itself arises. To assume uniform rates of profit of all branches of production or all firms, is not to 'solve' the transformation problem. It is to assume that the problem to be solved does not really exist.

Marx therefore raises the transformation problem only in the third volume of *Capital*, because it is only there that the problem of capitalist competition, of 'many capitals' is dealt with. The first two volumes deal with 'capital in general', where there is no place for that problem. Capitalist commodity production, viewed in the light of the existence of 'many capitals' and their mutual competition, implies firstly, that production is not only production of commodities with exchange value realized through sale, but also production for profit, each firm being forced to strive to maximize profit under the pressure of competition.

Secondly, it implies that the objective motive forces and the objective results of the subjective motivation of capitalist entrepreneurs must be uncovered, and cannot be automatically derived. For example, the fact that each firm takes decisions in order to maximize profits might very well lead to results in which the overwhelming majority of firms will in fact realize less profits than if they had not all taken that decision, yet some will profit more.

Thirdly, it implies that the objective source of profit must be uncovered. In the same way as price is the money-form of value (in the last analysis based upon abstract human labour), profit is the money-form of surplus-value, that is value produced by labour-power over and above its own costs of reproduction. To take profit for granted in the sphere of circulation, and not look for its sources in the sphere of production, is not only logically and analytically inconsistent. It leads again to problems of incommensurability. For it is enough to represent profits as the social surplus product, that is as a sum of commodities (additional fixed means of production plus additional circulating capital in the form of gold plus luxury consumer goods), to see that the problem of a common measure of 'profit goods', commodities in general, and gold, arises. And this leads back to the problem of value.

The final implication is that as capitalist production is a production for profit, and as profit is the money-form of surplus-value, capitalist gold production, that is not only the value of gold but also the rate of profit in gold mining, will influence the general level of profits. That the value of gold will influence the general price level and hence the general level of profits, at least in the short run, already flows from what has been said before about the influence of the value of gold upon the general price level. When a sudden strong decline in the value of gold, for instance after the discovery of new rich gold fields, causes a strong rise in the general price level, this does not influence all prices equally and in the same time span. Generally, one can assume that prices of consumer goods, both mass consumer goods and luxury goods, as well as raw materials and intermediary products used in gold mining, will rise before and more quickly than prices of fixed means of production, be it only because the latter do not need to be constantly or totally replaced.[11] So in the short run, department II and parts of department I will witness a stronger rise in prices than department I as a whole, the organic composition of capital will tend to decline, and the general rate of profit will rise. This will be even more so if the rise in wages in all of industry and agriculture lags behind the rise in prices of consumer goods, which means that the rate of surplus-value increases simultaneously with the decline in the organic composition of capital. The long-term effects on the average rate of profit of the general rise in the price level triggered off by a sharp decline in the value of gold will be examined later in this article.

As to the effects of a sharp decline in the value of gold on the rate of profit in gold mining, and on the general rate of profit, at this stage of the analysis it is sufficient to state the following. Gold has many functions besides being a medium of exchange. One of them is to act as a means of hoarding, of anticipating future demand, by embodying the equivalents of future, anticipated and yet to be produced commodities. In this function, nearly all currently produced or produceable gold will always find buyers (we shall see later that this is not true in an absolute sense; this is why we use the term 'nearly'). Therefore, if through the discovery of new rich gold fields, the value of gold (the amount of socially necessary labour embodied in gold) is suddenly sharply decreased, but at the same time most of the old gold fields continue to produce, then the richer gold fields will yield high surplus-profits in the form of differential mineral rents. These high surplus-profits obviously increase the total mass of profits in gold mining as against the total capital invested in that branch, at least in the short run, as capital investment cannot increase as quickly as these rich windfall profits. Therefore the average rate of profit in gold mining will tend to increase sharply and, all things remaining equal, the general rate of profit will likewise increase, albeit not in the same proportion. Thereby, a general supplementary influx of capital into gold mining will be induced.

## Capitalist Gold Production and the Operation of the Law of Value

After the birth of the capitalist mode of production, gold production remained for a long time essentially handicraft production, with a few instances of manufacturing capital organizing larger-scale output. Only with the discovery of the rich South African goldfields did capital really start dominating gold production, making extensive use of wage-labour and modern machinery. As long as gold production was essentially petty-commodity production, empirical facts didn't raise any basic problem for the theory that gold exchanges at value level against commodities whose value has been transformed into prices. Indeed, one might well wonder whether Ricardo's mistaken quantity theory of money didn't find its basic roots in this perculiarity of gold production.

The situation changed when gold production in turn was capitalistically organized. This implied that capitalists investing their capital in gold mining expected to realize at least the average rate of profit existing in a given country for a given period. Gold production being commodity production, as is the case for all other commodities, at first sight it should be the weighted average productivity of gold mining which should determine the value of gold. However, like grain production in nineteenth-century Britain, gold production is commodity production under special circumstances: those of 'structural scarcity' which cannot be overcome by short-term or medium-term inflows of capital into the particular branch of production concerned. Given the special nature of the commodity gold, which implies that it is not only a means of circulation but also the general embodiment of human wealth in a market economy (a general social reserve fund, a means of hoarding, frozen anticipated future demand), nearly all gold which can be physically produced will find a purchaser on the market. Therefore, capital invested in the least-productive gold mines in operation will fetch their owners the average rate of profit, that is, will determine the social value (price of production) of gold. Capital invested in more productive gold mines will fetch its owners surplus-profits taking the form of differential mining rents.

The average rate of profit is not stable for longer periods in a given country. It fluctuates as a function of fluctuations in the organic composition of capital, in the average rate of surplus-value and in other partially independent variables in society as a whole, independently of what happens in gold production or inside gold mines. If there is a sudden rise in the average rate of profit in society as a whole, to which production costs in the least productive gold mines cannot adjust immediately or rapidly, the rate of profit of capital invested in those gold mines will decline below the social average and they will eventually be closed. Capital will flow out of gold mining towards other branches of industry. Gold production will fall below what is technically possible. That is why, in spite of its quality as a general or universal commodity, not all gold which could be produced actually will be produced—only nearly all.

In the opposite way, when there is a sudden fall in the average rate of profit in society taken as a whole, which cannot lead immediately or very rapidly to a reopening of closed gold mines for obvious technical reasons, the rate of profit in gold mining will rise above the social average. Even the least productive gold mines still in operation will fetch the owners of capital invested in them surplus profits in the form of differential mining rents. Capital will flow away from other branches of production into gold mining and exploration for new gold mines will be intensified. This will also lead, with an inevitable time-lag, to production being restarted in previously closed mines where production costs prevented owners fetching the average rate of profit. This influx of capital into gold mining will continue till the rate of profit in the least-productive gold mines in operation is equal to the social average rate of profit.

Given capitalistically organized gold mining, the general process towards the equalization of the rate of profit through capital flows between different branches of industry therefore applies to gold-mining as well. Gold mining cannot excape this specific mode of operation of the law of value under capitalism through the mechanism of capital movements in search of higher profits, different as it is from the law's operation through simple exchange under pre-capitalist conditions. This remains true even though gold, as a general equivalent, enters the process of circulation with a value and not with a price. For like all other commodities, it cannot enter the process of circulation without being produced, without first leaving the process of production. What happens in that process of production is pre-determined by capitalists' profitability (expected and realized profit, interacting with each other, determining investment), that is in the last instance by average conditions (costs) of production and by the equalization of the rate of profit.

Therefore, the law of value rules gold mining through the fluctuations in the cost of production in that branch of the economy, which are determined by the fluctuations in the general wage level,[12] by the general level of prices of machinery, energy, raw materials and auxiliary products indispensable for industrially organized gold mining, and by the general level of the rate of interest. All these elements of gold production costs are largely unaffected by the intrinsic productivity of this or that gold mine, except in an extremely indirect way, which we need not analyse here. But all these elements co-determine the price of production (value) of gold. We say 'price of production' because we have seen that gold mining is subordinated to the general laws of the process towards equalization of the rate of profit, which are expressed in the formation of prices of production.

It is through this nexus—the determination of the value (price of production) of gold by its own *varying* costs of production—that gold becomes part and parcel of general capitalist commodity production, and that the general laws applying to all capitalist commodity production, above all the laws determining the value (price of production) of all commodities, apply to the 'universal commodity' too. This is the precise reason gold *can* become a 'universal commodity', a 'general equivalent' for the value of all commodities, which *can* therefore express their value in gold and then enter the circulation process with a price, which is nothing but their value (price of production) expressed in gold.

Throughout the nineteenth century up to the First World War, and after that, from the Bretton Woods Agreement to Nixon's proclamation of the inconvertibility of the dollar in 1971, the practical mechanisms through which the law of value applied to gold mining were obvious. The leading capitalist powers' central bank, first the Bank of England, then the US Federal Reserve System, bought, or was ready to buy, all produced gold at a fixed price of £3 17s 10½d or $20 an ounce before 1914, and $35 an ounce from 1933 to 1969. In reality, this formula is of course unscientific. It should read: the 'gold contents' of £1 and of $1 (the quantity of gold each banknote was representing) was fixed at respectively, 1/3.89 of an ounce of gold for one pre-1914 pound, and 1/35th of an ounce of gold for one pre-1969 dollar.

All gold mines producing at costs of production which did not fetch their owners the socially average rate of profit at the above 'purchase price' for gold, tended to get closed. Conversely, during periods of general crisis of over-production, when the socially average rate of profit was rapidly declining, the rate of profit in gold mining tended to rise above the average because of this fixed 'purchasing price', that is the fixed 'gold contents' (gold representation) of convertible banknotes. There would be an influx of capital into gold mining and gold production would go up while general commodity production went down. Hence the anticyclical nature of gold production and of capital investment in gold mining.

In those periods in which the paper currencies of many (or most) capitalist countries were inconvertible, and central banks no longer offered a fixed purchasing price for gold so that each paper currency represented a constantly changing quantity of gold, free market prices of gold played more or less the same role as the previously fixed price played before. This is especially obvious in the 1970s, leading to a situation where the gold content of paper currencies (the quantity of gold each paper currency represents) adapted itself in the long run to the free-market price, even officially, through the revaluation of the value of the central banks' gold stocks in terms of this free market gold price.

There is no circular reasoning involved here, as these free-market prices of gold are in the last analysis nothing but the reciprocal of the general rate of inflation of inconvertible paper currencies (which represented constantly declining quantities of gold).[13] And the ups and downs of this general rate of inflation are closely dependent on the general state of the capitalist economy, on fluctuations in the average rate of profit and, through this mediation, on fluctuations in production costs in gold mining.

## Fluctuations in the Value of Gold and Fluctuations in the General Price Level

As said before, the general price level of commodities is determined by the correlation of divergent or potentially divergent values, that is in the last analysis divergent or potentially divergent trends in the productivity of labour in general commodity production on the one hand, and gold production on the other hand. As commodity prices are the expression of commodity values in the value of gold, both of which are largely independent variables, we get the following table where $\pi$ stands for productivity, $\Delta\pi$ ($= \partial\pi/\partial t$) its rate of change with time, and $|\Delta\pi|$ is the absolute magnitude of $\Delta\pi$.

Figure 1

| Variants | (a) Productivity of Labour in Gold Mining | (b) Productivity of Labour in Industry and Agriculture | General Price Level |
|---|---|---|---|
| 1 | $\Delta\pi_a = 0$ | $\Delta\pi_b = 0$ | Static |
| 2 | $\Delta\pi_a = 0$ | $\Delta\pi_b > 0$ | Falling |
| 3 | $\Delta\pi_a = 0$ | $\Delta\pi_b < 0$ | Rising |
| 4 | $\Delta\pi_a < 0$ | $\Delta\pi_b = 0$ | Falling |
| 5 | $\Delta\pi_a < 0$ | $\Delta\pi_b > 0$ | Falling |
| 6a | $\Delta\pi_a < 0$ | $\Delta\pi_b < 0; |\Delta\pi_b| = |\Delta\pi_a|$ | Static |
| 6b | $\Delta\pi_a < 0$ | $\Delta\pi_b < 0; |\Delta\pi_b| > |\Delta\pi_a|$ | Falling |
| 6c | $\Delta\pi_a < 0$ | $\Delta\pi_b < 0; |\Delta\pi_b| < |\Delta\pi_a|$ | Rising |
| 7 | $\Delta\pi_a > 0$ | $\Delta\pi_b = 0$ | Rising |
| 8 | $\Delta\pi_a > 0$ | $\Delta\pi_b < 0$ | Rising |
| 9a | $\Delta\pi_a > 0$ | $\Delta\pi_b > 0; |\Delta\pi_b| = |\Delta\pi_a|$ | Static |
| 9b | $\Delta\pi_a > 0$ | $\Delta\pi_b > 0; |\Delta\pi_b| > |\Delta\pi_a|$ | Rising |
| 9c | $\Delta\pi_a > 0$ | $\Delta\pi_b > 0; |\Delta\pi_b| < |\Delta\pi_a|$ | Falling |

In other words, the general price level is rising when $\Delta\pi_b < \Delta\pi_a$, falling when $\Delta\pi_b > \Delta\pi_a$, and static when the two are equal. The most interesting cases, from a theoretical and historical point of view, are cases 7 and 9c. This refers to a sudden radical decline in the value of gold through the discovery of a new gold field, a so-called gold bonanza.[14] Through what concrete mechanisms does the sudden fall in the value of gold lead to a general rise in the price level?

### Gold Production and Price Revolutions

In order not to complicate the answer by the side issue of balance of payments fluctuations, let us assume all gold production occurs in a single region of a single country and constitutes the exclusive output of that region. A sudden increase in gold production in that region will lead to various consequences, all having equal (or similar) results.

Firstly, there will be a rapid internal migration of labour (gold miners and gold explorers) into that region, who will have to be fed and who will spend their wages (or surplus-profits) partially on luxury goods. Hence there will be a sudden inflow of consumer goods, both mass consumer goods and luxury goods, into the gold-mining region. As output cannot be increased immediately and in the same proportion, the market prices of all consumer goods will rise simply through a temporary imbalance of supply and demand for these goods. There will also be a near-immediate influx of capital into the gold-bonanza area.[15]

Secondly, under capitalism, a general increase of 'embodied social wealth' (monetary demand, either immediate or frozen, that is, held back for future expenditure) will occur in the whole country, since gold is, as the general equivalent, immediately differentiated purchasing power. Not all the increased gold output is being spent immediately inside the gold-mining region itself: part of it flows out into the rest of the country. Thereby, a general imbalance of demand and supply occurs, and market prices, which have initially risen only for specific commodities flowing into the gold mining districts, will tend to rise throughout the economy.

Thirdly, this general rise of market prices is a deviation (and an increasing deviation) from the value (prices of production) of all commodities other than gold. These values were determined by conditions of production existing in all branches of production previous to the sudden gold bonanza and, with regard to prices of production, by the process towards equalization of the rate of profit resulting from capital flows previous to the gold bonanza. But such a deviation of the market prices of commodities from their values cannot persist for long. Essentially, it will be changed through what occurs—or does not occur—in the field of production and in that of capital movements. And here, only two basically different hypotheses are possible.

Either the decrease in gold's value has been relatively limited, as has been the increase in general social demand embodied in the growth of the gold stock existing in the country after the discovery of the gold bonanza. In that case, the inflow of capital into gold mining, and the reopening of unproductive mines following such a bonanza, will lead to an increase of gold output at much higher costs of production than the bonanza gold, the general increase in the price level adding of course to the rise in the cost of gold production.[16] There will be a process towards equalization of the rate of profit between gold mining and all other branches of production and a general petering-out of the price increases of all commodities. This will be at a slightly higher level than before the discovery of the new gold mines or at the previous price level, depending on whether the long-term determinants of the value of gold have been slightly changed (whether the long-term value of gold has declined slightly) or not changed at all in the period following the bonanza discovery.

One of the mechanisms through which this could occur would be a general crisis of overproduction, following the short-term boom induced by the gold bonanza. This would mean that the general increase in social demand in the country, caused by the arrival of supplementary gold from the gold bonanza region, had led to a general increase of investment and output which rapidly ran out of steam, because the increase in the value of gold was only limited, no large new markets appeared, no cumulative increase in labour productivity (no new technological revolution) occurred throughout the economy, and no basic force appeared to stop the trend towards a normal cyclical decline of the average rate of profit.

If however the decrease of the value of gold was massive and of such a magnitude as to make a similar decrease in the value of all industrial and agricultural commodities impossible in the medium or even long term—for instance a decrease in the value of gold of 50%, which would need an annual rate of increase of productivity of labour in industry and agriculture of 7% to be neutralized within ten years—then the rise in the general price level would become permanent. The increase in the mass of gold flowing into the country would induce a general boom of investment and output for a long period, initiated by the long-term increase in purchasing power of the gold-mining region, and unable to be met just by liquidation of existing stocks of other commodities. If a long-term boom is initiated in this way, there is no reason to assume that it would immediately trigger off a cumulative technological revolution. It would thus start at the previously existing levels of productivity of labour in industry and agriculture. Only after the initial impetus had spent itself, and the boom became threatened by declining rates of profit and rapidly increasing competition, would the incentives for a general overhaul of technology become overwhelming. This, in turn, would lead to a new wave of capital accumulation and investment which would prolong the boom.

At the same time, the rate of increase of productivity of labour in industry and agriculture would now grow, that is the value of all other commodities would tend to decrease, while the massive inflow of capital into gold mining would tend to bring into operation old, less-productive mines. It would thus tend not only to stop the rapid decrease in the value of gold, but even to increase it slightly, although not to the level preceding the bonanza; the bonanza's very scale with total gold output produced at radically lower production costs, would rule this out. Eventually, the decrease in the value of industrial and agricultural commodities would catch up with the stabilization of the value of gold, and the general level of prices would then decline. The mechanism of this adjustment would obviously be a grave crisis of over-production, or even a long slump.

We can therefore conclude that only big gold bonanzas, which radically decrease the value of gold, can induce a long-lasting rise in the general price level. It is significant that in the long debate on the explanation of the sixteenth-century price revolution in Europe, which started with the publication of E. J. Hamilton's *American Treasure and the Price Revolution in Spain* (Harvard, 1934), nobody, with the honorable exception of the French Marxist Pierre Vilar (*Or et Monnaie dans l'Histoire*, Paris, 1974), has studied whether the real correlation is not between the decline of the *intrinsic labour value* of gold and silver on the one hand and the price rise in consumer goods (in the first place wheat) on the other hand, instead of between the *quantities* of gold and silver imported into Spain and thus into Europe, and the increased price indices. An examination of the empirical data gives much weight to this Marxist interpretation.

According to tables computed by Braudel and Spooner, the silver prices of wheat in Europe, that is the value of wheat measured against the value of silver, remained stable till around 1550 and started to rise only after that date. This more or less coincides with a technological revolution in silver mining: the introduction of the mercury amalgamation process into Mexico and Peru, which strongly depressed the value (production costs) of silver, especially when local mercury instead of European mercury could be used. Only from that point on did the 'silver price of wheat' really take off, increasing by nearly 300% in the course of fifty years. What had happened before was a parallel rise in the price of wheat and the price of silver expressed in debased currency, whose silver content had been drastically reduced in a process similar to that of paper money inflation.

Likewise when one examines what happened previously with the value of gold, one notices that sheer plunder and the use of slavery drastically reduced the production costs of gold. In the Central American Isthmus, a black slave in the beginning of the Spanish colonization in the early sixteenth century produced as much as four grammes of gold a day. Hence an initial rise in the price level of other commodities. But this bonanza quickly petered out. In the Macuiltepec mines in Mexico, directly administered by Cortez himself, output per slave declined to four grammes a month and gold production became so onerous that slave labour was actually transferred to plantations which appeared more profitable. Only then did the silver boom start, with its subsequent results in price revolution.[17]

We can also show that the mechanisms of the price rise pass through successive stages: first, a rise in market prices deviating from prices of production for commodities immediately exchanged against gold; then a rise in market prices for all commodities other than gold, again deviating from prices of production; next a change in the price of production (value) of all commodities through changes in investment and in production techniques, but within strict limits, so that the rise in the average productivity of labour cannot catch up with the big rise in productivity of labour in gold mining (a short-term boom); and finally a growing decrease in the price of production of all other commodities through a long-term increase in the productivity of labour in these sectors, which can only occur during a long wave of an expansionary nature. This then will lead in turn to a new decline of the general price level as a result of a big slump.

History has, in our opinion, confirmed this scenario in at least two cases concerning industrial capitalism. The general price increase in the sixteenth century, as a result of cheaply produced and plundered gold and silver in the Americas predates the industrial revolution, and has therefore to be studied in a more complex context. The first case was the California Gold Rush of 1848 and the second, the Rand bonanza of the 1890s, to which the Alaskan and Australian bonanzas added a small supplement.

But in order not to be misunderstood, we would like to add immediately that in both cases, the gold bonanza was not the basic cause of the long-term boom, and neither was the technological revolution. The gold bonanza was only the initiating force (and one among several, at that), while the technological revolution was the force which gave the boom a cumulative, lasting character. The basic cause of the turn from a long-term wave with a stagnating trend into a long-term wave with an expansive trend was each time a sudden sharp rise in the average rate of profit, resulting from the combined operation of all, or at least most, of those forces which counteract the basic tendency towards a decline of that rate.[18]

## Gold Production and the Transformation Problem

We can now tie together all the elements of the analysis in order to clarify some of the methodological questions raised by the so-called transformation problem. We have stressed the basic contradiction of capitalistically organized gold production. On the one hand, gold, including capitalistically produced gold, enters the circulation process as value and not as price. It is exchanged against all commodities on the basis of its value, even if some time-lag occurs before that value can be correctly ascertained. Marx and Engels stressed that, precisely because the value of all commodities is only measurable in gold and not directly in labour-time (which, under commodity production, is not automatically 'socially necessary labour-time'), it is a fluctuating and uncertain entity. Only when commodity production is abolished, under socialism, and measurement of all goods can be made directly in actually spent labour time, because all human labour spent in production will be immediately social labour, and recognized as such by the collective associated producers, can 'value' disappear, along with the need to express labour spent in gold.[19] On the other hand, gold production is capitalistically organized gold production. Its value is therefore unstable, because as in all other branches of production there is a tendency in gold mining towards revolutions in technology and constant changes in the productivity of labour under the pressure of the search for surplus profits.

On a historical level, therefore, gold mining is subordinated to the general laws of the flow of capital between all branches of the economy: capital flowing into gold mining when the rate of profit of the marginal mines is above the socially average rate of profit; capital flowing out of gold mining when the rate of profit in the marginal mines falls below the social average. From this basic contradiction of capitalistically organized gold mining, two key conclusions follow regarding the transformation problem. First, prices of production cannot be prices in the current, common-sense meaning of the word, that is prices as they appear in the market place (we would call them gold prices, as distinct from market prices, which are these gold prices modified by short-term fluctuations in supply and demand). Such gold prices, that is prices which express the value or price of production of other commodities in the value of gold, can only result from a study of what happens simultaneously in general commodity production (a problem raised by Marx in the third volume of *Capital*) and in gold production. And such a study of the influence of gold production (of variations in the value of gold) does not appear at all in the third volume of *Capital*.

It is true that volume 3 encompasses some analysis of the problems of paper currencies and credit (in chapters 21 to 35). But these chapters are all subsequent to those dealing with prices of production and hence the transformation problem. Their intent is essentially to explain the basic problem of the third volume, that is the redistribution of total surplus-value produced by all productive labour between all different sectors of capitalists. This is treated in separate aspects. Thus, the part of the third volume of *Capital* dealing with the equalization of the rate of profit which includes the transformation problem, deals with the redistribution of surplus-value between industrial capitalists, while the part dealing with money and money-capital is concerned with the redistribution of profits between industrial capitalists and banks (or between industrial profit and interest).

Fluctuations in the value of gold cannot, however, be studied before the laws of equalization of the rate of profit are established. For we have seen that by and large, again with all the reservations flowing from the specific nature of gold, the universal commodity, variations in the value of gold depend upon the general movements of capital, determined by the establishment of the average rate of profit and the deviations therefrom. Thus, to introduce the problem of the variations in the value of gold, and their influence upon the general price level, in the first part of the third volume, would have been logically and methodologically inconsistent. It would assume that a problem had already been solved which it was precisely the function of that part of *Capital* to solve.

We can therefore conclude that prices of production are different and apart from prices (e.g. market prices) in the current sense of the word. As the subtitle of the first section of the third volume of *Capital* clearly indicates, the purpose of that analysis is essentially, if not exclusively, to study the transformation of surplus-value into profit, making an abstraction of 'price problems' in the fundamental sense of the word, that is of the correlation between changes in the value of commodities including surplus-value and the changes in the value of gold. It is true that chapters 6 and 10 of the third volume deal with market prices and market values. But it is clear that what these chapters are concerned with are exclusively variations in the *relative prices* (values, prices of production) of *different categories of commodities* (raw materials, machinery, labour-power) and their effects upon the average rate of profits, and not the influence of variations in the value of gold upon the general price level, that is, prices in the strict sense of the term.

In other words, throughout the third volume of *Capital* Marx assumes a stable value for gold, whereas in his general theory of money in the *Contribution to a Critique of Political Economy*, as well as in the first part of the first volume of *Capital*, he stresses many times the variability of the value of gold. Is this a logical inconsistency?

Not any more than the 'inconsistency' which Joan Robinson thought she had discovered between the first volume, assuming stable wages, and the third, stressing the variability of wages. It is just a further application of Marx's general method of approaching step-by-step the explanation of the concrete phenomena appearing at the surface of capitalist society, starting from elementary categories which have first to be fully clarified—including being checked against phenomena and historical evidence—before they can be used as efficient stepping stones for the analysis in general. Before variations in the value of gold, largely influenced by capital mobility between different branches of production, and governed by deviations from the average rate of profit, can be studied, the formation and very existence of that average rate of profit has to be ascertained.

It is perfectly admissible to study the process towards equalization of the rate of profit (the famous transformation problem) while making an abstraction from variations in the value of gold, assuming *for the time being* a stable value of gold, and postponing the study of the variations in the value of gold to a later stage of the analysis, provided one does not mistake prices of production for gold prices or market prices, and also provided one understands that the whole transformation problem concerns the transformation of values, and of values only (measurable only in gold). And this is the methodological weakness of most of the critics of Marx's solution of the transformation problem.

They forget that, for the reasons already given, prices of production cannot be and are not prices in the current sense of the word, but only transformed values, that is results of the redistribution of surplus-value between different capitalists, and not results of what happens in the circulation process as a result of the exchange of commodities embodying various proportions of surplus-value against money (gold). The transformation problem deals with the problem of capital movements, of capitalist competition through capital movements, and not with the problem of measurement (expression) of values and prices of production of commodities through the value of gold.

From that point of view, which corresponds to the inner logic of Marx's *Capital* as a whole, as well to an understanding of his method of gradual approximation, the study of real price (gold price) fluctuations, as well as the study of real market-price fluctuations, has no place in the third volume. One might think Marx was not interested in these problems and had banned them from *Capital* altogether. That is the opinion of those who believe that he did not really intend to write more than three volumes of *Capital* and that he had changed his initial plan for six volumes. Those who believe, as we do, that he stuck to his initial plan, will say that on the contrary the study of real (gold) price fluctuations, as well as the study of real market-price fluctuations, was postponed by him to the sixth volume which deals with competition on the world market. But both groups will have to recognize the obvious fact that the study of fluctuations in the value of gold is excluded from the third volume, and, for that reason alone, prices of production (and the whole transformation problem) cannot be treated as concerning prices (gold prices) in the Marxist as well as in the current sense of the word.

### Time Schedules, the Transformation Problem and the Role of Money (Gold) in the Circulation Problem

We have had occasion, at different points of this analysis, to stress the key role of time lags in the concrete operation of capital movements between gold mining and commodity production in general. These time lags are at the basis of the concrete process towards equalization of the rate of profit, a process which results precisely from its negation, from differences between real rates of profits in different branches of production. In that sense, as in many others, Marx's *Capital* had discovered key elements of a detailed theory of the industrial cycle and of crisis almost three quarters of a century before they were integrated into academic economic theory.

But the understanding of how capital movements, inflows and outflows of capital, really operate between different branches of production, is at the basis of the transformation problem. And what has been stated for gold mining can be stated for all industry—including the special form of industry which mechanized agriculture has become—as a general law. The very durability of fixed capital imposes a time lag between the appearance of a higher than average rate of profit in certain branches of production, and the disappearance of these higher rates through the influx of capital and increased investment in these branches.

Once we have understood this, we understand that the basic logical objection raised by critics of Marx's solution of the transformation problem, that in Marx's transformation tables inputs are calculated in values whereas outputs are calculated in prices of production, is largely irrelevant, represents a false problem. What these critics do not understand is the structural difference between inputs and outputs in capitalist production, governed by the rules of competition and the anarchy of the market appropriation of amounts of profit (fractions of socially produced surplus-value).

*Under normal conditions of capitalist production, inputs are data.* The capitalist buys machinery, raw materials and labour power, at a given price. This price cannot change through what happens as a result of the new reproduction cycle, which begins when he has already bought these inputs. Prices of already-bought machinery do not change because of what occurs at the end of that new cycle of reproduction, which might or might not establish new values of commodities, new (gold) prices as a result of the expression of these new values in a changed value of gold, and new average rates of profit.

One might object that while the point on the previously established price of machinery is well taken, it does not apply to prices of raw materials and the level of wages, which fluctuate on a much more short-term basis. But there is again a misunderstanding at the basis of this objection. What we are talking about is not the fact that prices of inputs vary on a long-term or short-term basis. It is the fact that such prices are data even if they fluctuate from week to week. These data cannot be changed through the end-result of a new cycle of reproduction which is finalized much later. And that is what the process towards equalization of the rate of profit and the transformation problem is all about.

We have deliberately used the formula 'cycle of reproduction', not 'cycle of production'. For the process towards equalization of the rate of profit can only occur after all new commodities have not only been produced but have also been sold or remained unsold, that is, after the realization process is over. And even then an important time-lag occurs, for the different capitals invested in different branches of production must have had time to react to the different rates of profit appearing at the end of the reproduction cycle of the realization process.

The outputs, in order to be measured by prices of production, have to reflect the *new* average rate of profit, which only appears *after* the realization process and after the reactions of the 'many capitals' to the different rates of profit resulting from the whole cycle of reproduction. It therefore stands to reason, that, whatever may be the short-term fluctuations of prices of inputs, they depend upon a *different* process of reproduction than the one which gives rise to the output prices of production under study.

It is therefore sufficient to treat the inputs themselves not as values but as prices of production *resulting from the previous cycle of reproduction*, to exclude logically the need for any 'feed-back' between inputs and outputs. That is the basic methodological objection to the criticism addressed to Marx's solution of the transformation problem, which is precisely that he supposedly overlooked a feedback problem which does not exist in the framework of the very mechanisms of the tendency towards equalization of the rate of profit he was studying.

When we study the reproduction cycle, as the unity of a production cycle and of a realization cycle, we note the decisive role played by the circulation process of the produced commodities, leading to partial, total or over realization of their 'original' values at the end of this process. Realized values are always values realized in money, that is in gold, during the circulation process.[20]

For that very reason the sum total of gold prices (values, prices of production, effectively exchanged against gold) will always tend to deviate somewhat from the sum total of values (prices of production) expressed in gold before they enter the circulation process, that is at the end of the production process.[21] This is not only true for the reason indicated in Anwar Shaikh's contribution to this volume. It also follows from two other fundamental reasons:

The first is that in the process of circulation there occurs a constant inflow or outflow of gold, independent of its role as means of circulation, for reasons linked to the inner logic of capitalist production and capitalist accumulation, so aptly analysed in the second volume of *Capital*. Capital accumulation is in fact impossible without such autonomous movement of money capital, as we have already recalled in our introduction to the second volume of *Capital*.[22] This means that there will never be a complete identity between the sum total of commodity values and money (gold) in circulation, only an asymptotic one. And these deviations of the total amount of (gold) money in circulation (taking into account fluctuations in the velocity of circulation of money) from the total sum of values of commodities in circulation leads to short-term gold price deviations, which imply that the total sum of the realized gold price of commodities differs slightly, either above or below, from the total sum of values expressed in gold when they leave the process of production.

The second reason is that prices of production of commodities, that is, cost prices plus the average rate of profit calculated upon total advanced capital in the course of production, when they leave the process of production and enter the process of circulation, are based upon the average rate of profit as it existed at the beginning of the process of production and as it lives in the consciousness of the capitalist class (cost price plus a given percentage of profit, say 15%). The sum total of the prices of production of all commodities when they leave the process of production incorporates a given amount of surplus-value which, measured in gold, is unchangeable in the process of realization. But the realization of the values of all commodities can reveal, at its end, a substantial decline or increase in the rate of profit, as a result of a massive devalorization of capital and destruction of value in a crisis or depression. The sum total of realized values will deviate from the sum total of produced values, not because surplus-value has mysteriously appeared or disappeared in the circulation process, but because values have been *destroyed* after their production.

Both cases do not refer to a deviation of the sum total of profit from the sum total of surplus-value, nor to a deviation of the sum total of values from the sum total of prices of production, but to a deviation of the sum total of realized equivalents, that is of the gold prices of all commodities from the sum total of both their values and their prices of production as measured (anticipated) when they have been produced but before they have been sold. Sudden autonomous changes in the value of gold during a full cycle of reproduction of capital can also precipitate such deviations.[23]

What lies at the bottom of this problem is simply the fact that commodity values, both intrinsically because of constant revolutions in production techniques and in the productivity of labour in commodity production, and as a result of changes in the value of gold, can be expressed in different quantities of gold at the beginning and end of a cycle of reproduction of capital. This means that the values of the commodities and their expression in gold can have changed during that cycle, because of what actually occurred in the process of production of commodities in general, as well as in the process of gold mining. But these changes remained hidden from the owners of the commodities (and the owners of gold and money). They cannot be known, because they result from overall social processes and not from what happens in each branch of production, not to say in each individual firm. They can only reveal themselves at the end of the realization process when a new average rate of profit appears, is calculable, and again becomes a living reality in the capitalists' consciousness, influencing their future investment decisions.[24]

In that sense, there are unsolved problems in the way Marx deals with the transformation problem in the third volume of *Capital*, but they are not those raised by his neo-Ricardian critics. They are alluded to by Marx himself in *Capital* and in his other basic economic writings. And they can be solved within the framework of a strict application of his labour theory of value and of his theory of surplus-value as surplus labour and nothing else.

# Value and Price of Production: A Differential Approach

## Pierre Salama

The transformation of values into prices of production presents well-known problems. While Bortkiewicz's claimed correction to Marx overcomes some difficulties, it renders Marx's own conclusions more fragile, and calls into question the need for a transformation.

Although von Bortkiewicz's correction is well known, as is the debate it provoked,[1] it is still worth noting that he uses a model based on simple reproduction. Marx uses no such model, either in chapter 9 of the third volume of *Capital*, where he presents his solution to the transformation problem, or in the following chapter in which he discusses its economic significance.[2] Though von Bortkiewicz gives a three-sector model whose sectors are interlinked through exchange, Marx neither uses an input–output model, nor imposes an equilibrium condition. He presents five branches of production which are not interlinked through exchange.

Improvements to von Bortkiewicz's solution and the correction of his errors have led to a disaggregation of his three sectors into 'n' branches.[3] Notwithstanding, these improvements do not bring the method employed into any closer correspondence with Marx's method. Marx's mathematical illustration in chapter 9, using five sectors, does not pretend to represent society. This is why these sectors are not interlinked.

This point is not made to avoid criticism but to show that the proposed corrections occupy a different conceptual framework. The use of an input–output model leads to a search for a *numéraire*. This *numéraire* must have certain properties, the result of restrictive conditions imposed on the equations with the aim of preserving the double equalities of prices with values, and of profits with surplus-values. These conditions weaken the pertinence of Marx's analysis. If one of them were not fulfilled, the sum of profits could differ from that of surplus-values, and there could be other sources of value. These conditions appear to make Marx's reasoning more coherent, but in fact have exposed it to considerable criticism.

One important aspect of these conditions has attracted little attention.[4] Commodities are measured in units of labour-time, and these commodities are then exchanged for each other. But it is incoherent for these commodities to be exchanged and measured in units of labour-time. There cannot be an exchange of type C-C within an analysis of Marx's type. Exchange expresses a metamorphosis of commodities and is necessarily of the type C-M-C. In other words, the distinction between value and exchange-value is essential. One refers to a quantity of abstract labour, and the other to a quantity of an equivalent. The two cannot be confused.

Confusion between value and exchange-value leads to an important bias. The problematic is that of real prices and the search for a *numéraire*. The distinction between value and exchange-value means that commodities are expressed in money terms even before money causes them to circulate, which renders absurd the search for a *numéraire*. The purpose of this article is to reconsider the transformation problem within this latter problematic.

## I. Value and Exchange-Value

The commodity has two aspects: use-value and exchange-value. The first definition of exchange-value is descriptive. It is the 'proportion in which values in use of one sort or another are exchanged for those of another sort.'[5] We can establish the relation $Q_1A = Q_2B$ between commodities A and B, but this relation is the point of departure for differing interpretations. It can be conceived as an equality, in which case the problem of measure becomes primary. This seems an obvious interpretation, but it leads to problems which, if they are to be overcome, call for dubious formulations.

This relation can, however, be conceived other than as an equality, leading to a radically different interpretation. Two questions are relevant here: the first consists in asking why there should be such a relation; the second involves asking on what exchange is founded. Why do commodities exchange? Why can't they be arrested in motion? Why can they be apprehended only through their multiple metamorphoses?

The answer to this question is simple. For the same individual, use-value and exchange-value simultaneously constitute two contradictory aspects. For a given individual the commodity can be either one or the other. Losing, for the individual, its use-value aspect, it can be used as a carrier of value for the acquisition of another commodity. The commodity is contradictory.[6] This contradiction is resolved through the circulation of commodities, which is why they can never be arrested in motion. That is why a commodity is already money even before it is converted into money. It incorporates its own future because this is one of the aspects of its being.[7] The logical genesis of money can be demonstrated starting from this simple relation.

It is not enough though to show why commodities circulate. We must also show what allows them to circulate—the foundations of exchange. If two commodities can be exchanged, and hence merge into each other, it is because they have something in common.[8] This something is abstract labour. We are not dealing with any kind of labour, nor with labour which would be the common factor between several specific labours. Marx commented that one of his two greatest discoveries was precisely that of abstract labour. This abstract labour is 'an abstraction realized in the reality of exchange'.[9] It is an abstraction which refers to the real; it is a real abstraction. In this sense, it cannot be confused with concrete labour, for in the same way that use-value and exchange-value are two contradictory aspects of a commodity, concrete labour and abstract labour are both contradictory.

In exchanging, commodities only express the fact that abstract labour has been accumulated to produce them. They are 'metamorphosed into identical sublimates'.[10] 'All these things now tell us is that human labour-power has been expended to produce them, human labour is accumulated in them. As crystals of this social substance, which is common to them all, they are values—commodity values.'[11]

The concept of abstract labour is deduced from the need to understand the foundations of exchange-value. It is the value substance. To paraphrase Rosdolsky, we could say that the sequence exchange-value–abstract labour—value, simply asserts that each one of these categories is transcended and cannot be fully comprehended in the preceding ones.[12] Behind exchange-value, therefore, is hidden value. Let us summarize what has just been said with the help of a small diagram.

The market price seems to result naturally from the interplay of supply and demand. The commodity is taken as given, a product of labour. This is stage 1 on the diagram. When we reflect on the commodity, it appears under a double, contradictory aspect. The analysis of this contradiction leads to the concept of value. This is

Figure 1

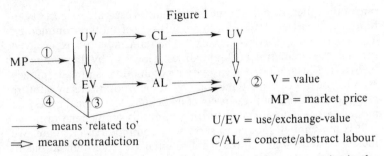

⟶ means 'related to'

⟹ means contradiction

V = value

MP = market price

U/EV = use/exchange-value

C/AL = concrete/abstract labour

stage 2 on the diagram. We have now reached a turning point in the analysis, for reflection on the reasons behind exchange and on its foundations have led us to introduce a new concept: value. Exchange-value, a relation of exchange between two commodities (first definition) becomes a form of value (second definition). Exchange-value 'is a form of appearance of a content which must be distinguished from it. This content, which must be considered as the foundation of exchange-value, is value.'[13]

Exchange-value is more than it seemed to be in the first instance. It is more than a simple quantitative relation, 'the proportion in which different exchange-values exchange between each other'. It is the form of value, the form of something which transcends it and makes it appear as something which it is not. Thus the relation $Q_1A = Q_2B$ is far from a representation of an actual exchange.[14] The '=' sign does not stand for equality.[15] It means that $Q_1A$ expresses itself in $Q_2B$. 'The expression of value itself lies in the relation between the two commodities. The relation which value constitutes, although dependent on the action of an agent or of agents ... is an objective relation.'[16]

Exchange-value is hence not what it is. It is a relation without being one, for it only appears to be a relation. It is not an actual quantitative relation, because it does not involve actual exchange, but only logical exchange. $Q_1A$ does not exchange against $Q_2B$ but is expressed in $Q_2B$. The '=' sign means 'is expressed in'.

The exchange-value of a commodity is the quantity of something. This thing expresses the value of this commodity, its value being the 'socially necessary' abstract labour. The magnitude of value is the quantity of this abstract labour. Thus $Q_1A = Q_2B$ is a logical relation of exchange and not an actual one, for $Q_1A$ is not in fact exchanged against $Q_2B$. This relation allows us to unveil the secret of value and the causes of its appearance as exchange-value. But it is more than that.

'Money is, and is not. In fact, initially there is neither the presence of money, nor pure and simple absence of money. There is the germ of money. This germ is the equivalent simple form which the commodity B takes or, more precisely, the commodity B in its equivalent form. The commodity which is found in its equivalent form is certainly not in its money-form, but this is no less true for the fact that this form is absolutely (or purely and simply) absent.'[17] It is hence starting from this relation that money is logically deduced. It is the *genesis* of money.[18] This is why, in fact, 'commodities are expressed in gold even before it circulates them.'[19] When the simple form is developed into the general form, $Q_1 A$ is expressed as a general equivalent (money-form).

A number of points flow from this analysis. First, 'the use-value [of the equivalent] becomes the form of appearance of its opposite, value.'[20] Second, 'concrete labour becomes the form of manifestation of its opposite, abstract human labour.'[21] And third, 'concrete labour ... possesses the characteristic of being identical with other kinds of labour ... Consequently, although, like all other commodity-producing labour, it is the labour of private individuals, it is nevertheless labour in its directly social form.'[22]

Exchange-value is hence 'the concrete private labour-time needed to produce that commodity which serves as a general equivalent and which incarnates abstract social labour into which private labour-time is transformed.'[23] Exchange-value is thus no longer a quantitative relation but an equivalent quantity. It is the form of value. We have arrived at stage 3 on our diagram.

What immediately presents itself to us is the market price. This remains to be explained. The market price certainly fluctuates according to variations in supply and demand, but these variations take effect around an axis. This is why it can be said that the market price is only *fixed* by the market, while its *determination* depends on the quantity of socially necessary abstract labour-time. This latter constitutes the axis around which prices pivot. The market price is hence also a form of value. Being fixed in a market it expresses constraints (*sanctions*). The market thus indicates whether too much, or insufficient, abstract labour, has been spent on their production. This in return acts on the magnitudes of values. Although appearing as the product of a realized exchange relation, the market price expresses as the magnitude of value, 'a relation of production, the intimate link that exists between a given article and the portion of social-labour that is needed to give birth to it.'[24]

It is the progression shown on the diagram from 1 to 3 and finally to

4 that lets us reach this essential conclusion. If, on the other hand, we confine ourselves to the first definition of exchange-value, if the chain of reasoning is halted at stage 1, then the problem of measure will be treated as primary, without producing the means for dealing with it. The analysis of measure demands first of all the analysis of commensurability. If we treat the problem of measure as primary, we are led to look on the circulation of commodities as an exchange $C_1$-$C_2$, and to introduce a *numéraire*, at the very point where money already exists.

*Measure and Exchange*

$Q_1 A = Q_2 B$ expresses the value of A in terms of B. This does not involve a symmetrical relation, a relation of equality, for the order is important. $Q_1 A = Q_2 B$ means something other than $Q_2 B = Q_1 A$. This approach, different from those which predominate, has important consequences. If $Q_1 A = Q_2 B$ is treated as an equality, there is no discussion about why exchange takes place and on what it is founded. The commodity, taken as given, remains. It becomes a natural, historic fact.

Let us consider now the relation $Q_1 A = Q_2 B$ where the left-hand side represents the quantity of labour carried out by a worker and the right-hand side the remuneration he or she receives. If we ended our interpretation with the most immediate aspect of this relation (equality), we would say that the quantity of labour carried out was worth so much money. Money would appear to become autonomous. The fact that the value of a 'quantity of labour' ($Q_1 A$) is expressed in money terms seems to confer on this money the natural quality of representing it.[25] If we go no further than the usual interpretation (equality), we would mistake appearance for reality, prevented from understanding that this interpretation masks the relations of production.

Conversely, if we adopt my proposed approach, we can avoid such errors and impasses. When we consider the nature of the wage relation, the wage becomes the price-form of the value of the commodity labour-power.[26] The study of the forms of value is primary, leading to the study of fetishism. The objectification of production relations is not a subjective fact. It has a material basis, proceeding from the generalization of commodities. The relation is not that of a quantity of effective labour against a quantity of money. The relation is that between the quantity of labour needed to reproduce this particular commodity—labour-power—and a quantity of money. The passage from the first relation to the second has not been demonstrated. It is not necessary to demonstrate exploitation: it is at the outset a fact. One does not demonstrate what exists.

The first question that must be asked is: why do the exploited workers not discern their exploitation spontaneously? The primary problem is not therefore that of the secret of surplus-value, but that of its camouflage. In this way we can show why the workers do not spontaneously perceive their exploitation as a process of surplus-value extraction. As a consequence, we can explain the mechanism of surplus-value, having already explained why it does not appear as such. Exploitation is explained through the distinction between labour carried out and labour needed to reproduce the labour force. It is explained, not demonstrated. It is imposed.

I indicated that Marx did not use an input–output type model to expound the transformation problem. This is because he envisaged an exchange of the type C-M-C and not C-C. The commodity would have been immediately expressed in money terms and it would have been absurd to look for a *numéraire*, invariable or not. The analysis of the forms of value allows us to understand the errors into which this type of interpretation leads. But this analysis also has a positive aspect to it. It allows us to understand the real meaning of transformation.

In chapter 10 of the third volume of *Capital*, Marx studies the economic meaning of transformation. This chapter is the one most commonly ignored by commentators. The exposition deals with the cycles of capital, Marx bringing to the fore the metamorphosis of commodities, its preconditions and implications. In distinction from the methods followed in the preceding chapter (the exposition of the 'model'), the conception here is immediately dynamic.

The rejection of a static approach, of an equilibrium approach, makes the interpretation of transformation more complex. As Aglietta notes: 'Economic theory cannot establish a measure outside of equilibrium, because its presuppositions demand that measure should be unique, an expression of the homogeneity of space.'[28]

We must take into account structural changes and the passage of time in which they can take effect. This modifies our objectives. The transformation of values into prices of production takes on a double goal: explaining why the capitalists constitute a common 'free-masonry', and understanding the real movement of capital. The problem of measure is not the primary one. Its place is taken by that of the cycle of conditions for the metamorphosis of commodities.

## II. A Transformation: an Alternative Approach

Elsewhere I have shown what inquiries follow as soon as a different interpretation of transformation is proposed.[29] These inquiries are of two types and are situated at two different levels of abstraction: the first concerns the meaning to be given to the equalization of profit rates; the second concerns capital's cycles and their adverse effects.

### Competition, Value and Price

The *tendency* to the equalization of the rate of profit has a status analogous to the tendency of the rate of profit to fall. It is not a datum. It is incessantly called into question. In chapter 10, Marx treats equalization as a result which constantly negates itself and reproduces itself: 'The really difficult question here is this: how does this equalization lead to a general rate of profit, since this is evidently a result and cannot be a point of departure?'[30] Equalization is not (only) the result of competition. Competition executes the internal laws of capital and makes them imperative for each individual capitalist. But it does not forge these laws: it realizes them. Competition is situated at the level of many capitals. Hence, 'So as to impose the inherent laws of capital upon it as external necessity, competition seemingly turns all of them over. *Inverts them.*'[31]

If one explains equalization through capital movements as Sweezy does, for example, then one takes the inverse for the real.[32] Capitals do not emigrate from branches with a high organic composition of capital, for which the rate of profit in a value schema is low, towards branches with a low organic composition. To explain transformation by the emigration of capital towards the labour-intensive branches to the detriment of the more mechanized ones is to refuse to face the reality of the movement of capital. One cannot explain, by means of competition, passage from a situation in which differing profit rates prevail (a value schema) to a situation with equal rates of profit.

Such a conception has two further major defects. It attributes to prices of production a status analogous to market prices. Prices of production are deduced from capital movements and their effects, via the intermediary of modifications of demand and supply, on the rate of profit.[38] It also situates the understanding of prices of production at the same level of abstraction as that of value. Thus, the question of value is situated at the level of the first volume of *Capital*, in which 'capital in general' is defined. The treatment of prices of production should be situated at another level of abstraction, dealt with in the third volume, and concerning 'many capitals'. Certainly, 'capital in general' and 'many capitals' do not constitute independent concepts. In order to grasp what is essential to the movement of 'many capitals', we must first of all analyse the laws applicable to 'capital in general'— that is to say, begin from the totality in order to arrive at its component parts, without, however, reducing them to the totality. But to place the value schema on the left-hand side and prices of production on the right-hand side, and link them by means of equality, is to attribute to each component part the same level of abstraction.

Conversely, if we treat the '=' sign as meaning first and foremost 'expresses', we opt for a different interpretation. The left-hand side (value) is expressed in the right-hand side. Prices of production become the application of the law of value at the level of 'many capitals'. The equalization of rates of profit is not a fact. Competition prevents it being attained. Rates of profit are different in each branch. Nevertheless we cannot treat differentials between profit rates as an initial hypothesis. Marx's commentators have often omitted to consider the term 'tendency'. In doing so, they make the same mistake as those who want to see in the historic evolution of profit rates the confirmation of a tendential fall in the rate of profit.

The rate of profit is different in each branch. These divergences express the fact that demand and supply cannot coincide in any one of these branches, and express the existence of constraints. The tendency to the equalization of profit rates is useful in explaining the reproduction of divergences, and the equalization of the rate of profit is as a result constantly called into question. This process translates the working of this law and its countervailing tendencies. But it would be a mistake to think that only competition, through the constraints that it overcomes and through those it produces, can explain this process of elimination and creation of divergences between profit rates.

Capital tends to go where the rate of profit is highest, and in so doing tends to reduce profit differentials. Competititon manifests this evolution. To say this is banal. Much more difficult, however, is to reply to a prior question: why are profit rates higher in certain places? To ask this question is immediately to introduce the temporal dimension of structural change into the analysis.

Equalization of profit rates is not a fact at the level of market prices. We must, however, make the hypothesis that it is at the level of prices of production. It is the product of a different process from that described by competition. It expresses a process of sanction.* This process is exclusively located at the level of production. Differentials between profit rates are created at the level of the sphere of conversion, where commodities are transformed into money, and this differential influences production conditions.

## The Transformation Process in the Real World

It is interesting to analyse the transformation of individual values into market values. This is what Marx does in chapter 10 of the third volume of *Capital*. It allows us to disentangle the method which should be followed if we wish to understand the transformation of values into prices of production, since 'what we have said here of market value also holds for the price of production, as soon as this takes the place of market value.'[34]

The concept of market value in the third volume of *Capital* corresponds to that of exchange-value in the first volume. But exchange-value concerns only a commodity manufactured using a single productive combination. Market value relates to a commodity produced using a variety of different productive combinations. Each commodity acquires an individual value and the market value is the weighted average of these different individual values. The market value of a commodity is hence determined by two factors: by the technical conditions of production in each enterprise; and by the allocation of capital between these enterprises.[35]

The market value 'imposes' itself on different factories. The magnitude of value is the quantity of socially necessary abstract labour-time. This is what it expresses and is brought into effect by means of different sanctions. It the individual value is superior to the market value, labour has been wasted. The enterprise has to undergo transfers of social surplus-value, to the benefit of other enterprises which are in the inverse situation.

It is important here to remark that this sanction does not appear in the market, but before the market is reached. It is a fact of production. In this sense, it is different from that which Marx demonstrates in the first volume of *Capital*, when he analyses the relation between

* (*Translator's note:* The French word *sanction* is used by Salama in a precise technical sense which the reader must interpret from its use in the text, where I have translated it using the English word 'sanction' as there is no exact English equivalent. The word has connotations of a penalty or fine, as in law, which is applied *post hoc* but which is known to the transgressor in advance and thereby (presumably) affects her or his actions. It is also used in the sense of the English word 'ratify'.)

exchange-values and market prices. This sanction is hence situated at a certain level of abstraction.[36] The way Marx deals with this question is sometimes ambiguous, notably when he writes: 'If demand is only marginally predominant, it is the individual value of the unfavourably produced commodities that governs the market price ... If demand is weak in relation to supply, the favourably situated part, however big it might be, forcibly makes room for itself by drawing the price towards its individual values.'[31]

These prescriptions seem to exclude the need for a concept of market value, and hence the need for a sanction (constraint) in relation to production. Sanctions at the level of production do not exclude sanctions at the level of exchange. This is expressed in the divergence between market values and market prices, and tends to influence the new conditions of production. The cycle of productive capital allows us to demonstrate the sequence involved:

Figure 2

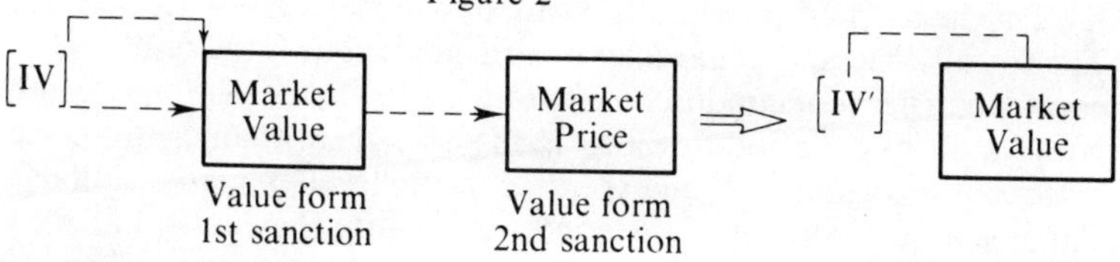

IV = Individual Value
MP = Means of Production
L = Labour

$$P \left\{ \begin{array}{l} MP \\ L \end{array} \right. \quad C+c \longrightarrow M' = M+m \quad \| \quad M \ldots P' \left\{ \begin{array}{l} MP' \\ L' \end{array} \right.$$

The socially necessary character of abstract labour becomes a result of the combined effect of conditions of production and conditions of exchange, as soon as the analysis is situated at the level of 'many capitals'. It is these considerations that will permit a different treatment of the transformation of values into prices of production.

Now we can understand the interest in the distinction between the equalization of profit rates and the tendency towards equalization. The equalization of profit rates expresses, at the level of 'many capitals', a phenomenon analogous to that which we have just described when dealing with individual values and market values. It expresses a sanction which is a fact of production. It translates into transfers of surplus-value between branches. The tendency towards equalization of profit rates expresses something else. Supply never being equal to demand, market prices are different from market value (exchange-value). They fluctuate around it and can influence it. The market penalizes wastages of labour, which reflect back on the rate of profit.

The category which corresponds to value, at the level of 'many capitals', is that of price of production. The category which corresponds to exchange-value is that of market price of production.[38] The market prices hence fluctuate around the 'market price of production' and influence it. Inequalities between supply and demand lead to a differential between profit rates. The tendency towards the equalization of profit rates is a result which negates itself and in doing so reproduces itself. It is situated in a relation with equalization, expressing at one and the same time inequalities between supply and demand, and the effects of capital movements resulting from them. Hence it expresses sanctions operating at the level of the market.

The market price is thus not simply the result of a sanction at the level of the market, but equally a sanction at the level of production. The socially necessary character of abstract labour is the result of the combined effects of conditions of production and conditions for the conversion of commodities into money. In such a conception, the price of production is value expressed at the level of 'many capitals'. There is an enrichment of the concepts because they are situated at this new level of abstraction.

This enrichment leads to a series of new inquiries. Sanctions at the level of production express the general level attained by the productive forces in society at a given moment. Sanctions at the level of circulation express social conditions for exchange. Differential profit rates are a result of this second sanction. It is not enough, however, to explain the existence of this differential: its specific reproduction must also be explained. The interplay of supply and demand is insufficient to explain the particular orientation of capitals towards what is, or will become, the key sector in the economy. The specific configuration of this differential must therefore be explained.

Numerous works have tried to respond to this question.[39] It seems to me that the state should be introduced. But the state's actions cannot be dealt with as a supplementary factor, added to the effects of competition. The state tries to act so as to modify the working of the tendency towards the equalization of profit rates. These modalities, their continuity, should lead us to inquire after the status of the state in relation to the law of value, that is to say, to call into question Marx's plan for *Capital*. Such an undertaking, which we have sketched elsewhere, goes beyond the scope of this article.[40]

# Constant Returns and Uniform Profit Rates: Two False Assumptions

## Jesus Albarracín

Since Sraffa's book *The Production of Commodities by Means of Commodities* appeared in 1961, and in particular since the 1966 debate on the validity of marginalism, a generation of economists has tried to resuscitate Marx's analytical schemata, enriched by modern mathematical techniques. In the light of this 'new political economy', Marx's thinking has been analysed minutely. Sraffa's followers claim to explain positively how a capitalist economy works and criticize Marx from this standpoint.

Many of their criticisms are old ones in a new guise, but their mathematical wrappings are worthy of study by Marxists because valid analytical instruments can be obtained from them for developing Marx's economics. Moreover, since neo-Ricardian postulates are becoming influential among socialist and communist parties, and because a section of official economics is casting a glance at the classical economists, these criticisms must be dealt with on their own terrain and, where possible, in their own language.

This piece discusses two crucial assumptions which underlie the neo-Ricardian construction and which correspond neither to the real world nor to Marx's own analysis. These are the assumptions of a uniform rate of profit and of constant returns to scale.[1] I investigate the mathematical effects of dropping these two hypotheses.

For this purpose I construct a mathematical system through which I present the most general fundamentals of neo-Ricardian analysis. This entails certain omissions and simplifications and none of the authors in this current can be fully identified with this presentation. No current is homogeneous and the differences between Sraffa and Morishima or Steedman are significant enough to excite important controversies.

Nevertheless, lest I am accused of setting up a 'straw person' to demolish, I insist that we can make a theoretical critique only by looking at shared fundamentals rather than concrete peculiarities. My aim is to present these in their pure state without dressing or adornment.

## I. The Fundamentals of Neo-Ricardian Analysis

### 1. Definitions

We assume m commodities, produced in two departments. Department I produces the n means of production and department II the m − n consumables. For now we assume no capitalist consumption so that these are destined for the workers, who for their subsistence get, per worker and production period, $b_i$ units of commodity i. These they acquire with a wage paid by the capitalists.

Each commodity can be produced in a finite number of ways but in our treatment only one, which may be an 'abstract' process comprising a linear combination of other processes, is used for each commodity. The n production processes in use will be termed the technology.

$X_j$ units of commodity j are produced in each production period, using material inputs $X_{ij}$ (i = 1, ..., n, j = 1, ..., m) and $L_j$ hours of labour. At least one $X_{ij}$ is strictly positive.

The capitalists introduce all necessary material inputs at the beginning of the production period, and these disappear during production. Their turnover period is therefore average and we ignore fixed capital for now. Labour is applied throughout the production period, at the end of which the product is available.

We assume a homogeneous labour force. For production to take place total hours worked must be less than total labour hours available. We use $\bar{N}$ for the number of workers and $\bar{T}$ for the maximum hours of work per production period they will accept. N is the actual number employed and T the actual hours worked per worker per production period, so that $N \cdot T \leqslant \bar{N} \cdot \bar{T}$.

The means of production used in production must be no greater than what is produced, and enough consumables must be produced to buy the labour-power used in production. At the end of each productive period all used-up means of production, and consumables advanced to the workers, are restored.

We denote net production of commodity i by $Y_i$ (i = 1, ..., m). Thus, for means of production

$$\sum_{j=1}^{m} X_{ij} + Y_i = X_i \qquad (i = 1, ..., n) \qquad (1)$$

and for consumables

$$b_i N + Y_i = X_i \qquad (i = n+1, \ldots, m) \qquad (2)$$

$Y_i$, the accumulation needed to increase production, is the net product of commodity i but not the surplus appropriated by sector i capitalists, since appropriation takes place in circulation. Distribution between capitalists cannot be ascertained independently of the proportions in which commodities exchange.

Let $P_j$ be the price of commodity j, $P_0$ the price per hour of labour and $R_j$ the surplus (in price terms) of capitalist j. Then for each $j = 1, \ldots, m$

$$\sum_{i=1}^{n} X_{ij} P_i + P_0 L_j + R_j = P_j X_j \qquad (3)$$

Let $r_j$ be the rate of profit on the price of the means of production used and wage advanced in sector j. Then for each $j = 1, \ldots, m$

$$\left( \sum_{i=1}^{n} X_{ij} + P_0 L_j \right)(1 + r_j) = P_j X_j \qquad (4)$$

But $P_0$, the hourly wage, will be

$$P_0 = \frac{1}{T} \sum_{i=n+1}^{m} P_i b_i \qquad (5)$$

Equations (4) and (5) form a system of $m + 1$ equations in $2m + 1$ variables, namely the m prices, m profit rates and the wage.

## 2. Two Fundamental Assumptions

Two basic problems must now be solved: to specify a law governing the variation in output corresponding to variations in inputs, and to eliminate degrees of freedom and so solve the equations. I shall show that two of the assumptions which are central to the neo-Ricardians' solution are those of constant returns to scale and equal profit rates.

With constant returns to scale a proportional change in inputs induces the same proportional change in outputs and the functions are homogeneous of the first degree. $X_{ij}$ can be replaced by $a_{ij} X_j$, where $a_{ij}$ is the input per unit output of commodity i in sector j.

The resulting equation system is, as we shall see, a convex set, permitting a mathematical treatment not otherwise possible given the state of our understanding of the material.

Letting $l_j$ be the quantity of labour used in producing one unit of commodity j, we define

$$\mathbf{A}_I = \begin{bmatrix} a_{11} & \cdots & a_{1n} \\ \vdots & & \vdots \\ a_{n1} & \cdots & a_{nn} \end{bmatrix} ; \mathbf{A}_{II} = \begin{bmatrix} a_{1n+1} & \cdots & a_{1m} \\ \vdots & & \vdots \\ a_{nn+1} & \cdots & a_{nm} \end{bmatrix} ;$$

$$\mathbf{L}_I = \begin{bmatrix} l_1 \\ \vdots \\ l_n \end{bmatrix} ; \mathbf{X}_I = \begin{bmatrix} X_1 \\ \vdots \\ X_n \end{bmatrix} ; \mathbf{Y}_I = \begin{bmatrix} Y_1 \\ \vdots \\ Y_n \end{bmatrix} ; \mathbf{P}_I = \begin{bmatrix} P_1 \\ \vdots \\ P_n \end{bmatrix}$$

$$\mathbf{L}_{II} = \begin{bmatrix} l_{n+1} \\ \vdots \\ l_m \end{bmatrix} ; \mathbf{X}_{II} = \begin{bmatrix} X_{n+1} \\ \vdots \\ X_m \end{bmatrix} ; \mathbf{Y}_{II} = \begin{bmatrix} Y_{n+1} \\ \vdots \\ Y_m \end{bmatrix} ; \mathbf{P}_{II} = \begin{bmatrix} P_{n+1} \\ \vdots \\ P_m \end{bmatrix}$$

$$\mathbf{B} = (b_{n+1}, \ldots, b_m)$$

$$[\mathbf{I} + \mathbf{R}] = \begin{bmatrix} 1+r_1 & \cdots & 0 \\ \vdots & \ddots & \vdots \\ 0 & \cdots & 1+r_m \end{bmatrix} = \begin{bmatrix} \mathbf{I} + \mathbf{R}_I & 0 \\ 0 & \mathbf{I} + \mathbf{R}_{II} \end{bmatrix}$$

Whence

$$\mathbf{X}_I = \mathbf{A}_I \mathbf{X}_I + \mathbf{A}_{II} \mathbf{X}_{II} + \mathbf{Y}_I \tag{6}$$

$$\mathbf{X}_{II} = \mathbf{B} \cdot \mathbf{N} + \mathbf{Y}_{II} \tag{7}$$

If we suppose, as do the neo-Ricardians, that competition equalizes profit rates, then we can let $r_i = r$ for all $i = 1, \ldots, m$ and $\mathbf{I} + \mathbf{R}$ will be a scalar. Equilibrium prices will be determined by the following system:

$$\mathbf{P}_I = (\mathbf{I} + \mathbf{R}_I)(\mathbf{A}_I{}'\mathbf{P}_I + \mathbf{P}_0 \mathbf{L}_I) \tag{8}$$

$$\mathbf{P}_{II} = (\mathbf{I} + \mathbf{R}_{II})(\mathbf{A}_{II}{}'\mathbf{P}_I + \mathbf{P}_0 \mathbf{L}_{II}) \tag{9}$$

$$P_0 = \frac{1}{T} \mathbf{B} \mathbf{P}_{II} \tag{10}$$

If we set $w = 1/T$ then w can be considered the real wage per hour (the inverse of the work needed to acquire the wage bundle). Dividing by $P_0$ we have, finally,

$$\mathbf{P}_I/P_0 = (\mathbf{A}_I'(\mathbf{P}_I/P_0) + \mathbf{L}_I)(1 + r) \qquad (11)$$

$$\mathbf{P}_{II}/P_0 = (\mathbf{A}_{II}'(\mathbf{P}_I/P_0) + \mathbf{L}_{II})(1 + r) \qquad (12)$$

$$l = w\mathbf{B}(\mathbf{P}_{II}/P_0) \qquad (13)$$

a system of m prices expressed in terms of the wage; a rate of profit r; and w. With w determined and **B** known we would have a solution for m relative prices and the profit rate. However, prices, the wage and the rate of profit are simultaneously determined, so that the distribution of the surplus is still not independent of the relations of exchange. We can thus derive an equation which relates r to w. This is the price-factor frontier, whose genesis and characteristics can be found in any textbook on linear models.

This does not, however, complete the solution. Variations in the profit rate or the wage can induce variations in the exchange rates $P_i/P_0$, and we cannot say if these are caused by the characteristics of the commodity whose price we are considering or that of the commodity taken as *numéraire*. If absolute prices $P_i$ could be derived directly this problem would not appear. In general we can determine only the proportions in which commodities exchange. This matters because of the characteristics of the unit of account under capitalism (gold). But here we are chiefly concerned with the fact that a valuation system is needed: a system such that the value of a commodity will not change when distribution does.

It is useful, before embarking on the main analysis, to examine the two main choices taken by the neo-Ricardians in dealing with this problem. The root of the problem is that different profit rates imply different sets of prices. However, there exist two singular points to which prices can be referred: point A on figure 1, which corresponds to the maximum profit rate $r^*$; and point B, which corresponds to zero profits. If each $P_i$ is referred to one or other of these singular points we shall know, when $P_i/P_j$ changes, to what this change is due, and we shall be able to deepen our explanation of prices and the profit rate.

I shall show that point A corresponds to the option chosen by Sraffa in his original work, while point B is that taken by Morishima, Steedman and the later neo-Ricardians. Moreover, the first system

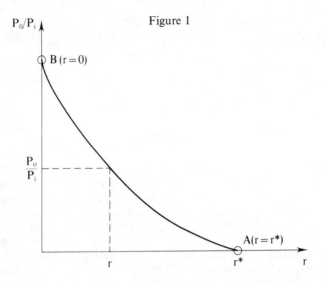

Figure 1

reveals itself on analysis to be one in which prices are a measure of the labour they can command, whereas the second is one in which they are a measure of labour incorporated.

## 3. A System of Commanded Labour Values

Let us suppose we are at point A, that is $P_0 = 0$ and $r = r^*$. Let us denote the prices obtaining by $\mu$. Then, from (8) and (9), prices will be given by

$$\mu_I = A_I' \mu_I (1 + r^*) \tag{14}$$

$$\mu_{II} = A_{II}' \mu_I (1 + r^*) \tag{15}$$

Since $P_0 = 0$, equation $m + 1$ has no meaning. No commodities are destined for the workers and all department II production is surplus production. We have $m + 1$ variables and m equations, so that only relative values can be obtained. Now, from (14)

$$\mu_I' = \mu_I' A_I (1 + r^*) \tag{16}$$

whence

$$\mu_I' \left( \frac{1}{r^*} \right) = \mu_I' A_I (I - A_I)^{-1} \tag{17}$$

Since r* is the inverse of the dominant characteristic root of the matrix $A_I(I-A_I)^{-1}$, there will be a semi-positive characteristic vector $\bar{X}_I$ for which

$$\{I - r^*A_I(I - A_I)^{-1}\}\bar{X}_I = 0 \tag{18}$$

whence

$$\{I - A_I(1 + r^*)\}\bar{X}_I = 0 \tag{19}$$

that is

$$\bar{X}_I = A_I\bar{X}_I(1 + r^*) \tag{20}$$

That is, we can find weights $K_i = \bar{X}_i/X_i$ such that for all sectors, with these weights applied to production levels, the surplus of each commodity will be in the same proportion as the used up means of production. This is a different system to the real system, in the sense that the commodities enter it in different proportions. The vector of department I surplus in this system is

$$A_I\bar{X}_Ir^* = \bar{X}_I - A_I\bar{X}_I \tag{21}$$

and since $A_I\bar{X}_I = \bar{X}_I/(1 + r^*)$, we have

$$A_I\bar{X}_Ir^* = \frac{\bar{X}_Ir^*}{(1 + r^*)} \tag{22}$$

Prices in this system are independent of $P_0$ and r since, for example, in sector I, $\mu_I$ is the characteristic vector of $A_I(I - A_I)^{-1}$ and so for all $P_0$, r

$$\mu_I = A_I\mu_I(1 + r^*) \tag{23}$$

By the same token the value of the surplus is also independent of $P_0$ and r.

Premultiplying (21) by $\mu_I'$, we have a value for the surplus in such a system:

$$S = \mu_I'A_I\bar{X}_Ir^* = \mu_I'\bar{X}_I\left(\frac{r^*}{1 + r^*}\right) \tag{24}$$

But in this system it is still true from (11) that

$$\mu_I = (A_I'\mu_I + P_0L_I)(1 + r) \tag{25}$$

even though $\mu_I$ is independent of r and $P_0$. Transposing and postmultiplying by $\bar{X}_I$ gives

$$\mu_I'\bar{X}_I = (\mu_I A_I \bar{X}_I + P_0 L_I'\bar{X}_I)(1 + r)$$

$$= \left\{ \mu_I \bar{X}_I \left( \frac{1}{1 + r^*} \right) + P_0 L_I'\bar{X}_I \right\}(1 + r) \tag{26}$$

whence

$$\mu_I'\bar{X}_I \left( 1 - \frac{1 + r}{1 + r^*} \right) = P_0 L_I'\bar{X}_I(1 + r) \tag{27}$$

whence

$$\mu_I'\bar{X}_I = \{ P_0 L_I'\bar{X}_I(1 + r) \} / \{ (r^* - r)/(1 + r^*) \} \tag{28}$$

and substituting, using (22) and (28), into (24), the value of the surplus, gives

$$S = \mu_I'A_I\bar{X}_I r^* = \frac{P_0 L_I'\bar{X}_I(1 + r)r^*}{r^* - r} \tag{29}$$

whence

$$\mu_I'A_I\bar{X}_I r^*(r^* - r) = P_0 L_I'\bar{X}_I(1 + r)r^* \tag{30}$$

that is

$$r = r^* \left\{ 1 - \frac{P_0 L_I'\bar{X}_I}{\mu_I'A_I\bar{X}_I r^*}(1 + r) \right\} \tag{31}$$

which in Sraffa's terminology is

$$r = R(1 - w(1 + r))$$

provided we assume that $L_I'X_I = L_I'\bar{X}_I$, that is, that the quantity of labour is the same in both systems. ($P_0 L_I'X_I$ = total wages in the real system and in the standard system.)

If we take as *numéraire* the value of net production in this system, that is if we make $\mu_I A_I\bar{X}_I r^* = 1$, then all prices in the real system will be measured in terms of a *numéraire* which does not vary with $P_0$ and r. We have in fact chosen as *numéraire* a composite commodity made up from a basket of commodities of the real system in proportions $K_i$. This is equivalent to including, in the prices system of department I, the equation

$$r = r^*(1 - P_0 L_I'\bar{X}_I(1 + r)) \tag{32}$$

With $\mathbf{P}_I$ determined and measured with respect to net natural product, $\mathbf{P}_{II}$ can be derived from the sector II equations. From (29) we get the labour which can be purchased with the net product:

$$\bar{L} = \frac{\mu_I' \mathbf{A}_I \bar{\mathbf{X}}_I r^*}{\mathbf{P}_0} = \frac{\mathbf{L}_I \bar{\mathbf{X}}_I (r^*(1+r))}{r^* - r} \tag{33}$$

Thus the standard commodity is such that with it one can buy a quantity of labour which varies inversely with the standard wage and directly with the rate of profit; and this is equal to the annual labour of the system when $r = 0$ and tends to infinity as $r \to r^*$. In this manner 'all the properties of an "invariable standard of value" are found in a variable quantity of labour, which, however, varies according to a simple rule which is independent of prices.'[2] This objective measure is the quantity of labour commanded. Point A, that is, the valuation of commodities as a function of their price when there are no wages, is equivalent to choosing a commodity whose net product, chosen as unit of account, is invariant with respect to distribution between wages and profits.

## 4. Values According to Labour Incorporated

Suppose we now start at point B and denote the relevant prices by $\lambda_i$. The price system becomes

$$\lambda_I = \mathbf{A}_I' \lambda_I + \mathbf{L}_I \tag{34}$$

$$\lambda_{II} = \mathbf{A}_{II}' \lambda_I + \mathbf{L}_{II} \tag{35}$$

$$1 = \omega \mathbf{B} \lambda_{II} \tag{36}$$

so

$$\lambda_j = l_j + a_{ij}\lambda_1 + \cdots + a_{nj}\lambda_n$$

is the quantity of direct and indirect labour employed in the production of commodity j. We have a system of m equations determining m values, which in this form would be the socially necessary labour to produce each commodity. Then

$$w\mathbf{B}\lambda_{II} = \frac{1}{T}(b_{n+1}\lambda_{n+1} + \ldots + b_m\lambda_m) \tag{37}$$

will be the value in terms of labour incorporated of the means of subsistence per worker and per hour of labour. Values can be expressed in terms of constant capital, variable capital and surplus value. We are in fact defining the rate of exploitation, as:

$$e = \frac{\text{surplus labour}}{\text{necessary labour}} = \frac{1 - w\mathbf{B}\lambda_{II}}{w\mathbf{B}\lambda_{II}} = \frac{T - \mathbf{B}\lambda_{II}}{\mathbf{B}\lambda_{II}} \tag{38}$$

manipulating this we get

$$(1 + e)w\mathbf{B}\lambda_{II} = 1 \tag{39}$$

and substituting in the value equations:

$$\lambda_I = \mathbf{A_I}'\lambda_I + (1 + e)w\mathbf{B}\lambda_{II}\mathbf{L_I} \tag{40}$$

$$\lambda_{II} = \mathbf{A_{II}}'\lambda_I + (1 + e)w\mathbf{B}\lambda_{II}\mathbf{L_{II}} \tag{41}$$

Now denote

Constant capital $\quad \mathbf{C_I} = \mathbf{A_I}'\lambda_I; \quad \mathbf{C_{II}} = \mathbf{A_{II}}'\lambda_I$ $\tag{42}$

Variable capital $\quad \mathbf{V_I} = w\mathbf{B}\lambda_{II}\mathbf{L_I}; \quad \mathbf{V_{II}} = w\mathbf{B}\lambda_{II}\mathbf{L_{II}}$ $\tag{43}$

Surplus-value $\quad \mathbf{S_I} = e\mathbf{V_I}; \quad\quad \mathbf{S_{II}} = e\mathbf{V_{II}}$ $\tag{44}$

This gives the expressions:

$$\lambda_I = \mathbf{C_I} + \mathbf{V_I} + \mathbf{S_I} = \mathbf{C_I} + (1 + e)\mathbf{V_I} \tag{45}$$

$$\lambda_{II} = \mathbf{C_{II}} + \mathbf{V_{II}} + \mathbf{S_{II}} = \mathbf{C_{II}} + (1 + e)\mathbf{V_{II}} \tag{46}$$

whose generic equation is:

$$\lambda_j = \sum_{i=1}^{n} a_{ij}\lambda_i + (1 + e) \sum_{i=n+1}^{m} b_i\lambda_i w e_j$$

$$= \sum_{i=1}^{n} l_{ij} + (1 + e) \sum_{i=n+1}^{m} \mathbf{V}_{ij} \tag{47}$$

From values obtained in this way we can pass on to prices. If $\alpha_j$ is the price of production of commodity j then

$$\lambda_j \alpha_j = \left( \sum_{i=1}^{n} C_{ij} \alpha_i + \sum_{i=n+1}^{m} V_{ij} \alpha_i \right)(1+r) \quad \text{for } j = 1, \ldots, m \qquad (48)$$

and in matrix terms:

$$\frac{1}{1+r} \begin{bmatrix} \alpha_1 \\ \vdots \\ \alpha_m \end{bmatrix} = \begin{bmatrix} C_{11} & \cdots & C_{n1} & V_{n+11} & \cdots & V_{m1} \\ \vdots & & & & & \\ C_{1m} & \cdots & C_{nm} & V_{n+1m} & \cdots & V_{mm} \end{bmatrix} \begin{bmatrix} \alpha_1 \\ \vdots \\ \alpha_m \end{bmatrix} \qquad (49)$$

a system with one degree of freedom in which we can derive the $\alpha_i$ by introducing one of the following normalization conditions:

(a) total value equal to total price

$$\sum_{i=1}^{m} \lambda_j X_j = \sum_{j=1}^{m} \lambda_j \alpha_j X_j \qquad (50)$$

(b) total surplus value equal to total profit

$$eV = \sum_{j=1}^{m} \lambda_j X_j \alpha_j - \sum_{j=1}^{m} \sum_{i=1}^{n} C_{ij} \alpha_i X_j - \sum_{j=1}^{n} \sum_{i=n+1}^{m} V_{ij} \alpha_i X_j \qquad (51)$$

(c) some particular $\alpha_i = 1$

With $\alpha_j$ known we know $P_j$. In fact $P_j = \alpha_j \lambda_j$. From the equation for $\lambda_j \alpha_j$ we have:

$$\lambda_j \alpha_j = \left( \sum_{i=1}^{n} a_{ij} \lambda_i \alpha_i + \sum_{i=n+1}^{m} \lambda_i \alpha_i l_j b_i w \right)(1+r)$$

$$= \left( \sum_{i=1}^{n} a_{ij} \lambda_i \alpha_i + \sum_{i=n+1}^{m} \lambda_i \alpha_i b_i w L_j \right)(1+r) \qquad (53)$$

and if $P_i = \alpha_i \lambda_i$, the former equation is merely the price equation:

$$P_j = \left( \sum_{i=1}^{n} \alpha_{ij} P_i - P_0 L_j \right)(1+r) \qquad (54)$$

since

$$P_0 = \sum_{i=n+1}^{m} b_i P_i w$$

We could thus have obtained prices directly, but the detour through which we obtained values has given us added information about the system we are trying to explain. It works as follows: from the definition of the rate of exploitation, we have, with some manipulation

$$w = [1/\mathbf{B}\lambda_{II}](1 + e) \tag{55}$$

If $e = 0$, then $w_{max} = 1/\mathbf{B}\lambda_{II}$. If $e > 0$ then $w < w_{max}$, and $e$ is maximum when $w_{min} = 1/T$. As a result the relation between $w$ and $e$ is that shown in figure 2. Furthermore, from the price system we can get the price-factor frontier $r = r(P_0)$ and, by some manipulation we can put this in the form $r = r(w)$.

Figure 2

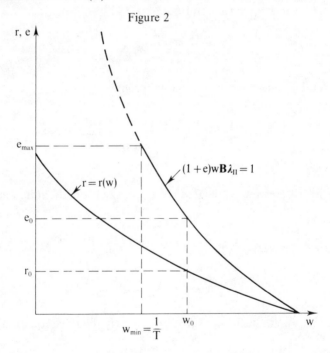

The way this works is as follows: given technical conditions, that is to say the matrices $\mathbf{A}_I$, $\mathbf{A}_{II}$, $\mathbf{L}_I$ and $\mathbf{L}_{II}$, values $\lambda_I$ and $\lambda_{II}$ are determined. Given $\mathbf{B}$, the class struggle will determine a point on the curve $(1 + e)w\mathbf{B}\lambda_{II} = 1$ such that $e_0$ corresponds to a real wage $w_0$ and, therefore, to a day's labour $T_0$. With w known, $P_i/P_0$ and r are determined.

## 5. *The Price System, Centre of the Problem*

In the preceding section we did more than determine values according to labour incorporated. We introduced e, the rate of exploitation. With it we did two things which are not strictly derived from the price system. First, we linked the surplus and production of department II with department I. This was not done in the first system, which treated as surplus everything remaining after replacement of the means of production, even though part of this is not a surplus since it is used to reproduce labour-power. This improvement means we can analyse the effect of variations in department II on department I. But we have also advanced our analysis of the determination of the rate of profit by referring it to labour values.

In Sraffa's original version, which is represented in the present text by equation (31), the rate of profit is inversely related to the share of wages in the standard net product, it exact quota being determined by the class struggle between workers and capitalists. But neither the relation between values and the rate of profit, nor its repercussions on prices, is evident. For example, to study the effects on profit of an increase in the working day or better technology in department II the analysis would have to go into details which, to say the least, would be extremely complicated.

Nevertheless the second model helps in the task, since in it the class struggle determines neither the wage nor the rate of profit directly, but via the rate of exploitation, that is to say the part of the working day which the capitalists appropriate. Therefore a rise in the latter, or a better technology in department II, would have repercussions for the profit rate which the model is capable of analysing.

Except for this point, however, both commanded and incorporated labour values are determined in the last instance by the price system. Neither the $\lambda_i$ nor the $\mu_i$ call for additional assumptions than that of constant returns to scale and equal profit rates. In order to solve the problem posed in equations (4) and (5), the neo-Ricardians are obliged to make these two fundamental assumptions and from them derive the main part of their analysis. But this is neither an alternative to Marx, nor does it correspond to the capitalist system, nor is it the only way to solve the problem. In what follows, therefore, we try to unravel their repercussions and establish that, since they undermine themselves, there is no other alternative to that given by Marx.

## II. The Importance of Constant Returns to Scale

The system (11), (12), (13), as we have seen, involves m prices plus $P_0$ and r. Hence there are $m + 3$ variables and $m + 1$ equations. Taking one of the commodities as *numéraire* we can reduce the system to a single equation relating $P_0$ (and hence w) to r, that is, to the so-called price-factor frontier.

This equation tells us that when the available technology in the economy is described by $A_I, A_{II}, L_I$ and $L_{II}$, a rise in the money wage in terms of any *numéraire* whatsoever implies a reduction in the rate of profit, although we may not know if it is a more or less proportional change and hence we do not know the shape of the curve. Thus, for the neo-Ricardians relative prices cannot be determined mechanically because an equation is missing and there is, therefore, an extra degree of freedom. The class struggle determines, in the last instance, a point on the price–factor frontier, and, with the last degree of freedom thus removed, relative prices and the price system are determined. Using implicit values in such a system (commanded or embodied labour, according to which we choose) we can study the characteristics of each one of the commodities, how profits are formed, and so on. But in all of this the assumption of constant returns to scale plays a role of transcendental importance.

### 1. The Effects of Demand on Prices

The assumption of constant returns is expressed in the constancy of the coefficients $a_{ij}$ and $l_j$ in the technical matrices $A_I, A_{II}, L_I$ and $L_{II}$. This is what guarantees that when all the inputs rise by X%, the product will rise in exactly the same proportion. It is precisely because of this supposition that the determination of relative prices, the wage and the profit rate is independent of supply and demand for the product, so that variations in this latter cannot lead to variations in prices or in distribution. Prices and quantities can be dealt with as two separate problems. But this is completely different from Marx's treatment and, even more important, from the way the capitalist system works.

If we drop the assumption of constant returns to scale the whole system becomes much more complicated. Suppose that, as in real life under capitalism, there are increasing returns to scale. This means production can be increased by, say, 10% by increasing the use made of the means of production and of labour by less than 10%. A speed-up in the pace of accumulation and hence a growth of demand would involve a slower increase in the production of the means of production. This would be expressed in the fact that the coefficients $a_{ij}$ will fall as production increases, that is,

$$\frac{\partial a_{ij}}{\partial X_j} < 0$$

It is enough for a single merchandise to exist with increasing returns to scale for the growth in demand for any commodity to cause some $a_{ij}$ to diminish. If the commodity whose demand is increasing is that for which there are increasing returns to scale, its $a_{ij}$ will diminish. If it is another, the demand for its inputs will grow, and for their inputs, and so on. Through this interrelation, since we have assumed that $A_I$ is indecomposable, the increase in demand will work its way through to the commodity with increasing returns to scale, so some $a_{ij}$ will diminish.

For the same reason, it is enough for demand to rise in sector II, even though within it there are no increasing returns to scale, for some $a_{ij}$ within sector I to fall. It is obvious that in the capitalist system many commodities will show increasing returns to scale. But, according to the theorem of Perron–Frobenius on the characteristics of semi-positive non-decomposable matrices, the dominant characteristic root of a matrix rises (or falls) when one of the elements of the matrix rises (or falls). So since r* (the maximum profit rate) is r* $= 1/\eta$ where $\eta$ is the dominant characteristic root of the matrix $A(I-A)^{-1}$, a rise in demand for one of the commodities implies a fall of some $a_{ij}$; which will lead to a fall in $\eta$ and thus a rise in r*, the maximum profit rate. A rise in demand, therefore, implies a displacement of the price–factor frontier to the right, so that the inverse relation between money wage and the rate of profit is broken, since a rise in wages can be associated with a rise in the rate of profit.

Therefore, with increasing returns to scale the determination of prices, of the wage and of the rate of profit is not independent of supply and demand, that is to say, of quantities. If the class struggle has any repercussions, not only on wages and profits, but on the demand for and supply of products—as in real life—prices in the neo-Ricardian schema remain indeterminate.

## 2. Constant Returns to Scale and the Organic Composition of Capital

The second reason the neo-Ricardians can derive a 'stable' relation

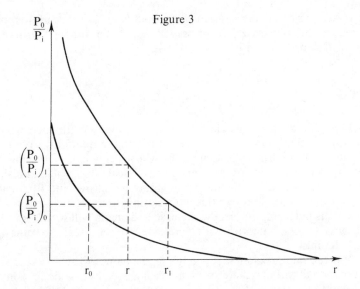

Figure 3

between wages and the profit rate is that they assume that the organic composition of capital for each commodity remains constant. Put another way, the assumption of constant returns to scale is expressed in the fact that the organic composition of capital (we shall call this the OCC) is constant for each commodity.

Sraffa assumes that the organic composition of capital remains constant in the standard system, because it has been constructed using the assumption of constant returns to scale. He makes a particular point of insisting that his model does not begin from this assumption. In principle, given that changes in organic composition only arise when the scale of production is changing, which does not concern Sraffa as he is dealing with static models, he would be right were it not for the fact that the assumption is used in constructing the standard commodity.

As we have seen, the standard commodity is composed of a set of products $\bar{X}_i$, each one of which is one of the components of the vector of production $\bar{X}$, which in turn is the characteristic vector corresponding to the dominant characteristic root of the matrix $A_l(I-A_l)^{-1}$. That is to say, to each maximum profit rate (which in turn is the inverse of the dominant characteristic root of the matrix $A_l(I-A_l)^{-1}$) there corresponds a vector of products of the standard system $\bar{X}$, which in its turn is the characteristic vector corresponding to this dominant characteristic root. As we have also seen, if returns to scale are not constant, r* will depend on the level of production through its effects on the $a_{ij}$. Therefore, $\bar{X}$ also will be a variable vector and the standard commodity cannot be determined independently of the level of production and the characteristics of increasing returns. In summary, if returns to scale are not constant, the dominant characteristic root is a variable, the characteristic vector associated with it likewise, and the standard commodity cannot be constructed since its composition will vary continuously.

But there is another way of looking at this. The standard commodity is a basket in which each one of the commodities is introduced in standard proportions. The system of valuation is the net product of this composite commodity which comprises the basket. We should recall that $K_i$ is the proportion in which the commodity $X_i$ has been introduced, so that:

$$K_i = \frac{\bar{X}_i}{X_i}$$

If returns to scale are not constant, any changes in the quantity of commodity i produced between the real system and the standard system—that is, any divergence of $K_i$ from unity—will involve changes in the inputs used to produce commodity i which will not be, in general, in the same proportion. If $X_j$ is produced by means of $X_{ij}$ (for $i = 1, \ldots, n$) a different quantity $\bar{X}_j = K_j X_j$ will be produced with $\bar{X}_{ij} = K_{ij} X_{ij}$, where all the $K_{ij}$ are not necessarily equal to $K_j$ or to each other.

The system defining the $K_{ij}$ will be

$$\sum_{j=1}^{n} X_{ij} K_{ij}(1 + r^*) = X_i K_i \qquad (\text{for } i = 1, \ldots, n) \qquad (56)$$

$$\sum L_i K_{0i} = L \qquad (57)$$

but, obviously, this system has no solution since there are $(n + 1)$ $K_{ij}$ for each commodity and for labour.

The only solution is thus to equalize these corresponding to each commodity j:

$$K_j = K_{ij} \qquad (\text{for } i = 0, 1, \ldots, n)$$

which assumes that for each commodity j we are making:

$$\frac{\bar{X}_j}{X_j} = \frac{\bar{X}_{ij}}{X_{ij}} \quad \text{(for } i = 1, \ldots, n\text{)} = \frac{\bar{L}_j}{L_j}$$

that is to say we are assuming variations equal in both inputs and outputs, and for this reason we are assuming constant returns to scale.

This method of calculating the standard commodity, implicitly using the assumption of constant returns to scale, presupposes the further assumption that the organic composition of capital of each commodity in the standard system is constant. Recall that using prices referred to the standard commodity, equations (14) and (25) give us

$$\mu_1 = A_1'\mu_1(1 + r)$$

$$\mu_1 = (A_1'\mu_1 + P_0 L_1)(1 + r)$$

giving

$$A_1'\mu_1 r^* = A_1'\mu_1 r + P_0 L_1(1 + r) \tag{58}$$

which means, for commodity j

$$r^* = r + P_0(1 + r)\frac{l_j}{\displaystyle\sum_{i=1}^{n} a_{ij}\mu_i} \tag{59}$$

But

$$\frac{l_j}{\displaystyle\sum_{i=1}^{n} a_{ij}\mu_i}$$

corresponds to (present labour)/(past labour)—since $a_{ij}$ can be reduced to its labour components—and is therefore equivalent to the organic composition of capital. Changes in the organic composition will bring about changes in $r^*$ and therefore the invariable standard of value will become variable.

However, this is only possible if $l_j$ and $a_{ij}$ are not constant, that is to say if constant returns to scale are not assumed. Thus, if we destroy the assumption of constant returns to scale and accept that the organic composition of each commodity is variable, then for each organic composition we will need a distinct standard commodity. But none of them can serve as a measure of changes in commodity prices brought on by changes in technology, since its own value will change at the same time as the rest of the commodities. The inverse relation between w and r will have been destroyed.

When values are constructed in terms of labour embodied something similar takes place in relation to the organic composition. It is obvious that in this case the neo-Ricardians are explicitly using the assumption of constant returns to scale, and it thus follows that the organic composition is constant. In fact from the value equations (40) and (41) we can derive the organic composition, which is

$$\frac{X_I'C_I}{X_I'V_I} = \frac{X_I'A_I\lambda_I}{X_I'L_Iw\lambda_{II}B} = \frac{X_I'A_I(I-A_I')^{-1}L_I}{X_I'L_Iw[A_{II}'(I-A_I')^{-1}+L_{II}]B} \quad (60)$$

that is for each commodity, as before, the organic composition can only vary if made to do so by changes in the $a_{ij}$ and $l_j$: in other words if returns to scale are not constant.

## 3. The Choice of Techniques and Demand

Having got to this point, it is appropriate to study the issue of alternative techniques. This is because a change in demand, leading to a change in the technical coefficients as a result of increasing returns to scale, can be treated as the adoption of a new technique. However, this does not solve the problem either.

Suppose that there are $\gamma_j$ alternative processes for producing commodity j, each with different technical coefficients $l_j$ and $a_{ij}$. We can assume that some of them involve smaller technical coefficients since their behaviour must produce the effect of constant returns to scale. Thus, if for each commodity j there are $\gamma_j$ different processes, for the economy as a whole there will be M alternative techniques, where

$$M = \prod_{j=1}^{n} \gamma_j$$

in sector I with an analogous quantity for sector II. Each set of M matrices which can produce the n means of production is a technology of the economy. It contains the technical knowledge which the neo-Ricardians call their 'book of blueprints' in which each page reflects a method of producing a commodity. The matrices of the technology will be called technique $\alpha$, technique $\beta$, and so on, with technical coefficients $a_{ij}(\alpha)$, $a_{ij}(\beta)$, using $a_{ij}(\cdot)$ for a general, arbitrary technology.

Let us suppose that in the economy technique X is being used. Then prices in department I will be, letting $P_i$ stand for $P_i/P_0$,

$$\mathbf{P}_1(X) = \mathbf{A}_1'(\alpha)\mathbf{P}_1(\alpha) + \mathbf{L}_1(\alpha)(1 + r) \tag{61}$$

Suppose the possibility exists of using technique $\alpha$, which is identical to $\beta$ except for those coefficients which refer to the production of commodity n. We can use prices in $\alpha$ to evaluate the cost of producing commodity n if the new activity is introduced. Technology $\beta$ will be adopted if

$$\left\{ \sum_{i=1}^{n} a_{ij}(\beta)P_i(\alpha) + l_j(\beta) \right\}(1 + r) < P_n(\alpha) \tag{62}$$

Hence, the price of n must fall, since if it does not, in this sector the rate of profit will be greater than that which holds in the rest of the economy and we are assuming that competition instantaneously equalizes profit rates. The price of everything else must also fall, since $a_{ni}(\alpha) = a_{ni}(\beta) > 0$, and for all commodities other than n $a_{ij}(\alpha) = a_{ij}(\beta) > 0$, that is to say $P_j(\alpha) \geqslant P_j(\beta)$. This process will continue and the new prices will be:

$$\mathbf{P}_1(\beta) = [\mathbf{A}_1'(\beta)\mathbf{P}_1(\beta) + \mathbf{L}_1(\beta)](1 + r) \tag{63}$$

The argument can be repeated one by one for each branch of production, establishing that there exists a technology $\eta$ such that prices are positive and the components of the vector of equilibrium prices $(P_i/P_0)$ will be a minimum when $\eta$ is used, so that

$$P(\eta) \leqslant [\mathbf{A}_1'(\cdot)\mathbf{P}_1(\eta) + \mathbf{L}_1(\cdot)](1 + r) \tag{64}$$

and therefore the money wage, in terms of any *numéraire* whatsoever, is a maximum.

Graphically this means, as there are various technologies, that the price–factor frontier is the envelope of those corresponding to each individual technology. Hence, given a profit rate $r_0$ the technology used will be that which minimizes $P_i/P_0$, that is, that which maximizes $P_0/P_i$.

All these results have been derived without taking into account the demand for production and they are a version of what is known as 'Samuelson's non-substitution theorem' which says that given an

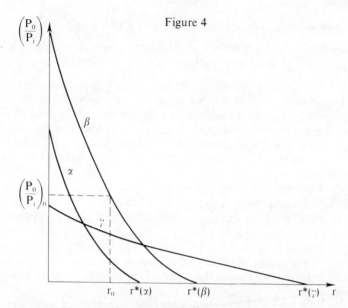

Figure 4

exogenous rate of profit for which there is at least one technology which gives positive prices, in competition prices will be determined by the rate of profit alone and are independent of the volume of production of each commodity. Furthermore, the money wage is determined by competition and depends only on the rate of profit.

If a rise in demand brings about a reduction of the coefficients $a_{ij}$ because of increasing returns to scale, a new technology will in general be chosen. In fact if $\alpha$ and $\beta$ are the technologies before and after a rise in demand, $a_{ij}(\alpha) > a_{ij}(\beta)$ if there are increasing returns to scale. Hence, $P_1(\alpha) > P_i(\beta)$ and therefore will be used. It is as if the 'map' of the price–factor frontier had been displaced to the right and, with it, the envelope.

The problem is that variations in demand will not have determined the technique chosen, since it will in reality be the same technique but on a larger scale. There will be a real change in the chosen technology only if $r$ changes or if one of the unused technologies has returns which increase faster than those in use, so that it appears on its right. But this latter possibility would definitively mean that the techniques used had changed not because of alterations in demand but because of changes in technical knowledge. Therefore, the choice of technology does not solve the problem posed for neo-Ricardian models by constant returns to scale.

## 4. *Increasing Returns, Wages and Profits in Late Capitalism*

Abandoning the assumption of constant returns, we have by now arrived at a series of conclusions which can be summarized thus:

(*a*) The level of production, and hence demand, affect the determination of values, whether we use commanded labour or incorporated labour. This is because the stability of the price–factor frontier, whose points of intersection with the axes are used as the basis of the two valuation systems, has been broken. This reveals a problem which the neo-Ricardians have made no attempt to solve whatsoever.

(*b*) The organic composition of capital, hence, changes with production and with demand. Its variations are basic to the understanding of the way capitalism works, and the neo-Ricardians do not even begin to look at it.

(*c*) Prices, wages and rate of profit are variables in a system which is no longer independent of supply and demand. The famous neo-Ricardian duality between the two problems of prices and quantities is broken.

(*d*) There is no single relation between wages (either monetary or real) and the rate of profit, because this relation can be seen to be affected by the level of production and hence demand. The mechanisms of distribution and, hence, the influence of the class struggle on prices, wages, profits, etc., is no longer so simple and mechanical as the neo-Ricardians claim. The neo-Ricardian conclusion that given technical conditions, the only determinant of the rate of profit is the wage level, is destroyed. The assumption of alternative technologies does not solve the problem.

In summary, if we do not assume constant returns to scale the changes which must be introduced are so important and so many that the neo-Ricardians' conclusions seem far less tenable. All elements of their model must be re-elaborated and many of the criticisms that they have addressed to Marx have become unsustainable.

## III. The Significance of Equal Profit Rates

One of the neo-Ricardian criticisms of Marx is that they establish a profit rate deduced from the price system which does not coincide with Marx's definition, $S/(C + V)$. Furthermore, as we have seen in section II.4, the transformation of values into prices of production is carried out in a system with one degree of freedom, which can be closed by assuming that total value is equal to total price, or that total surplus-value is equal to total profit, but not both. In fact, if both conditions can be imposed, the profit rate derived from the price system will be that defined by Marx, but this is mathematically impossible because the price system remains overdetermined.

As we have seen, for the neo-Ricardians, prices and profit rates are variables which, with w and **B** determined by the class struggle, for example, can be simultaneously determined from the system (14), (15), (16). In this system there are $m + 1$ equations and $m + 2$ variables (m prices, $P_0$ and r). Taking one of these as *numéraire* (gold, for example, which can be commodity m, for which $b_m = 0$) the system depends only on $A_I$, $A_{II}$, $L_I$ and $L_{II}$, that is, the rate of profit is determined by physical conditions of production and values do not figure at all in the calculation. Under these conditions the rate of profit as determined by Marx as $S/(C + V)$ does not coincide with r, the homogeneous profit rate of the system in terms of monetary prices. If $\rho = S/(C + V)$ following the neo-Ricardians' definitions of value:

$$(1 + \rho) = \frac{X_I'\lambda_I + X_{II}'\lambda_{II}}{X_I'(A_I'\lambda_I + L_I w X_{II}'B) + X_{II}'(A_{II}'P_I + L_{II} w \lambda_{II}'B)} \qquad (65)$$

whilst the rate of profit in the price system is

$$(1 + r) = \frac{X_I'P_I + X_{II}'P_{II}}{X_I'(A_I'P_I + L_I w P_{II}'B) + X_{II}'(A_{II}'P_I + L_{II} w P_{II}'B)} \qquad (66)$$

and these would only be equal if numerator and denominator were also equal, that is if total value is equal to total price (the numerator) and total surplus-value is equal to total profit (or, which is the same, total costs in value terms are equal to total costs in price terms).

If we impose on the price system the condition that $(1 + r) = (1 + \rho)$, that is, both conditions, automatically we will have made a variable disappear from the system so that it will still be overdetermined. If we impose one of the two conditions (total value equal to total price) the system will not be overdetermined, because we are not supposing that $(1 + r) = (1 + \rho)$, but it is significant that total surplus-value is not equal to total profit in the sense that r is not equal to $\rho$. And in general this need not occur, because for the neo-Ricardians it does not depend on the factors which determined r. Therefore, as we have seen in section II.4 we can transform values into prices, but only if we do not a priori impose $r = \rho$, and, therefore, that we do not assume that Marx's two conditions apply.

## 1. Average and Homogeneous Rates of Profit

These neo-Ricardian conclusions are derived from the assumption that competition equalizes all profit rates, that is, that which makes it necessary for the *homogeneous rate of profit of the system* to be determined at the same time as prices, once w and **B** are known. But if we do not make this assumption, that is, if we assume that each sector has a different profit rate, the rate of *average profit* is no longer determined simultaneously with prices, because the rate of profit corresponding to each sector bears on it. Under these conditions the average profit rate in the system can be equal to that defined by Marx, total surplus-value will be equal to total profit and total value will coincide with total price, without any incoherency appearing in the system.

The supposition that profit rates equalize through competition was not made by Marx, who spoke of a tendency towards equalization, but, most importantly, who derived no such thing as a complete equality from the working of the capitalist system. Normally, each sector has its own profit rate and, although the tendency is towards equalization, at each point in time it does not actually take place, so that capital, in moving from spheres with lower profits to spheres with higher, does not achieve such an equalization. Hence $(1 + r)$ is not a scalar but a matrix $(\mathbf{I} + \mathbf{R})$, in which the diagonal consists of the particular profit rates $(1 + r_i)$. The system is thus:

$$\mathbf{P_I} = (\mathbf{I} + \mathbf{R_I})(\mathbf{A_I}'\mathbf{P_I} + \mathbf{p_0}\mathbf{L_I}) \tag{67}$$

$$\mathbf{P_{II}} = (\mathbf{I} + \mathbf{R_{II}})(\mathbf{A_{II}}'\mathbf{P_I} + \mathbf{P_0}\mathbf{L_{II}}) \tag{68}$$

$$\mathbf{P_0} = w\mathbf{P_{II}}'\mathbf{B} \tag{69}$$

In this system, given w and **B**, we have $m + 1$ equations and $2m + 1$ variables (m prices, $\mathbf{P_0}$, the money wage and m rates of profit). Taking one of the prices as *numéraire* we then have $m - 1$ degrees of freedom, for which an infinite number of sets of $r_j$ can be found which give positive prices. Each one of these sets of profit rates gives rise to an average profit rate $\bar{r}$. This can be defined as

$$(1 + \bar{r}) = \frac{\mathbf{X_I}'\mathbf{P_I} + \mathbf{X_{II}}'\mathbf{P_{II}}}{\mathbf{X_I}'(\mathbf{A_I}'\mathbf{P_I} + \mathbf{L_I}w\mathbf{P_{II}}'\mathbf{B}) + \mathbf{X_{II}}'(\mathbf{A_{II}}'\mathbf{P_I} + \mathbf{L_{II}}w\mathbf{P_{II}}'\mathbf{B})} \tag{70}$$

that is

$$\frac{\displaystyle\sum_{j=1}^{m}X_jP_j}{\displaystyle\sum_{j=1}^{m}\left(\sum_{i=1}^{n}X_{ij}P_i+L_jwP_{II}'\mathbf{B}\right)} \tag{71}$$

and since

$$\sum_{i=1}^{n}X_{ij}P_i+L_jwP_{II}'\mathbf{B}=\frac{X_jP_j}{1+r_j} \tag{72}$$

it follows, finally, that

$$\frac{1}{(1+\bar{r}_j)}=\sum_{j=1}^{m}\left\{\frac{X_jP_j}{\displaystyle\sum_{i=1}^{m}X_iP_i}\right\}\frac{1}{(1+r_j)} \tag{73}$$

Each set of $r_j$ determines an average profit rate and each average profit rate will be associated with an infinite number of sets of $r_j$. Suppose $\bar{r}$ is equal to r, that is, the average profit rate is equal to the hypothetical homogeneous profit rate. There will be infinitely many sets of $r_j$ which will satisfy this condition and amongst them there will be just one in which $r_j = r$, the neo-Ricardian solution to the problem. But, obviously, there is no need to assume that $\bar{r} = r$, because there is no reason why the different $r_j$, being influenced by their corresponding prices of production, should be the profit rates which would exist if the system were perfect. Thus, not only does $r_j$ not need to be equal to r, but this procedure is not even valid as a method of approximating to the real numerical value of prices, since it refers everything to a homogeneous profit rate which does not have to be equal to the average of the system and which, therefore, has nothing to do with the real world, but with the theoretical preoccupations of the neo-Ricardians. They are therefore choosing a particular case which might occur, but which is one amongst infinitely many possibilities. The neo-Ricardian solution avoids the problem simply by ignoring it.

Alternatively, we could assume that $\bar{r} = S/(C+V)$, that is the average profit rate defined by Marx. This is a possible solution and, as before, there will also be an infinite number of $r_j$ which make $\bar{r} = S/(C+V)$ and, in this case, total value will be equal to total price and total profit to total surplus-value.

A priori this is no more arbitrary than the neo-Ricardian solution. Furthermore, although this is not the place to deal with this theme, since in some sense it relates to the controversy at another level, this solution is more correct because it derives the operation of the law of value from the fact that $S/(C+V)$ is the rate of profit in terms of society's human resources for all of society, which is known a priori when values are known (to the extent that the surplus is known) and the particular $r_i$ only divide this surplus between the various sectors.

## 2. Steedman's Example

Steedman uses an example in his book to show that the rate of profit obtained in a price system is not that which Marx defines as $S/(C+V)$.[3] This example, which seems categorical, is nevertheless a particular case of a more general solution. Furthermore this case is the least 'reasonable' of all such. Steedman's example is as follows:

|  | *Iron* | *Labour* |  |
|---|---|---|---|
| 1. Iron | 28 | 56 | $\rightarrow$ 56 of iron |
| 2. Corn | 12 | 8 | $\rightarrow$ 8 of corn (of which 5 for the workers) |
| 3. Gold | 16 | 16 | $\rightarrow$ 48 of gold |
| Total | 56 and | 80 |  |

Supposing with Steedman that the rate of profit is homogeneous across the three sectors, the price system is:

$$\begin{aligned}(1+r)(28P_1+56P_0)&=56P_1\\(1+r)(12P_1+8P_0)&=8P_2\\(1+r)(16P_1+16P_0)&=48\\80P_0&=5P_2\end{aligned}\tag{74}$$

where $P_0$ is the wage in money terms, defined by the real wage per hour of work $(5/80)$ and $P_2$ the price of corn in terms of gold (taken as a *numéraire*).

The solution to this system is

$$\begin{aligned}P_1&=1.7052\\P_2&=4.2960\\r&=0.5208\\P_0&=0.2685\end{aligned}$$

unit values are

$$56\lambda_1 = 28\lambda_1 + 56\lambda_1 = 2$$
$$8\lambda_2 = 12\lambda_1 + 8\lambda_2 = 4 \qquad (75)$$
$$48\lambda_3 = 16\lambda_1 + 16\lambda_3 = 1$$

The rate of profit, according to Steedman's interpretation of Marx, is

$$\rho = \frac{S}{C+V} = \frac{80 - 5\lambda_2}{56\lambda_1 - 5\lambda_2} = 0.4545$$

which, as Steedman shows, does not coincide with the profit rate obtained in the price system.

If we suppose that the real wage (5/80), instead of being given, is a variable, we can see why this happens. The price system becomes

$$(1+r)(28P_1 + 56P_0) = 56P_1$$
$$(1+r)(12P_1 + 8P_0) = 8P_2$$
$$(1+r)(16P_1 + 16P_0) = 48 \qquad (76)$$
$$P_0 = \omega P_2$$

a system in which there are five variables ($P_0, P_1, P_2, \omega$ and r) and only four equations. By successive elimination we can get an expression relating $\omega$ to r, which is

$$\omega = \frac{1 - 0.5(1-r)}{(1+r)^2 + (1+r)}$$

which is denoted by the term 'price factor frontier' in figure 5.

The rate of profit on Marx's definition is

$$\rho = \frac{80 - \omega \cdot 80\lambda_2}{56\lambda_1 + \omega \cdot 80\lambda_2} = \frac{10 - 40\omega}{14 + 40\omega}$$

and therefore

$$\omega = \frac{24 - 14(1+\rho)}{40(1+\rho)}$$

which is also shown in figure 5. Therefore for $\omega = 5/80$, which is the value it takes in Steedman's example, the two values for the rate of

Figure 5

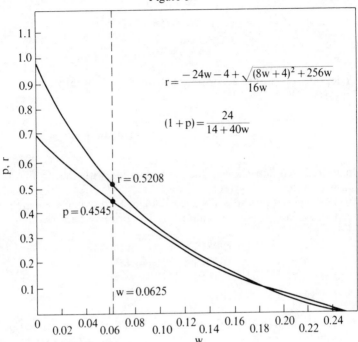

$$r = \frac{-24w - 4 + \sqrt{(8w+4)^2 + 256w}}{16w}$$

$$(1+p) = \frac{24}{14 + 40w}$$

profit r (that obtained in the price system) and $\rho$ (that defined following Marx) do not coincide.

However, insofar as we drop the supposition that the rate of profit is homogeneous, that is to say that each sector has its own profit rate, the 'price–factor frontier' ceases to be just a curve and becomes a family of curves, each of which corresponds to a combination of rates of profit, so that the equality of the average rates of profit in the price system and in the values system can be restored. Under these conditions, Steedman's solution corresponds to one of the curves in this family for which in general $r \neq S/(C+V)$, because he has chosen an r for which this is so.

In effect, Steedman uses in his example an economy of the type:

|  | Units used of: | | |
|---|---|---|---|
|  | Iron | Labour | Production |
| 1. Iron | $x_{11}$ | $L_1$ | $\rightarrow x_1$ of iron |
| 2. Corn | $x_{12}$ | $L_2$ | $\rightarrow x_2$ of corn, of which B are for workers |
| 3. Gold | $x_{13}$ | $L_3$ | $\rightarrow x_3$ of gold |
| Total | $x_1$ of iron | L of labour | $\rightarrow x_1$ of iron, $x_2$ of corn and $x_3$ of gold |

If we suppose that the rate of profit is not homogeneous in the three sectors, the price system will be:

$$(x_{11}P_1 + L_1P_0)(1 + r_1) = x_1P_1$$
$$(x_{12}P_1 + L_2P_0)(1 + r_2) = x_2P_2 \qquad (77)$$
$$(x_{13}P_1 + L_3P_0)(1 + r_3) = x_3$$

$$P_0 = \left(\frac{B}{L}\, P_2\right) = \omega P_2$$

where $P_1$ and $P_2$ are the prices in terms of gold, $P_0$ the money wage and $\omega = B/L$ the real wage, that is to say the goods put at the disposition of the workers for an hour's labour.

Given that we are working with a strictly static system, taking into account the criticisms which we have made until now of the assumption of constant returns to scale, and in order to facilitate the calculations, it is convenient to define

$$a_{ij} = \frac{x_{ij}}{x_j} \qquad \text{and} \qquad l_j = \frac{L_j}{x_j}$$

But remember that if we depart from a static analysis, $a_{ij}$ and $l_j$ are variables and not constants. The price system can now be given as:

$$(a_{11}P_1 + l_1\omega P_2)(1 + r_1) = P_1 \qquad (78)$$

$$(a_{12}P_1 + l_2\omega P_2)(1 + r_2) = P_2 \qquad (79)$$

$$(a_{13}P_1 + l_3\omega P_2)(1+r_3) = 1 \tag{80}$$

and the average rate of profit as

$$1 + \bar{r} = \frac{x_1 P_1 + x_2 P_2 + x_3}{x_1 P_1 + L\omega P_2} \tag{81}$$

a system in which there are more variables than equations and therefore, there are an infinite number of solutions. Let us carry out some operations on it in order to analyse it. From (78)

$$P_2 = \frac{1 - a_{11}(1+r_1)}{l_1\omega(1+r_1)} P_1$$

and from (80)

$$P_1 = \frac{l_1(1+r_1)}{(1+r_3)(l_3 + (l_1 a_{13} - l_3 a_{11})(1+r_1))} \tag{82}$$

that is, the rate of exchange of iron for gold does not depend on w, the real wage, but on the proportions in which labour, $l_1$ and $l_2$, enters in both. It follows that

$$P_2 = \frac{1 - a_{11}(1+r_1)}{\omega(1+r_3)(l_3 + (l_1 a_{13} - l_3 a_{11})(1+r_1))} \tag{83}$$

Substituting the two values of $P_1$ and $P_2$ in (79) gives

$$(1+r_2) = \frac{1 - a_{11}(1+r_1)}{\omega(l_2 + (l_1 a_{12} - l_2 a_{11})(1+r_1))} \tag{84}$$

and doing the same in (81) gives

$$(1+\bar{r}) = \frac{x_2 + (x_1 l_1 \omega - x_2 a_{11})(1+r_1) + l_3\omega(1+r_3)x_3 + (l_1 a_{13} - l_3 a_{11})x_3(1+r_1)}{\omega L + \omega(x_1 l_1 - La_{11})(1+r_1)} \tag{85}$$

The system (82) to (85) is equivalent to the primitive system (78) to (81), but now all the variables are expressed as a function of the rates of profit in the two sectors 1(iron) and 3(gold).

In Steedman's example

$$
\begin{array}{llll}
x_{11}=28 & L_1=56 & x_1=56 & B=5 \\
x_{12}=12 & L_2=\phantom{0}8 & x_2=\phantom{0}8 \\
x_{13}=16 & L_3=16 & x_3=48
\end{array}
$$

and substituting these values we get:

$$
P_1 = \frac{1+r_1}{(1+r_3)(0.\dot{3})+0.1\dot{6}(1+r_1))} \tag{86}
$$

$$
P_2 = \frac{1-0.5(1+r_1)}{\omega(1+r_3)(0.\dot{3}+0.1\dot{6}(1+r_1))} \tag{87}
$$

$$
1+r_2 = \frac{1-0.5(1+r_1)}{\omega(1+(1+r_1))} \tag{88}
$$

$$
1+\bar{r} = \frac{8+(56\omega-4)(1+r_1)+16\omega(1+r_3)+8\omega(1+r_1)(1+r_3)}{80\omega+16\omega(1+r_1)} \tag{89}
$$

Let us analyse this system. $P_1$ is always positive whatever the values of the rates of profit; $P_2$ is always positive, provided:

$$
1-0.5(1+r_1)\geqslant 0
$$

that is

$$
(1+r_1)\geqslant 2
$$

that is

$$
r_1 \geqslant 1;
$$

and in order for $r_2$ to be positive the requirement is that $(1+r_2)\geqslant 1$, and therefore that

$$
1-0.5(1+r_1)\geqslant \omega+\omega(1+r_1)
$$

that is

$$
(1+r_1)\leqslant \frac{1-\omega}{\omega+0.5}
$$

and since $\omega=B/L=5/80=0.0625$ $r_2$ will be greater than 1 if $(1+r_1)\leqslant 1.\dot{6}$; hence all the variables are positive if $0\leqslant r_1 \leqslant 0.\dot{6}$ whatever the value of $r_3$.

Finally, the equation (89), for the particular case of $\omega=0.0625$

taken by Steedman, is

$$(1+\bar{r})=\frac{8-0.5(1+r_1)+(1+r_3)+0.5(1+r_1)(1+r_3)}{5+(1+r_1)}$$

and clearing up,

$$(1+r_1)=\frac{8+(1+r_2)-5(1+\bar{r})}{(1+\bar{r})-0.5(1+r_3)+0.5}$$

For each value of $\bar{r}$ we shall have the geometrical position of those pairs of values of $r_1$ and $r_3$ which satisfy the price equations. All values of $r_1$ between 0 and 0.6 give positive solutions, whatever the value of $r_3$ and provided that $\bar{r} \geqslant 0.35$.

Of all possible solutions, Steedman chooses one: that in which $r_1 = r_2 = r_3 = 0.5208$ and therefore, he is choosing a particular case. Any small deviation whatsoever of the rates of profit $r_1$, $r_2$ or $r_3$ will bring us towards the solution of the price system ( values, prices of production, intrinsic market prices, etc.).

This brings us to one of the peculiar characteristics of Steedman's example. In this example there is only one commodity for the workers (corn) and, for this reason, we can speak of a real wage in terms of goods: $\omega = B/L$. But if there was more than one such commodity we would need a valuation system in order to talk about a real wage. Prices cannot serve because they give the money wage. So the real wage must be determined by values. But, with values known, there is no reason why the real wage should be determined by them and not by the average rate of profit.

In the second place, in Steedman's example the average rate of profit $\bar{r} = \bar{\rho} = 0.4545$, so that if $r_{\text{gold}} = \bar{r} = 0.4545$, the rate of profit in the corn-producing sector is negative. It is reasonable to expect that when the profit rate in the gold-producing sector is equal to or greater than the average, the system would give positive results. But in the example this does not happen because he has posited an unusual capitalist system, in which the organic composition of capital of the corn-producing sector is greater than that of the gold-producing sector, which in turn is greater than that of the iron-producing sector. Under these conditions, a small rise in the rate of profit in iron would imply a very pronounced fall in that of the corn sector, and thence the paradoxical result we have noted. Thus the example does not correspond to what one should expect of a capitalist system.

## IV. The Neo-Ricardians and the Transformation Problem

In section I.4, we examined the neo-Ricardian version of the transformation problem, and in section III their criticism of Marx, starting from this version. As can be seen, although dressed up in new clothing, these are the criticisms already made by von Bortkiewicz, and we can sum them up as follows:

(*a*) The transformation of values into prices of production must be done as on page 178ff; that is, transforming inputs and outputs and not as Marx did it, where he only transformed values into prices of production, but not inputs.

(*b*) With things looked at in this way, the determination of prices through values is an unnecessary detour ($X_j$ to be determined first by $\lambda_j$ in order then to calculate $P_j = \alpha_i \lambda_j$).

(*c*) Furthermore the profit rate of the price system does not coincide with that given by Marx in terms of value, and total value cannot equal total price at the same time that total surplus-value equals total profit, since the system would then be indeterminate.

Our criticisms of this criticism of Marx, expressed in the preceding pages, was designed to dismantle the theoretical bases on which the neo-Ricardian analysis rests and which make these conclusions possible. We have seen that this whole analysis rests on two fundamental assumptions: the existence of constant returns to scale and the equality of profit rates. If we destroy both suppositions, the neo-Ricardian analysis must be substantially altered and in my view the criticisms of Marx will be unsustainable.

# The Negation of 'Negative Values'

## Sungur Savran

Within the multi-faceted critique directed at Marx's theory of value by those economists who base themselves on the work of Piero Sraffa, there is an area which has intrigued many if only because of the singularity of its very terms. I am referring to the debate on so-called 'negative values' and 'negative surplus-value', a debate initiated by Ian Steedman in 1975,[1] and since then a central feature of his critique of labour values.[2] To many, it seemed that since the extension of the Marxist theory of value to various fields (i.e. joint production and fixed capital) yielded such absurd results, there certainly had to be something irredeemably wrong about it. Given the impeccable nature of Steedman's mathematical argumentation, there seemed to be no escape route. The contradictions simply had to be admitted.

The truth is that the *mathematical* argumentation that leads to these results is based on a fallacious reconstruction of the *theoretical* structure of Marx's concept of value. It can be shown that in both cases, the demonstration rests on the inacceptable replacement of Marx's concept with another which is totally alien to it. The anomalies reached in this manner are then falsely presented as resulting from Marx's own theory. My purpose in this article is to argue that these anomalous results have no relationship to Marx's theory of value.[3]

### 1. Social Values

What I will do is to show that, contrary to his claims, Steedman reaches negative values and negative surplus-value through the application not of Marx's concept of value but of a totally erroneous and caricatured version of it.

In order to do this, one has to reduce the situation depicted by Steedman to its true dimensions. This situation is not joint production pure and simple, as would have been the case if two commodities were produced by a single process. It is a situation where each of the two commodities in question is produced using two different processes, this is to say, there are prevalent in society two different production methods for each commodity. If, therefore, Marx's theory of value is to be applied to the situation in question, as Steedman claims to do, one has to follow Marx's own method of dealing with such questions. This is briefly what we shall first have to review.

In the first volume of *Capital*, where he investigates commodity and 'capital in general', that is capital in its sole relationship to wage-labour, Marx abstracts from the relations among different producers of the same commodity. Hence, the effects of these relations are excluded by the nature of the level of abstraction. In the investigation of the 'isolated commodity' of the first volume, the labour embodied in the commodity has to be socially necessary, no more, no less.[4] That which determines socially necessary labour is defined as 'the conditions of production normal for a given society'.[5] This first definition of socially necessary labour is, therefore, abstract: in other words, it is not explained how the category 'normal' is determined in the concrete. This category is indifferent to the various conditions of production that may exist in real life, be they conditions of average, high or low productivity with respect to the situation prevalent in society.

In the third volume, on the other hand, where the relations between various capitals are included in the investigation, the competition among producers within a single branch of production can no longer be abstracted from. This, of course, results in the analysis of situations where different capitals produce the same commodity with methods of differing productivity.

The concept of socially necessary labour is now subject to new determinations, beyond that generality appropriate to the level of abstraction made in the first volume. It is, in other words, made concrete. It now turns out that in a branch of social production where various capitals produce under different conditions of productivity, the social (or market) value of a unit of the commodity produced in this branch is determined by the division of the whole quantity of labour expended in the branch to the total mass of commodities produced in the branch. Commodities under different conditions of production have distinct individual values which are equalized, through a process, in the social value of the commodity.

In the context of this general approach, Marx investigates the effect which different conditions of production have in determining social value. A detailed analysis of this investigation is unnecessary for our purposes. What is important is the fact that, in different circumstances, different conditions of productivity may influence or determine social value. That is to say, social value can be determined by those producers who work at the lowest or highest levels of productivity, as well as those who work at average levels. It is, therefore, absurd to contend, as Steedman does in his debate with Morishima, that 'in his mature works, Marx repeatedly asserted that ... he would define the value of [a] commodity by reference to the average conditions of production and not by reference to the most (or least) favourable conditions.'[6]

That Steedman distorts Marx's position on this question should not obscure the even more important fact that for Marx the same commodity, when produced with different methods, has a multiplicity of individual values, none of which is in general equal to the social value of the commodity. The latter comes about only as a result of a process of equalization.

We are now ready to evaluate Steedman's claim that what he applies to the case of joint production is Marx's theory of value. Before embarking upon a detailed critique of Steedman's procedure, it is useful to point out that the result of negative surplus-value is entirely contingent upon the existence of negative values, so that, once the concept of negative values is done away with, there remains no problem to be solved with respect to negative surplus-value.

A second point of considerable importance is that, in the example which Steedman constructs,[7] which analyses a situation where two commodities are produced jointly by two different processes, one of the processes represents a higher productivity of labour. That is to say, one process is more productive than the other.

Using Steedman's example, if one compares the two processes, the net product (in Sraffa's sense) of the first process contains one unit of each commodity, while the net product of the second contains three units of the first commodity and two of the second. This is no mere coincidence. It has been proved that negative values can only arise under such conditions. In other words, an absolute difference of productivity between the two processes is a necessary condition for the appearance of such negative values.[8] Hence, if it can be shown that Steedman's method is inappropriate in this specific case, then the question of negative values will totally disappear.

Figure 1

| | Inputs | | | Outputs | | Net product | |
|---|---|---|---|---|---|---|---|
| | Com- modity | Com- modity | | Com- modity | Com- modity | Com- modity | Com- modity |
| | 1 | 2 | Lab. | 1 | 2 | 1 | 2 |
| Process 1 | 5 | 0 | 1 | 6 | 1 | 1 | 1 |
| Process 2 | 0 | 10 | 1 | 3 | 12 | 3 | 2 |

## 2. The Equalization Process

Once this has been established, we can now proceed to investigate Steedman's example in the light of Marx's framework. In a system of one-product processes, given the values of all other commodities, the individual values of a certain commodity produced under several different conditions can be determined by recourse to the individual processes. With joint production, on the other hand, it is not possible to 'read off' individual values from individual processes, since at least some processes produce more than one commodity. Nevertheless, where an absolute difference exists between the two processes with respect to productivity, one fact can be established unequivocally: that the individual values of both commodities cannot be simultaneously equal for both processes. For instance, if the individual values of the first commodity are equal in the two processes, those of the second are necessarily unequal, and vice versa. Of course, in all probability, the individual values of both commodities will be different for the two processes, but as a special case one of the two commodities may have identical individual values in the two processes. However, even in such a case, this cannot be true for both commodities at the same time.

The proof is simple. Pick a commodity at random and assume that its individual values in the two processes are equal. Once due deduction is made for this commodity, the quantity of labour that remains for the second commodity in the first process is necessarily smaller than that remaining in the second process. This is because, in the second process, a greater amount has been produced of the first commodity, so that whatever value is allocated to this commodity in the first process, more has to be allocated in the second. On the other hand, more has been produced of the second commodity in the second process than in the first. Therefore, to determine the value of the second commodity, a smaller amount of labour has to be divided into a larger number of units in the second process. Hence the individual value of the second commodity is necessarily smaller in the second process than in the first. Equality between individual values in the two processes is not possible for commodities simultaneously.

This result is very important, for it implies that in the context of an absolute difference in productivity between the two processes, the individual values in the two processes of at least one of the commodities are unequal. Hence a method consistent with Marx's has to investigate the method of equalization of these two distinct individual values. Steedman claims that he is applying Marx's method to his own special case. Yet what he does is to ignore this difference between the individual values (which has conclusively been proved) and to declare, through the use of simultaneous equations, their equality. Thus he totally sets aside Marx's own analysis regarding the determination of social value. Whereas Marx speaks of a process of equalization between distinct individual values, with Steedman these lose their quality of distinctness only to be assumed equal from the outset. Hence the existence of negative values. These arise as a result of the forcible equalization of distinct and unequal magnitudes.

It has, therefore, been shown that in the unique case where negative values can arise, Steedman has reached them by applying a theory of value different from Marx's. Hence the futility of his allegation that Marx's theory of value leads to self-contradictory results in the context of joint production. It is a caricature of the Marxist concept of value that leads to these absurdities. Of course, as has already been noted, once the existence of negative values is disproved, so is the existence of negative surplus-value, so that there is no contradiction in either the theory of value or the theory of surplus-value developed by Marx.

Although it has already been proved that Steedman's method of simultaneous equations is patently inappropriate for representing Marx's method, it may still be necessary to dwell upon Steedman's own claim that the former method is in fact due to Marx. Since the method of simultaneous equations does not occur in Marx's own voluminous work, Steedman bases his claim on Marx's calculation of value through the addition of that part of constant capital used, variable capital and surplus-value. In either of the following cases, it can be regarded as appropriate to express this method of calculation through the use of simultaneous equations: firstly, if each commodity is produced by a single method or, secondly, if individual values have already been reduced to social values. However, if and when there exist more than one method of production for a commodity, it is impossible to determine the social values of this commodity simultaneously with the others by the use of a system of equations.

There are two reasons for this, one theoretical, the other formal. The theoretical reason is that this method assumes equal individual values where there are only unequal magnitudes. The formal reason is, very simply, that if two production equations are included in the system but in both cases the same identical value is attributed to the commodity, the number of equations will exceed the number of unknowns and the system will be indeterminate. Hence the method of simultaneous equations is inappropriate for the reduction of distinct individual values into one social value. Note that this is true even in the general case, before joint production is introduced. Not being valid in the general case, naturally it cannot be extended to Steedman's case. Therefore Steedman's claim that he is applying Marx's method to joint production falls to pieces. The 'difficult' problems of negative values and the coexistence of positive profits with negative surplus-value are no more than pseudo-problems that arise from mistaking mathematical relations for real relations.

One final point before we leave the matter. Not only is the method applied by Steedman to the analysis of joint production not Marx's method, but, equally, this method is itself internally inconsistent. According to Steedman, value is determined by the labour embodied in commodities, which in its turn is totally dependent upon the method of production used. In his own example, two different methods of production are used for the production of each commodity and, consequently, the quantity of labour embodied in the commodity is different in the two processes. The value of the commodity when produced in one process should therefore be different from that of the same commodity when produced in the other. Steedman contradicts himself by assuming these different, individual, values of the commodities to be equal.

## 3. Fixed Capital

A third area where Steedman claims to have shown an inconsistency is in Marx's treatment of fixed capital. This question is also important because the significance of joint production for the theory of value has been defended not on the grounds of 'pure' joint production but on the contention that joint production is the only method of satisfactorily dealing with fixed capital. In what follows, both contentions will be seen to be wrong. Limitations of space do not permit the reproduction of Steedman's arithmetic examples. The interested reader is referred to the relevant chapter of his book.[9]

Steedman's point of departure is the observation that value depreciation with respect to time may not be linear, for example a machine may turn out to be less efficient in the first year of its life and more efficient in the following years. He admits that Marx is aware of this fact but assumes linear depreciation as a first abstraction. He claims, however, that once this first level of abstraction is abandoned, Marx's method of treating fixed capital, namely the transfer of value to the final product, can lead to self-contradictory results. To show that this is the case, he constructs an example where the same machine of different ages is used by different capitals. His first step is to reach two different values for the same commodity, produced by the use of these machines of differing ages, through the application of Marx's method. What is more, both of these values are different from the 'correct' value, calculated by the use of the net product method. Therefore, concludes Steedman, the use of this method within Marx's theory of value leads to internally inconsistent results.[10]

According to him the correct method of calculation is to attribute different values to machines of different ages and solve the problem by means of a system of simultaneous equations. In other words, it is to treat fixed capital as a joint product. This does lead to consistent results but also to other sorts of bizarre consequences. Depending on the case, either the depreciation quota, that is the value transferred from fixed capital to the final product, or the value of fixed capital at the end of the period may turn out to be negative.[11] Hence even in those cases where it does not lead to unacceptable results, the theory of value ends up in a state of contradiction with its bases.

The problem seems serious indeed. Negative value transfer or a negative value for the used fixed capital is contradictory with the fundamentals of Marx's treatment. As Marx says, 'the means of production can never add more value to the product than they themselves possess independently of the process which they assist.'[12] This is contradicted by a negative value for fixed capital, for what this implies is, in effect, that fixed capital imparts to the final product more value than it possesses and thereby acquires a negative value. On the other hand, the value of the means of production 'is determined not by the labour process into which it enters as a means of production, but by that out of which it has issued as a product.'[13] This is in blatant contrast with negative value transfer. What happens in such a case is a flow of value from the product to fixed capital, or, in other words, the determination of the value of fixed capital by that process into which it has gone as a means of production.

All these important results are obtained, however, on the basis of unsound arguments. To show that this is the case, it is better to start with the second of Steedman's calculation methods. As in the case of joint production, this allegedly correct method relies on the forcible equalization of the unequal individual values of different species of a commodity produced under different conditions. It is of course very easy to show that individual values are not equal: different degrees of efficiency having been assumed for the different ages of the machines, equal numbers of living labour will produce unequal quantities of the commodity in the different cases. This of course implies unequal individual unit values.

What should have been done, on the contrary, is to admit the inequality of individual values and to investigate the process of the formation of social value. The answer to this correct question is not difficult to provide, since as 'the means of production transfer their value to the product only in so far as they lose their exchange-value along with their independent use-value',[14] they impart to each unit that can be produced during their lifespan the same amount of value. Which means that the basis of Marx's conception is linear depreciation not with respect to time but with respect to use-value. In this case, the value of each such unit is equal in magnitude. During those years in which the means of production are less or more efficient than average, individual value rises above or falls below social value. In the first case, the capital in question receives a lower rate of profit than average, in the second, it is the opposite that holds. But calculated over the whole lifespan of the instrument, the rate of profit of both the branch and the individual capital that uses this instrument is equal to the general rate of profit.

The application of Steedman's allegedly 'correct' method is not only inconsistent with the bases of value theory, it also produces absurd results. To take but a single instance, if this method is adopted but the example is modified, the value of the commodity will fluctuate from one year to another.[15] That this result is absurd in the context of the theory of value is obvious, for the products of the various years will have different social values even though all are produced under what Marx calls 'normal' conditions prevalent in society. But this is secondary. What is of primary importance is that Steedman has arrived at negative-value transfer and negative fixed-capital value not by applying Marx's method but by abandoning it. Therefore, these results have nothing to do with Marx's theory of value.

Once this is understood, it is easy to see that value calculation according to Marx's own method, that is value transfer to the final product proportional to use-value depreciation, is totally consistent and adequate. It was already noted that Steedman obtains three different values for the same commodity through the application of this method. Once it is grasped that two of these three values are the individual values related to two different production processes, it is very simple to explain firstly, why these values are not equal to each other, and secondly, why both of them are distinct from and not equal to the third, which is social value. In fact, far from being the symptom of an inconsistency, this result is a perfect manifestation of the logical conherence of Marx's work in its totality. The analysis of fixed capital merges here into the analysis of the formation of social value in the context of the existence of different methods of production for a commodity. Steedman's allegations, both of inconsistency and of the necessity of the method of joint production in the treatment of fixed capital, fall to pieces on careful examination.

## Conclusion

The argument presented in this article shows that the anomalous results reached by Steedman in his treatment of joint production and fixed capital have no bearing on Marx's theory of value, for they are derived on the basis of a total misrepresentation of the relevant aspects of this theory. Once this is seen, the mystique that surrounds the concepts of 'negative values' and 'negative surplus-value' vanishes. Non-existent in theory, 'negative values' are revealed to embody wasted intellectual labour in practice.

The rebuttal of the allegations concerning joint production and fixed capital removes yet one more foundation of the post-Sraffian critique of the Marxist theory of value. Of modest importance on its own, this result is significant insofar as it contributes to the all-sided demise of this supposed critique.

# The Logic of the Transformation Problem

## Alan Freeman

### 1. Introduction

Since Bohm-Bawerk first criticized Marx's transformation of values into prices of production, almost everyone who has tried to correct or refute Marx's value theory has claimed it is logically flawed. The post-Sraffians are the most emphatic. Steedman writes that the 'central objection' to Marx's approach is that 'even if input prices are transformed, Marx's solution is internally inconsistent.'[1] His argument, which has almost no empirical component, stands or falls on its logical critique. As he himself says, his case 'is the conclusion of an argument in logic; should anyone wish to challenge it, they must do so either by finding a logical flaw in the argument or by rejecting explicitly and coherently one or more of the assumptions on which it is based.'[2]

A footnote adds:

> 'The present type of argument has been examined, in various forms, by many different writers over the last eighty years. The same conclusions have always been reached and no logical flaw has ever been found in such arguments.'[3]

My limited but perhaps ambitious aim is to identify and demarcate this logical flaw.

### 2. The Argument in Outline

Steedman makes two charges: inconsistency and redundancy. The first allegation dates from von Bortkiewicz. It says that Marx's transformation cannot be applied to a self-reproducing economy without dropping one or other of his famous equalities and his expression for the rate of profit. There is a logical contradiction between hypotheses and results, so the hypotheses must be wrong.

Post-Sraffian writers have developed this idea, for example with claims that labour values lead to negative values, and so on. Nevertheless, what distinguishes writers such as Steedman from all Marx's 'interpreters' and 'correctors' is their use of the second charge: redundancy. They have a distinctive creed, pursued with Jesuitical zeal, and which prescribes that political economy must be reconstructed without labour values.[4] Steedman's argument is succinct. He says that values are not needed to calculate prices and therefore they are not needed at all, because they do not 'determine' prices.

There are four reasons why I shall concentrate on this second charge:

First, the redundancy charge has not been 'studied for eighty years' and is a distinct logical issue from that of inconsistency, deserving separate treatment.

Second, there is no need to repeat Farjoun, Savran and Giussani's refutations of many inconsistency charges. For the same reason I do not propose to adopt the more general joint production framework,[5] the arguments applying *mutatis mutandis*. Third, I wish to re-assess the way in which Marx's equalities have been translated into mathematical terms using simultaneous equation systems, and show that in the sense most important to Marx's analysis, his equalities do hold, even within such systems. But this different interpretation calls for a critical assessment of the post-Sraffian view of causality, the central issue being what 'determines' prices in the real world.

Most important, however, the charge of redundancy is actually the only basis in logic for rejecting labour values. This is not always understood, but becomes clearer if we ask how scientific progress, which constantly encounters contradiction and inconsistency, takes place.

In general two different 'paradigms', or programmes of scientific inquiry, can result from a formal inconsistency. One involves critical revision—reworking existing theory to remove the inconsistency by changing either its hypotheses or the way they are formulated. The other involves critical rejection—transcending the theory as a whole. Within logic as such there is no basis for settling on one or other choice on the grounds of inconsistency. If one assumes $1 + 1 = 4$, one can deduce $1 = 3$, which contradicts an axiom of number theory. Most mathematicians have not rejected number theory, but the hypothesis that $1 + 1 = 4$.[6]

The normal scientific reason for throwing out a theory is that a new one explains the known facts better. Indeed, if inconsistency were sufficient ground to reject an entire theory, the neo-Ricardian school would be obliged to discard their own theory which contains many inconsistencies, some openly conceded and others brought to light in this volume.

Hence the thrust of this paper. Its argument, in outline, is as follows:

(*i*) The post-Sraffian refutation of labour values cannot be dissociated from a particular formalization (mathematical representation), namely a simultaneous equation system with a uniform profit rate in which input prices are equal to output prices.

(*ii*) This involves 'simplifying assumptions' which turn out to be axioms—indispensable elements of the theory—because without them the neo-Ricardian solutions for prices and profit do not exist. These axioms are incompatible with a real commodity economy and Marx's theory of labour values. Above all they cannot model real causality or real determination, because: (a) They abstract from independent movements in time of economic quantities. Both in reality and in Marx's theory, these movements are the actual causal mechanism through which value magnitudes are transformed into prices. (b) They cannot model capitalist behaviour because they abstract from the real quantities which determine capitalist actions, above all differential profits.

(*iii*) Real causality is therefore replaced by algebraic calculation based on these (false) axioms. The result is a profoundly unscientific theory—in fact idealist—because prices are allegedly determined by metaphysical constructs and not the behaviour of independent private producers.

(*iv*) Further advance demands a different formalization of labour value theory and a critical rejection of simultaneous equation models. The independent variation over time of all economic quantities, particularly differential profit rates, must be given the status Marx himself assigned them, namely that of mechanisms of the law of value.

(*v*) If this is done in accordance with Marx's own suggestions there is every reason to suppose that though new contradictions will certainly emerge, the 'inconsistencies' that arise in the Sraffian formalization will not exist. The alleged inconsistencies in labour value theory turn out to result from the hidden assumptions of this formalization, not from the theory as such.

## 3. Origins of a Fundamental Error

Sraffa prefaces his work with a statement of intent. He says: 'The investigation is concerned exclusively with such properties of an economic system as do not depend on changes in the scale of production or in the properties of "factors"... The reason is obvious. The marginal approach requires attention to be focussed on change ... In a system in which, day after day, production continued unchanged in these respects, the marginal product of a factor (or alternatively the marginal cost of a product) would not merely be hard to find—it just would not be there to be found.'[7]

This is more than a restriction of the field of study, for in no real economy does production, day after day, continue unchanged in any respect whatsoever. Sraffa, however, did not claim to present a model of the real workings of a real economy, but concentrated his fire on the internal inconsistencies of the marginalists. He therefore considered it legitimate to abstract from the process of change.

For Steedman the same assumptions take on an enhanced role, since he claims to lay the foundations of a new system of political economy. A founding principle, among those he challenges his critics to refute, is the following: 'The capitalist economies considered are always in a self-reproducing state, whether reproduction be 'simple' or 'expanded' (stationary or growing).'[8]

The term 'self-reproducing' here does not just mean that if the economy is here on Monday, it will also be here on Tuesday. Sraffa and Steedman both repeat a construction which von Bortkiewicz uses when he sets out to solve the alleged 'feedback' failure of Marx's transformation, and which lies at the basis of all such presentations of labour value theory. That is, they say the prices paid for goods at the beginning of a cycle of production are the same as those charged for the same goods at the end of the same cycle. They forcibly equate the results of production to its premises. In short the economy does not merely reproduce itself; it reproduces itself identically. Its past, present and future are locked in a self-sustaining circle.

This is most obvious in relation to prices. Following Steedman, let $\mathbf{p}$ be the price vector, $\mathbf{r}$ the scalar profit rate, $\mathbf{A}$ the matrix of production, $\mathbf{w}$ the real wage, $\mathbf{a}$ the labour employed in each industry, and $L$ the total labour available. The equation

$$\mathbf{p} = (1+r)(\mathbf{p}\mathbf{A} + \mathbf{w}.\mathbf{a}/\mathbf{L}) \qquad (1)$$

is a special case of a more general equation, namely

$$\mathbf{p}^{t+\delta t} = (1+r)(\mathbf{p}^t\mathbf{A} + \mathbf{w}.\mathbf{a}/\mathbf{L}) \qquad (2)$$

where $\mathbf{p}^t$ are prices at time t. The hidden assumption is that $\mathbf{p}^t = \mathbf{p}^{t+\delta t}$.

Without this we would not have a solvable simultaneous equation system at all but a set of n relations connecting $2n + 2$ variables, relating prices now to prices then.

It is less clear that a similar, but not identical constraint applies to quantities. Neo-Ricardian assumptions require all goods to be consumed; that is, there are no unconsumed stocks, no build-up or decline of use-values in circulation, either of goods or money. In fact the simultaneous equation method, in general, reduces to a treatment of flows, rather than stocks, of commodities.

It might appear that this still leaves room for expansion, provided this is matched either by increased capitalist consumption or by demand arising from investment to meet such consumption. However, matters are not quite so simple if we consider the course of events over time when a new demand arises in the economy. Suppose, say, production increases in the cornflakes sector, either to meet a new demand or in anticipation of it. This creates a demand for inputs of cornflake-making equipment and materials; say, corn and iron. But such a demand cannot be satisfied immediately, because all existing output is allocated to existing consumption, either productive or unproductive.

Within the model as it stands, since these inputs are needed before new production can begin, they cannot be supplied in time to make the extra cornflakes unless the iron and corn manufacturers increase their production in the relevant proportions. Indeed, strictly speaking the extra corn and iron would have to be produced in the previous reproductive cycle to be ready in time, reversing the actual economic sequence and endowing the people concerned with clairvoyance as well as omniscience. Even then, the problem is not solved, since it is unclear where the iron or corn producers can get their own surplus inputs from. Thus the sins of the sons are visited on the fathers, since for all time the economy must already have been preparing itself for the coming cornflake boom.

It may appear that a reduction in production at least is possible. Not so simple; it will lead to temporarily unsold stocks of surplus goods. But unsold goods means a reduction of money profits since it reduces money income. However, profits are already fixed at the same time as the price, and like the price may not vary over the period of reproduction.

These and similar difficulties may be averted only by assuming that production rises everywhere at once in such proportions as perfectly to balance out inputs and outputs. Insofar as changes in the scale of production are even conceivable, they impose a most peculiar condition, namely that the economy must change all at once or not at all. An unbalanced economy with surplus supply or demand in particular sectors destroys the formal derivation of prices.

Clearly this is at best an abstraction. But it is not a real abstraction. It is an idealization, justified on the basis that more sophisticated analysis can dispense with the simplifications later. An obvious question therefore arises: what happens if these simplifications are dropped? A second question presents itself: what are their logical consequences as they stand?

To answer both questions, we should ask how these simplifications enter the calculation of prices and profits. We have already noted that a solution depends on equating $\mathbf{p}^{t+\delta t}$ to $\mathbf{p}^t$. Can we drop this assumption? No, because without it there are simply too many variables, and no solution exists. Moreover if one did exist, its meaning would be open to question since it would imply that $\mathbf{p}^t$ were determined by events in the future.

But the same argument applies if we try to relax the many other built-in assumptions. In particular, we cannot allow profit rates to become non-uniform, and the matrix $\mathbf{A}$ cannot be made up of less or more columns than rows; that is, there must be exactly as many producers as products.[9] Nor can any of these quantities actually vary while reproduction is going on, for the same reason as prices. Any adjustment to the parameters of the economy must take place in some nether or aetherial region which is not actually part of the space-time continuum occupied by the economy, unless like Joshua we can halt the sun and moon in the sky while the awful business is done.

If any of these assumptions are dropped, instead of an exact determination of $\mathbf{p}$, $\mathbf{w}$ and r we are left with a collection of relations between a large number of variables out of which no definite determination can in general be made, notwithstanding the interesting or insightful relations which can be established between the variables concerned.

There is an instructive way of looking at this, which the non-mathematical reader can omit, moving to the next section, if necessary.

Let us write the equation relating $\mathbf{p}^{t+\delta t}$ to $\mathbf{p}^t$ in a slightly more general form:

$$\mathbf{p}^{t+\delta t} = \mathscr{F}(\mathbf{p}^t, \delta t) \tag{3}$$

where $\delta t$ is the time interval under consideration, usually the period of production. Or, bringing all the parameters involved into the expression,

$$\mathbf{p}^{t+\delta t} = \mathscr{F}(\mathbf{p}^t, \mathbf{r}^t, \mathbf{A}^t, \mathbf{w}^t, \mathbf{a}^t, L, \delta t) \qquad (4)$$

where now $\mathbf{r}^t$ is a vector of not necessarily equal profit rates.

Two directions of development now suggest themselves. The only fully general mathematical approach would be to derive equations relating $\mathbf{r}^{t+\delta t}$, $\mathbf{A}^{t+\delta t}$, and so on, to the values of all other parameters at time t, and thus derive a differential equation

$$\mathscr{G}(D, \mathbf{p}, \mathbf{r}, \mathbf{A}, \mathbf{w}, \mathbf{a}, L) = 0 \qquad (5)$$

where D is the differential operator $\delta/\delta t$. A solution to this equation, together with the appropriate boundary conditions, would in theory define the motion of an economy in time. In my view such an approach, though untried and difficult, is closer to the general method of Marx.

It is instructive to view Sraffa's solution as a second direction of development arising from his desire to abstract from motion. However the method he uses is unnatural. It arrests the moving process neither by recording economic quantities at a particular moment like a photograph, nor by averaging over time, as Marx does. Instead it imposes the boundary condition

$$\frac{\partial}{\partial t}(\mathbf{p}, \mathbf{r}, \mathbf{A}, \mathbf{w}, \mathbf{a}) \equiv 0 \qquad (6)$$

for all time and all values of the parameters, corresponding to a particular degenerate case of (3): static equilibrium. It eliminates motion by commanding it to cease.

To do this, the post-Sraffians use one of a class of theorems known as 'fixed-point' theorems. These tell us that under very general conditions, if $\mathscr{F}$ is a function which maps a variable X onto the domain from which X is chosen, then there exist one or more values of X, say X*, for which

$$X^* = \mathscr{F}(X^*) \qquad (7)$$

In this case the domain of X is the space of possible values of p. Moreover, if we impose a particular condition on $\mathbf{w}$, $\mathbf{r}$, $\mathbf{A}$, and $\mathbf{a}$, we can obtain non-zero, positive values of $\mathbf{p}$ which turn out to be independent of **w** and **r**. The construction also yields a functional relation between **A**, **a**, **w** and **r** if we demand, as we must, that the price vector be non-zero, and be exactly determined, i.e. neither under-determined (too many price solutions) or overdetermined (only zero solutions).

This functional relationship is equivalent to specifying the operator $\mathscr{F}$ as a function of **p** with parameters **r**, **A**, **w**, **a**:

$$\mathscr{F}_{(r,A,w,a)}(\mathbf{p}) = \mathbf{p}[(\mathbf{I} + \mathbf{r})(\mathbf{A} + \mathbf{a}.\mathbf{w}/L)] \tag{8}$$

and requiring it to map **p** strictly onto the set of all prices; that is, it must not add or remove any degrees of freedom from **p**. In more familiar terms, the number of equations must equal the number of variables. One way of satisfying this is to add two conditions:

(i) the profit rate must be scalar and uniform.

(ii) the matrix **A** must be non-singular and hence, in general, square. There must, in other words, be as many producers as products.

These conditions guarantee a unique price vector provided **A** represents an economy producing a physical surplus. The condition for unique prices to exist is that

$$\mathbf{p}[(\mathbf{I} + \mathbf{r})(\mathbf{A} + \mathbf{a}.\mathbf{w}/L) - \mathbf{I}] = 0 \tag{9}$$

for some positive p, which implies

$$\det[(\mathbf{I} + \mathbf{r})(\mathbf{A} + \mathbf{a}.\mathbf{w}/L) - \mathbf{I}] = 0 \tag{10}$$

or, since **r** is a scalar,

$$\det[(1 + r)(\mathbf{A} + \mathbf{a}.\mathbf{w}/L) - \mathbf{I}] = 0 \tag{11}$$

and **p** becomes the dominant characteristic vector of $(\mathbf{A} + \mathbf{a}.\mathbf{w}/L)$, with characteristic root $1/(1 + r)$. If wages are paid *post factum* as in Sraffa this becomes

$$\det[(1 + r)\mathbf{A} + \mathbf{a}.\mathbf{w}/L - \mathbf{I}] = 0 \tag{12}$$

with a determinate but slightly different relation between **r** and **w**.

These particular solutions suit the post-Sraffians since they yield a relation between the uniform profit rate and the wage which is independent of **p**, so that both **p** and the wage-profit relationship can be treated as functions of **A** and **a** (the 'technical conditions of production') and independent of each other.

What happens to this solution and its properties if either condition (i) or (ii) above is dropped? This is studied by Albarracín and by Farjoun in this volume. If **r** is not scalar its relation to **w** is no longer independent of **p**, as Albarracín shows, for then relation (10) will give solutions for **p** which depend on the distribution of the elements of **r**. But it is unclear in any case in what sense the system is 'determined', as none of the quantities involved can be exactly calculated.

If **A** is not square or is otherwise singular it ceases to yield unique magnitudes either for **p** or for the wage-profit relation, as Farjoun points out. The maximum profit rate becomes arbitrary and ceases to bear any relation to the 'physical surplus' it is supposed to represent.

These are not mere simplifying assumptions. Without them the solution is not just different or more complex, but *ceases to exist*. The neo-Ricardian construction in general simply stops working. This is not necessarily catastrophic for Sraffa because his restrictions are related to his limited aims. For the post-Sraffians it has far more serious implications, since for them simultaneous equation systems are the foundation of a new system of political economy, to replace labour values. Within their system, these simplifications are in reality structural elements of the theory: axioms. We now turn to the study of their consequences.

## 4. Price, Supply, Demand and Markets

One of the interesting modern advances in von Bortkiewicz-type equation systems is the discovery, through successive advances by Winternitz, May and Seton,[10] that under the assumption of constant returns to scale, prices do not depend on the scale of production, that is, on the quantity of goods produced in each sector.

It is relatively easy to show from what has already been said that prices in neo-Ricardian systems are generally independent of the quantity of goods produced, and vice versa. This is hardly surprising, since it coincides with Sraffa's general aims. The point is related to the issue of constant returns to scale, which Albarracín in this volume discusses at greater length. Sraffa does not explicitly assume constant returns to scale for parts I and II of his work because no assumption concerning scale appears necessary, though he concedes it to be involved in part III where he discusses the choice of technology.[11]

The assumption is repeated by Steedman when he studies the

'allocation of labour',[12] which in his treatment is equivalent to the scale of production, since under constant returns to scale, production in each sector must everywhere increase in proportion to the employment of labour.

The independence of price from scale of production emerges if we consider Steedman's formulation of the equation system, where he specifies that 'the gross output of each commodity be unity by a suitable choice of units.'[13] This is formally the same as specifying the technological matrix **A** in the normal input–output manner as a matrix of inputs needed to produce one unit of output. Under constant returns to scale, such an equation system clearly does not change with the scale of production, because the elements of the matrix **A** are constants, along with **a**. If production in, say, sector 5 doubles, then the fifth equation is simply multiplied by 2, so that it is in effect the same equation.

Insofar as the scale of production is determined, there is an interesting duality. It would be given by an equation of the form

$$\mathbf{Y} = \mathbf{X} - \left( \mathbf{AX} + \frac{\mathbf{w.a}}{L} \right)$$

where **Y** is the vector of surplus available for investment or capitalist consumption, and **X** is the vector of the quantity of output in each branch of production. This is in turn independent of the price structure, so that prices are determined independent of quantities and quantities are determined independent of prices.

It might be argued that if **A** varies with changes in **X** (or **a**), that is, if we drop the assumption of constant returns to scale, then the above equations will be interrelated via variations in A or a. Precisely: but under such conditions there is no longer a unique solution for **p**, **w** and **r**, as we have yet another unmanageable system relating, in this case, $n^2 + 2n + 1$ quantities through n equations. Moreover, it becomes absurd to suppose that p will remain constant over time if the scale of production changes over time. The neo-Ricardian construction is not general enough to study such a system.

The independence of price and quantity in the calculation has some unpleasant consequences. We should recall that Steedman says values cannot affect prices, on the grounds that they are not needed to calculate them. But in his system the scale of production need not be known to calculate prices and nor need prices be known to calculate the scale of production. It follows by Steedman's own logic that the price of a good cannot affect how much of it is produced or consumed, nor can the quantity of goods produced affect their prices. This is an extraordinary conclusion, since in real life these two things have an enormous effect on each other.

Moreover, even discarding Steedman's logic, there is a still more intractable difficulty. If we try to modify the system so that there is a relation between supply, demand and prices, for example by dropping the assumption of constant returns to scale, we find that prices are doubly determined: once by the simultaneous equation model, and once again—differently—by the effects of supply and demand. This is logically impossible, since even in dialectical logic a quantity cannot simultaneously possess two magnitudes.

This adds up to a bald fact: that the interplay of market forces plays no role, and can play no role, in such models. *The market is absent*, in that its mechanisms—the interplay of supply, demand, and movements in prices and profit—are logically incompatible with the post-Sraffian universe.

## 5. Marx, Markets and Money

By now a vociferous objection will probably have been lodged. Marx himself constantly abstracts from the fluctuations of market prices and frequently explains values and prices of production as 'long term averages' of price movements. Moreover, he explicitly rejects the idea that variations in supply and demand objectively determine the magnitude of prices, the central issue on which labour value theory stands opposed to what has become neo-classical marginal theory.

However, there are two different concepts of determination involved, and two entirely different interpretations of a 'long term average'. In consequence both movements in market prices and the effects of supply and demand do play a role, in Marx's theory, as *mechanisms* of the law of value. Moreover this relates directly to the issues raised by Mandel, Giussani and Salama concerning the role of money and the private character of capitalist production.

The neo-classical interpretation of the average or 'natural price' is that of equilibrium—the level which prices would attain if all variation were to cease. This is a view of price which both neo-classical and neo-Ricardian theory hold in common, and which distinguishes both of them from Marx. Consider, for example, the following passage:

'The value of commodities as determined by labour time is only their average value. This average appears as an external abstraction if it is calculated as the average figure of an epoch, e.g. 1lb of coffee equals 1s if the real average price of coffee is taken over 25 years; but it is very real if it is at the same time recognized as the driving force and the moving principle of the oscillations which commodity prices run through... The market value is always different, is always below or above this average value of a commodity. Market value equates itself with real value by means of its constant oscillations, never by means of an equation with real value as if the latter were a third party, but rather by means of a constant non-equation of itself... the two are constantly different and never balance out, or balance out only coincidentally and exceptionally. The price of a commodity constantly stands above or below the value of a commodity, and the value of the commodity itself exists only in this up-and-down movement of commodity prices. Supply and demand constantly determine the prices of commodities; never balance, or only coincidentally; but the cost of production, for its part, determines the oscillations of supply and demand,'[14]

This quite categorical view establishes that Marx by no means denies fluctuations in supply and demand a role in determining the *formation* of values and prices of production; and that his concept of long-term average is precisely what it says: the average of a varying quantity. In no sense is this identical or even comparable to the notion of an equilibrium price. This is scientifically correct, because in all but the simplest of oscillating systems the two magnitudes are numerically different. In mechanics they are different, for example, in any system in which energy of oscillation is transformed into energy of motion, that is, in which net mechanical work is performed. Thus the average behaviour of a surfboard being propelled by a wave is quite different from the behaviour of the same board in a calm sea.

Moreover, where fluctuations in supply and demand are discussed in Chapter 10 of Capital Volume 3, they are not simply noted and passed over, raised in order to be dismissed as so many interpreters imagine. Marx makes it clear that though the magnitude of prices and values are objectively constrained by the law of value, this law includes a mechanism—a qualitative and quantitative process through which commodities come to exchange against money at prices regulated by the labour embodied in them; and that this mechanism can also—as with absolute rent—play a quantitative role where there are natural obstacles that prevent the free oscillation of supply and demand balancing out over time.[15]

This underscores a crucial point about the way the word 'transformation' has been interpreted by Marx's correctors and detractors. The transformation of values into prices is not a calculation through which, given values, one can work out prices, but a process in the real world through which prices come into existence, quite independent of whether or not the mathematical tools have been developed to calculate the magnitudes involved. In Capital Volume 3 Marx attempts to describe this real process and comes to a definite conclusion on the relation between mechanism and results.

We can fruitfully regard his famous 'two equalities' as a judgement on this relation. While shortages and surpluses can give rise to divergence of market price from value,[16] they cannot create new value in and of themselves. They can play one of two roles. They can either enter the determination of value itself by passing judgement on labour which society has performed, and deciding whether or not it is surplus to requirements; or they can, with the formation of prices of production and the role of rents (not to mention merchant and banking profits) redistribute existing value between capitalists.

This outlook distinguishes him both from marginalists, who only see the mechanism, and the neo-Ricardians, who only see the results.

For the marginalists, the play of demand and supply is in some mysterious way the source of value instead of its regulator. They analyse only fluctuations, and not their objective context. This is like studying wave motion and ignoring the fact that there are definite global quantities associated with a wave: its velocity, amplitude, wavelength and energy, linked by definite objective relations which are more comprehensive than the movement of any particular particle in the wave's path and moreover the key to understanding how the wave connects up with the rest of the world. This is what one must study to see how a board will behave when struck by a wave. But equally one cannot solve the problem by pretending the wave does not exist, as the neo-Ricardian equation systems oblige us to do.

We can illustrate the preceding points with a simple extension to a Sraffian system, also useful in studying the transformation of values into prices, in which I try to make mathematical allowance for the existence of stocks in circulation and their relation to money profits.

We begin from the first surplus-producing economy cited by Sraffa on p7 of his book. This is as follows:

Figure 1

| 280 qr. wheat + 12 t. iron | → | 575 qr. wheat |
|---|---|---|
| 120 qr. wheat + 8 t. iron | → | 20 t. iron |

I choose such a simple system, Sraffa's most basic surplus-producing economy, because my aim is to show what happens to the most basic category of the Sraffian system—the maximum profit rate—during disequilibrium. I choose, without loss of generality, and for simplicity of illustration, a model in which labour exists only as a co-participant in the Sraffian 'surplus', so that 'profits' here actually represents a surplus to be shared between workers and capitalists, as explained by Guillén Romero in his piece. However, the points made apply equally well in the more developed versions of this system, as the reader can easily verify.

In the above system the rate of profit is 25% and the price of a quarter of wheat is equal to one-fifteenth of a ton of iron.

We now suppose a disturbance to this economy, resulting from a decision by wheat-producing capitalists to increase their supply of wheat by 20%. This decision is taken on an individual basis and without consultation or prior arrangement with the iron-producing capitalists. It is therefore only possible if there are already stocks of wheat and iron from which investment goods may be purchased. We assume that the capitalists possess such stocks, the size of which will in general be related to the time of circulation.

In order to present the analysis in its clearest possible way we assume that they possess these stocks initially in such proportions that the rate of profit remains uniform. The rate of profit will be lower since the capitalists must advance working capital to cover the costs of these stocks.

The absolute quantities of stocks of goods being processed, and tied up in circulation, are laid out below with the prices in brackets, measured in units of iron.

Figure 2

|  | Production | | Stocks | Advanced capital |
|  | wheat | iron | | |
| --- | --- | --- | --- | --- |
| wheat | 280 (18.67) | 12 (12) | 287.5 (19.17) | (49.83) |
| iron | 120 (8) | 8 (8) | 10 (10) | (26) |
| total | 400 (26.67) | 20 (20) | (29.17) | (75.83) |

If trading and production continue as before, the reduced uniform profit rate is 15.38%. Now consider the effects of the investment. Assume this happens at the same time that productively consumed goods are replaced after a productive cycle. Our table will now read

Figure 3

|  | Productive Capital | | Stocks | Advanced capital |
|---|---|---|---|---|
| wheat | 336 | 14.4 | 231.5 | |
|  | (22.4) | (14.4) | (15.43) | (52.23) |
| iron | 120 | 8 | 7.6 | |
|  | (8) | (8) | (7.6) | (23.6) |
| Total | 456 | 22.4 | | |
|  | (30.4) | (22.4) | (23.03) | (75.56) |

We cannot yet calculate profit on the new investment because nothing has been produced or sold. Assume a complete cycle of reproduction takes place, at the end of which all productively consumed goods are simply replaced without further investment. It is still not possible to determine sales, because we have not said how the 20% increase in wheat production will be absorbed by consumption. Nor can we; and this already reveals one of the problems. Nevertheless, let us make an assumption as close as possible to general neo-Ricardian principles, which is to assume that consumption (by both capitalists and workers combined) increases in proportion to the increase in wheat production, that is, also by 20%. We can now calculate sales as the sum of productive consumption and other consumption (replacement of used up inputs plus the wage plus capitalist consumption), as follows:

Figure 4

|  | Output | Sales | | | Costs |
|---|---|---|---|---|---|
| wheat | 690 | 456 | +210 | = 666 | |
|  | (46) | (30.4)+ | (14) | = (44.4) | (36.8) |
| iron | 20 | 22.4 + | 0 | = 22.4 | |
|  | (20) | (22.4)+ | 0 | = (22.4) | (16) |
| total | (66) | (52.8)+ | (14) | = (66.8) | (52.8) |

Profits can now be calculated in each sector along with a sectoral profit rate. Wheat sellers realize 7.6 in money profits on an advanced capital of 52.23; a profit rate of 14.5%. Iron sellers realize 6.4 in money profits on an advanced capital of 23.6; a profit rate of 27%. The average profit rate in the economy is 18.4%; the theoretical equilibrium maximum profit rate is exactly what it was before, namely 15.38%. These quantities are nowhere near each other.

The origin of the difference in profit rates is twofold; first, because of the increased demand for their output resulting from investment, iron producers have realized some of the capital previously tied up in stocks, whereas wheat producers have overproduced. Second, since iron stocks have diminished and wheat stocks have increased, the iron producers' profit rate is calculated on less advanced capital. This is not at all unrealistic and such effects figure in all capitalist balance sheets as a matter of course. In 1982, for example, British manufacturing industry recorded a book value of £36,567 m in stocks and work in progress of which £11,107 m were in finished goods.

It may be argued that our assumption about consumption has 'cooked the books' and that a different assumption will equalize profit rates. Yes: profit rates would be equalized at a consumption level of 307 qrs of wheat, representing a 75% increase. Which figure is the most arbitrary? Moreover whatever assumption is made, the iron-makers' profit will be 27%, nearly double the theoretical equilibrium.

The analysis above is in no sense intended to be a real analysis of a real economy nor even a correct approach to such. It is chosen to illustrate our basic point about simultaneous equation systems, which is that the standard solution simply ceases to exist in any meaningful sense once the equilibrium of the economy is disturbed, even as in this case by a relatively small amount. For example, above we assumed that goods continued to sell at the same price following the neo-Ricardian assumption. But there is in fact no a priori way to decide whether sales would actually take place at the indicated prices, whether the iron-makers would be able to put their prices up to reach an even higher profit rate, or whatever.

However, this is only half the story and the worst is yet to come. In principle, there is an escape route for the simultaneous equation method. Following a process analogous to Shaikh's iterative solution to the derivation of labour values,[17] we could 'follow through' the disturbance created by the new investment decision by assuming that in the next period there will be increased investment in iron production to cash in on the higher profits. Given stable technology, prices and quantities will converge to a new equilibrium in which prices are determined as before and the scale of production is determined by the (exogenous) demand for the physical surplus, i.e. by some form of combination of capitalist greed and the class struggle.

In essence, this is the argument that tends to be put forward by all who use simultaneous equation systems to represent real economies. They choose to ignore the process of attaining a new equilibrium on the basis that, provided it can be shown that such a convergence could theoretically take place, economists should study not the process but the end result.[18]

*But this convergence is absolutely not guaranteed if technology changes and continues to change while the adjustment process is going on*, above all if the changes in the deployment of technology are a product of the adjustment process itself and take place over a comparable span of time.

In the normal course of events—taking the above as an example—investment will be in more productive technology, so that for the same or comparable deployment of capital (in price terms), physically more goods will be produced. However, while investment in new technology is going on, the old technology is still in use. Investors in new processes can realize exceptional profits precisely because they can produce their goods more cheaply without having to pass on the cost reduction to their purchasers, as long as the market price is determined by costs of production in more backward sectors. If we assume in the above model that investment in wheat production started because a new wheat production process was discovered, and 50% more could be produced for the same investment, then of course the new wheat production process would yield still higher profits than the iron makers.

At this point the neo-Ricardian system ceases to offer any guidance whatsoever. If we stick to fixed prices, the iterative process simply does not converge. If we drop the assumption of fixed prices, there is no basis either for saying what the new prices will be or what the 'physical surplus' will be, or what profits will be, at least until the new production technique has completely displaced the old. But this cannot happen rapidly, if for no other reason that that only 25% of economic production is available for capitalist consumption, workers' consumption and investment all combined. Even assuming 10% of the entire resources of the economy go into investment, and half of this into investment in the new wheat production process, it would still take nearly ten reproductive cycles to replace one process by another. What happens in the ten intervening years? What happens if yet another technological advance comes along in five years time?

The distinctive weakness of simultaneous equation systems and particularly their post-Sraffian interpretation can be summarized quite concisely. In Sraffa's desire to abstract from all marginal effects and all process of change, a system has been created in which the economy has no means of reaching its ideal state. It has no economic mechanisms: only economic results. It is therefore incapable of studying the economic mechanism most characteristic of industrial capitalism, the central feature of the 'production of commodities by means of commodities', namely the pursuit of differential profit originating in differential rent derived from advances in labour productivity occasioned by technical advance. This is how values are actually transformed into prices of production under advanced, industrial capitalism. We now turn our attention to this process.

## 6. Price, Value, and Technological Change

It could be argued that so far we have only unearthed a secondary mechanism connecting market price movements to some form of 'natural' long-term average price, and that the variations concerned are all extremely short term and will cancel out over a period of production, so that for all practical intents and purposes constant prices are a reasonable approximation. It could be argued that since Marx himself abstracts for the most part from the market mechanism, the neo-Ricardian construction is simply Marx's under a cleaner and tidier guise.

This objection cannot be sustained if it can be established that in addition to short-term fluctuations in market prices, there are also medium and long-term movements in average prices interacting with supply and demand to shape the behaviour of a capitalist economy. Are there price movements with the same sort of time scale as variations in either $A$ or $a$? If so, the neo-Ricardian model collapses into vacuousness, since all quantities are changing with comparable periodicity, the system never settles down, and no simple mutual determination emerges at all. And indeed, both in reality and according to Marx, prices of production move as a function of technical change itself, that is, over the medium and long term.

Steedman's treatment of technological change makes a strange assumption, which has been less searchingly analysed than it ought. Capitalist choice is in effect treated as if all producers at once switched between two or more alternative technologies with two profit rates and two sets of prices. Yet no indication is given of the process of change itself. A series of bizarre consequences follow, not the least of which is that capitalists would be obliged almost instantaneously to liquidate their entire stock of fixed capital almost at will in order to embark on a new technique of production, without regard either to the time it takes to supply the new fixed capital required—that is, the rate of investment—or the effect on profits of suddenly liquidating old factories, tools and stocks which have not yet realized their value.

Furthermore, Steedman and others make equally strange assumptions about what influences capitalists when they choose a new technique. Investors decide, it appears, not by looking at the profits they will get now, while they are ahead of their competitors, but on the basis of the profit they will later get when their competitors catch up, using the very technique introduced to steal a march on these same competitors. Stranger still, entrepreneurs do not look at their own individual profit rate, but at the average profit rate in the sector as a whole and, indeed, in the economy as a whole.

But this does not at all approximate to the real process of technological change, and certainly not to anything Marx ever discussed. Why does a capitalist invest in a new technique? Why, for example, was car production automated? Not at all because of the average profit which Henry Ford expected the car industry to be making in fifteen years' time, but because by stealing a march on all his competitors, he could for an extended period sell cars for the same price as them but much less than they cost him to make, at a far higher profit rate than the prevailing average and higher than the average eventually attained. It is not the average profit in a sector which influences capitalists, but the prospect of making an exceptional profit while price is still determined by the backward producers in the market, because new technology has not yet augmented supply enough to make the price fall.[19]

Such exceptional profits can exist for some period of time because capital destined for investment is not in infinite supply but is also quantitatively restricted and cannot meet all available investment opportunities at once. Supply of every commodity is therefore restricted below the maximum possible using the newest technology. No single technology is ever, therefore, totally generalized.

Therefore, the normal condition of a capitalist economy is not at all that a single technology rules, but that a variety of technologies coexist along with a distribution of profit rates within, as well as between, sectors. The neo-Ricardian discussion of technical change introduces equilibrium considerations in the least appropriate place to do so. As fast as old technology is replaced by new, still newer technology is invented. The basis of production is, in Marx's words, 'continuously revolutionized'.

However, can simultaneous equation systems be modified to deal with this process? Not at all. The hidden axioms of the neo-Ricardian system, which we identified earlier, rule it out. First, there must be a uniform profit rate. Differential profits cannot act as a motor of change; they cannot even exist. Second, and even more devastating, the matrix of technical conditions of production is not allowed to introduce more than one functioning producer for each product.

Sraffa at least acknowledges this problem,[20] but falls back on a peculiar construction. If two producers coexist using different methods, then one is assumed to be producing a different commodity from another so as to get an extra equation. This second commodity must be 'non-basic', that is, must not enter the production of any other commodity.

It is very obliging of the producer concerned to show such respect for Mr Sraffa, but the idea is to say the least arbitrary. When you, I, or Mr Sraffa buy a pound of copper, we get a pound of a salmon-coloured malleable conductive substance and we neither know nor can find out whether it is basic or non-basic copper, whether it came from a backyard scrap firm or a third world copper-mine. This is the whole point about what a commodity is under capitalism; it acquires exchange-value because exchange abstracts from all the concrete labours which went to make it, so it becomes indistinguishable from all other commodities of the same type no matter where they came from.

If this were not so, if one paid a different price for copper depending on who made it and independent of its chemical or physical properties, and put it to different use depending on who one bought it from, then one would cease to have 'production by means of commodities' and would have production through a series of planned bilateral or multilateral arrangements. Price paid would cease to represent real transfers of money and would become instead a mere book-keeping arrangement, as it is within a large enterprise whose departments supply each other and charge each other 'shadow prices' fixed by decree and not by the market.

There is yet a third point. Sraffa's construction also serves to derive an 'independent standard of value'—the standard commodity—to use as a yardstick in comparing physical quantities of different commodities. Sraffa rightly criticizes neo-classical capital theory because it cannot establish any independent measure of the 'quantity of capital', whence its derivation of global quantities such as the marginal productivity of capital is next to meaningless.

But Sraffa's construction by no means escapes the problem. It is hard enough to use the standard commodity, as Sraffa acknowledges, to compare physical quantities of fixed capital in different systems, that is, systems employing different technologies. But if the technology of a single capitalist economy undergoes constant change, the standard commodity itself undergoes constant change even within that system, and no invariable measure of the neo-Ricardians' beloved 'physical quantities' exists.

This is precisely the importance of labour values. If we try to use 'physical quantities' to compare the results of production using different techniques, we find ourselves unable to do so because changes in technique invalidate Sraffa's construction of a standard commodity. If we try to use prices, we find the standard of measure varies over time in an unpredictable manner and in response to factors extraneous to production as such. Labour values behave differently. They do vary over time, but in a manner which we can keep strict account of, and which is rooted in production itself, because reflective of one of the most fundamental relations between human and machine—namely, the productivity of labour.

The value added to a commodity during production, critics often forget nowadays, is not a metaphysical quantity defined by a set of equations, but in the last instance a real quantity measurable with a stopwatch, even though it owes its existence to exchange. Every capitalist company keeps the most detailed record of its labour statistics. Even in the depths of capitalist crisis we can visit any functioning factory and make a plausible provisional estimate of the value it is adding to its product. Using backward extrapolation as Shaikh proposes in this volume we can make fair estimates, not just of value added but of the total value of any stock of use-values. To the extent that we are inaccurate, the problem is one of measurement and lack of data, not one of theoretical principle. We do not need to assume that the whole system can reproduce itself for this calculation; only that private exchange takes place on a sufficient scale to abstract from the concrete labours involved and thus establish exchange value, hence that the commodities involved should be capable of being sold for money. Values *exist* and are empirically measurable, redundant or not.

This is not substantively altered because we might include a correction in later accounts if we find that some of the labour was wasted because products went unsold. The initial statistics serve as the basis of valid calculations which can later be adjusted, just as any good capitalist bookkeeper will calculate provisional sales and profits without full knowledge of bad debts, returns, or the value of stock in hand, and will carry the difference between estimate and final figure over to the next accounting period as accrued costs or benefits. Nor is the principle altered if a commodity is devalued through technical change, and value thereby destroyed. On the contrary, this brings to light an important difference between value and the neo-Ricardian concept of dated labour. Dated labour measures the labour which has actually been expended on a commodity. If productivity does not change, this is theoretically the same as value.

However, suppose a car is made using presses made twenty years ago, when the presses required 100,000 hours of labour to construct. If the same presses or their equivalent are now made using 50,000 hours, then even the old presses will now pass progressively less value to the cars as the new presses come into use, eventually being found socially surplus to requirements as a result of technical progress. Iterative calculations with input-output matrices yield *values*, not dated labours, which could only be calculated (with difficulty) from a succession of input-output tables of different dates. Finally, the calculation of values is not invalidated if certain labours must be valued higher or lower than others either because of skills, or for other reasons, provided the difference is quantifiable.

Measurements of labour time are thus the best objective basis for studying technical change precisely because they are not derived from a future reproductive process which may well fail to work, but from the private circumstances of each individual producer as they arise from previous phases of reproduction.[21] What is Marx's presentation of technical change?

Its crucial component is identified by Savran in his piece, and touched on also by Salama: that is, the role of 'individual values'. Their existence, which cannot be comprehended by Steedman's derivation of value magnitude, is not just a convenient means of escaping criticism; it is the mechanism of superprofit.

Consider a single branch of production in which there are two capitals. One turns over values each year according to the following:

Figure 5

| Constant | Variable | Surplus-value |
| --- | --- | --- |
| 4000 | 1000 | 1000 |

producing, let us assume, 6000 units of use-value. The second turns over the same values but produces 7000 units of use-value because it has a higher productivity of labour. We have assumed an identical value-composition of capital only to illustrate our point and a more general treatment is perfectly simple.

According to Marx three circumstances can arise. If supply exceeds demand, social value will be determined by the most productive capital. If supply falls behind demand, value will be determined by the least productive producer. We will treat in this example the third and most general case of a balance between supply and demand; in this case the value of the 13000 produced commodities will be equal to the total labour time added or transferred in their production, namely 12000.[22] The average value of a unit of use-value is $12000/13000 = 12/13$. At this point it is convenient to define the inverse of this as the *specific productivity* in the sector concerned: $13/12$. (This is not the same as labour productivity, since it will vary with changes in the value of constant capital, though the two quantities are clearly and easily related.)

What is the individual value of the use-values produced by each capital? Simply the quantity of labour added or transferred divided by the quantity of use-values produced: for capital 1, this will be 1, for the second 6/7. Specific productivity of each capital is 1 and 7/6 respectively.

The differences in productivity will have an effect on profits. Suppose initially that goods exchange at their social value, that is, at $12/13$ per unit of use-value. Suppose for convenience that 1 unit of exchange value is priced at £1, that is, £1 represents one hour of abstract labour.

Capital 1 will realize $6000 \times £1 \times 12/13 = £5,538.46$, Capital 2 will realize $7000 \times £1 \times 12/13 = £6461.53$. The 6000 hours of labour added or transferred by capital 2 have yielded a differential rent of £461.53, or a *specific differential rent* of 7.6 pence per hour, 6.6 pence per unit of use-value sold. Capital 1 has suffered a negative differential rent of the same amount, equivalent to 7.1 pence per unit sold.

There is no essential difference if we move from values to prices of production. Let us assume that constant capital is divided into 400 in fixed, and 3600 in circulating capital in each case, again for simplicity, and that fixed capital turns over in ten years whereas circulating capital turns over four times a year. Assume variable capital turns over once a week.

In order to begin production, the two capitalists will require stocks of productive capital with the following values:

Figure 6

| Fixed constant | Circulating constant | Variable |
|---|---|---|
| 4000 | 900 | 20 |

In the case of variable capital, money sufficient to buy 20 units of value is advanced but the 'stock' possessed by the capitalist takes the form of hired labour-power, or the right to use the labourers' time—in our case, 40 units of such time. Strictly speaking, the 20 units of variable capital are advanced as money by the capitalist and maintained as commodities by the labourers in the shape of the week's purchases of food, clothing, and so on.

Let us assume that inputs were all bought at a specific price of £1 per unit of value. This assumption is for simplicity only and the essential results are no different if input prices differ from values. Assume the ruling rate of profit is 20%. Capital advanced is then £4920 for capital 1 and for capital 2, so that total capital advanced in the sector is £9840. The calculation can be followed through with the same essential results if input prices are higher or lower.

On the output of the sector, if the sectoral average profit is assumed equal to the global average of 20%, a mark-up on costs yields a price of £11808 for 13000 use-values, or 90.8 pence per unit. Individual sales will realize £5449 for capital 1, and £6358 for capital 2. The producers will calculate their individual annual profit rates by subtracting the money they spend over the preceding year, namely £5000 each, from their sales. This yields the following table, dividing by capital advanced to get profit rate:

Figure 7

| | Mass of Profit | Rate of Profit |
|---|---|---|
| Capital 1 | £449 | 9.1% |
| Capital 2 | £1358 | 27.6% |

This considerable difference results almost entirely from the productivity difference of 16.6%. In the next reproductive cycle things will change depending on a number of circumstances outside this analysis but not outside value analysis in general. If an individual profit rate of 28% is attractive enough for investment capital—that is, if there are not even higher individual rates of profit to be had elsewhere—new capital will flow into process 2, either because capital 2 invests its (much greater) profits in expanding production or because other capitals will get in on the act. The average composition of capital in the sector will fall at a definite rate related to the rate of investment; the specific productivity of the sector will rise and the social value of its product will in general fall, as will its price of production. Beyond a certain point, capital 1 will cease to yield any profit at all and will go bankrupt; in any case it will decline because its rate of profit is lower than that of capital 2, so that its owners will tend to disinvest, contributing to cheapening the output.

Finally, the output of this sector will, of course, gradually decline in value in a clearly measurable and definable way. As this happens, capitalists who use it as input will be affected, because their stocks of this commodity will be revalued; that is, value will be destroyed through technological obsolescence. If we want to keep track of all these processes, it then turns out that it is no longer sufficient, as in neo-Ricardian models, just to keep a record of capital turned over in a given period; one must keep a record of the stock of capital kept in each of the forms of capital identified by Marx: commodity capital about to enter production (C); productive capital (P); commodity capital seeking realization (C' and hence c); and not least, to study investment behaviour and price phenomena in their full complexity, some hypotheses and analysis must be made about the behaviour of hoards of the money-form of capital, M and M'.

All these quantities are in principle empirically measurable or deducible from empirically measurable quantities. They give us a measure of capital independent of price movements, though not of course fixed in time, and also traceable to empirically measurable quantities. Most important, however, they permit us to study precisely what neo-Ricardian systems do not, namely the movement of capital consequent on variations in individual profit rates.

The neo-Ricardians may object that the analysis does not allow us to calculate prices. Precisely so, but neither does Sraffa's analysis. In general, the whole idea of calculating prices, as we will discuss in the final section, is vain because prices, like values, are *data*. They are empirically given, the result of a complex process with a visible end result. The problem, if one wants to make useful predictions, is not to make bets on the end result, which can be more quickly ascertained from the nearest grocer, but to find out about the process which produced it. But, as we have established, price-value deviations are not the result of the aggregate masses of value in various parts of the economy, but result from the changes in these masses, from the process of capital movement. Of course, if one abstracts from this movement, one will be unable to find any connection between value and price, because one has abstracted from the process that produces prices in the first place. If one stops a clock, one will be unable to tell the time; this does not stop time passing.[23]

Two questions then remain. First, what are the factors which determine differences in profits, as opposed to their average values? Second, what is the relevance of Marx's two equalities, and his rate of profit formula, to the above analysis?

The first question yields an important answer. Despite deviations of average prices of production from average values, there is every reason to suppose that the deviation of individual values from average values is far greater, and that the movement of capital is ultimately determined by these differences. Value magnitudes, though disguised in the price form, can and do exert a decisive influence on the very factor from which the neo-Ricardians abstract—economic change.

The point can be studied both theoretically and empirically. A model, which space does not permit us to exhibit in full, can be constructed in which each sector comprises $b_i$ capitals $(i = 1, \ldots, n)$ with outputs $X_i^k$ $(k = 1, \ldots, b_i)$, requiring use-values to be advanced in the form of productive constant capital in quantities $U_{ij}^k$ $(j = 1, \ldots, n)$ and with turnover $T_{ij}^k$ (so that the quantity of a use value turned over in unit time will be $T_{ij}^k.U_{ij}^k$),[24] and variable capital sufficient to maintain a workforce of $L_i^k$ workers. Following the method just used we can define specific productivities $\tau_i^k$ and market shares $Z_i^k = X_i^k/X_i$ where

$$X_i = \sum_k X_i^k.$$

We can derive a formula for differential rent per unit of use-value

$$\rho_i^k = \frac{Z_i^k}{\tau_i^k} - \frac{1}{\tau_i} \tag{13}$$

A profit and price analysis can be defined using price-value multipliers $\lambda_i$, which it is convenient to write in the form $(1 + \mu_i)$.[25] Prices are of course the same for each of the $b_i$ capitals producing commodity i. Profits and prices are related through the formula

$$(1 + r_i^k(t))(K_i^k(t)) = (1 + \mu_i(t + \delta t))X_i^k/\tau_i^k$$

$$= (1 + \mu_i)V_i^k(1 - \tau_i\rho_i^k) \tag{14}$$

where $K_i^k$ is the price of advanced capital and can be calculated from prices and the quantities $U_{ij}^k$, $\tau_j$, $\mu_j$ as they stand at the beginning of production, and $V_i^k$ is the value of $X_i^k$.

In general $r_i^k$ is of course different from the surplus-value added in capital K. However, it then becomes relevant to find out the relative magnitudes of the different components of the deviation of $r_i^k$ from this surplus. In static models, attention has always focussed on the price–value deviation, and not on the deviation of individual value from average value. But in the above equation for individual profit there are two terms. One represents the price–value deviation, and one the variation in individual values. If the second turns out to be in general greater than the first, then the movement of capital will be dominated by value quantities even though in the aggregate quantities of production resulting from these movements, values are disguised as prices.

But this is in fact the case. A substantial amount of data exists, particularly the material collected by the US Bureau of Labour Statistics in the 1950s, the material from the European Productivity Association in the 1960s, and more recent studies, among others by Salter, in which inter-firm differences in productivity have been studied.[26] It turns out that differences in labour productivity in quite settled industries regularly amount to some 100–200%, vastly in excess of the deviations of price from value. With the introduction of a complete new technology such as the production line, or electrical power, differences in labour productivity can be quite phenomenal and out of all proportion to price-value deviations.

Indeed the US Bureau of Labour Statistics, which persists in the best interests of the capitalist class in collecting detailed figures on

labour productivity despite dogmatic attacks in the capitalist finan-
cial press, has seen fit to justify this in terms which all participants in
the value debate should frame in gold and install on their walls:

> 'The indexes (of labour productivity) do not measure the specific contri-
> bution of labour or of capital or of any other factor of production. Changes
> in the ratio between output and man-hours of work show the joint effect of
> a number of separate though interrelated influences such as technological
> improvements, the rate of operations, the relative contributions of
> production of plants at different levels of efficiency, the flow of materials
> and components, as well as the skill and effect of workforce, the efficiency of
> management and the status of labour relations.'[27]

## 7. Revisiting the Two Equalities

We now return to our starting point and to von Bortkiewicz's demand
for 'feedback'. I hope by now I have convinced the reader that there is
an insuperable logical error in his approach, which carries over into
the simultaneous equation method in general; and that it is illegitimate to equate the results of production to its premises, because this
imposes a forced abstraction from economic motion, and hence from
all the central characteristics of commodity production.

This does not mean that the results of production have no relation
to its premises. An economy emerges from its past and perforce gives
birth to its future. However, value theory must clear away the fog of
eighty years of confusion heaped on confusion and permit the past to
*produce* the future instead of the other way round. The discussion has
to be dragged from the eternal present and put back in the green
world of real history.

In my view, therefore, the question to be addressed is slightly
different from von Bortkiewicz's, and arises naturally from the
discussion: Given that the actions of private commodity producers
are socialized through exchange, how do the social results of
exchange in turn impose themselves on private individuals?

To see why the issue needs to be posed this way, let us look at the
theoretical movement involved in neo-Ricardianism. At first sight,
production is private and exchange is social, in that producers take
independent decisions, and only through exchange do they discover
they are part of a social organism, when the market passes judgement
on their actions. The marginalists leave the matter there, believing
without proof that the market can instantly reconcile all private
fantasies.

Nevertheless, scientific study reveals that the apparent privacy of production has limits. The social results of exchange enter production as soon as circulation broadens to include the means of production: when they become commodities. Producers must then pay apparently given prices, apparently given wages, content themselves with an apparently given average profit rate, and in general cannot exercise private control over their inputs. Therefore, says von Bortkiewicz, we must take the results of circulation as an immediate premise of production.

But this leads to the converse error. Reason displaces animal spirits as the guardian angel of a system which is neither wholly animal nor wholly rational. But not all that is rational is real. Though social constraints are imposed by previous history, capitalists still cannot and do not plan, because they still do not know, and cannot know, what will happen when they take their plans to market, which is anonymous and unconscious. Commodity production remains quintessentially private even in the epoch of monopoly, cartel, and state intervention. Fluctuations in supply and demand, and capital movements, even within definite constraints, still prevent the next price round matching up to capitalist expectations, and their best-laid plans go wrong.

However, these deviations from private plans are not arbitrary. They are arrayed on a definite lawlike framework. Capitalists cannot set fantastic prices or seek ludicrous profits, or they perish. There are limits on what they can do, and these limits are social. When venture capital pursues superprofit, only to find output prices collapse so that superprofit evaporates, it confronts the social effects of its private behaviour. Moreover these are not the social effects of exchange in general, but specific results of the circulation of aggregate capital: of what happens when social *aggregate* demand meets social *aggregate* supply in the market place. The neo-Ricardians assume a priori that these match. They do not; but the deviations between them are the key to economic motion.

These effects, studied and codified, constitute the formal closure of the mathematical systems I have exhibited, and make them decidable, i.e. make it possible to produce definite results from them, either in the form of a class of differential equation systems, or a class of computer simulations. But they also correspond to the way Marx himself approaches reproduction.

In Volume 2 of *Capital* Marx asks: how does circulation, which is regulated by exchange-value, lead to the distribution of commodities to producers for whom they serve as use-value?[28] How can an individual capital be sure of retrieving the factories, tools, raw materials, labourers it needs to resume production, when it does not itself produce them? Marx approaches the issue by looking at the totality of produced commodities and asking how they find their way from initial sellers to final buyers. He gives a precise solution in volume 2, where goods exchange at their value, but appears not to give one in volume 3, where they exchange at prices of production.

Is this an omission? Commentators have often failed to ask the obvious question: what *constitutes* a precise solution? The problem is that *at this level of concreteness, there is no single general solution to be derived solely from the conditions of production*, because the solution depends on the economy being studied including its conditions of circulation, distribution, class structure, and so on. Even with a widely shared technology, social reproduction takes completely different forms, for example, in Britain and in Germany—not least because of the different relations between the banks and industry.

Does this mean Marxism should cease to seek such precise solutions? Does it mean Marx 'forgets' the problem? In my view, not at all. For the social effects one must study in order to see how capitalist plans are reconciled with market reality are no more or less than the *competitive struggle between capitals for a share of the annually-produced surplus-value*, which is the subject matter of the whole of volume 3.[29]

This restores the proper and legitimate subject matter of both politics and economics, namely political economy; it connects up economics and politics and studies the class struggle in all its richness. Marx's concern, which I think is the only correct one, is to explain what lies behind the class struggle—not just between workers and capitalists, but between capitalists and capitalists—by showing how battles over rent, rates of interest, relative profits, battles to raise or lower prices, tariff and tax battles, and even wars, all repose on a common substratum: the battle for the redistribution of the spoils of exploitation, in its value form.[30] What I hope I have shown with the above argument is that this concern is not a narrow political concern which can be hived off from economics, as Steedman tends to do, but is on the contrary the only formally correct way to close the mathematical models we have been discussing; different structures and relations of class forces defining different ground rules for capital and price movements.

And this is what defines the scientific function of the famous 'two equalities'; not, as von Bortkiewicz and his successors would have it, as a device for calculating prices which are already known anyway, but as an analytic instrument for going *behind* these prices and finding out how they distribute the results of production to the capitalists.

What determines that any given capitalist cannot raise her or his rate of profit to 100%, 200% or 300%? What determines that if one individual profit rate goes up, others must go down? What determines that bankers, to take a topical example, cannot extract arbitrary debt repayments from Mexico or Argentina? Ultimately the fact that there is a finite and definite quantity of new exchange value produced each year, that a finite and definite proportion of it goes to the capitalists as a whole, and that try as they might they can do no more than redistribute this amongst each other. Thus supply and demand do not cause profits and prices to vary arbitrarily but within definite limits which can be mathematically prescribed.

This basic fact emerges even if one works directly from prices, even paper money prices. If total profits are £75bn and if the banks take £15bn and the merchants £25bn, then industry will take £35bn and no book-juggling can alter it. If, moreover, commercial capital has advanced £100bn and industry £200bn, then the gross average profit rate in commerce will be 25% and in industry 17.5%, again no matter how the books are juggled—even if the issue of fictitious capital disguises the fact for a period, only to vanish with the onset of crisis. And if industry forces commerce to cut its margins and thence its profits, it cannot thereby make more than £60bn, a profit rate of 30%, by any means at all.

To express this algebraically, if the mass of realized profits is P in price terms, being $P_1, \ldots, P_k$ for each of k capitals; and if these capitals, again in price terms, add up to $K_1, \ldots, K_k$ with $\sum_1 K_i = K$, the total advanced social capital; then there is a definite relation between profit rates and share of profit, namely

$$\sum_i r_i K_i = P = \sum_i P_i \tag{15}$$

But prices are not enough to express what is going on. Suppose there is an inflationary issue of paper money which doubles paper money prices. None of the profit ratios will change, nor will the ratios $P_i/P$, except insofar as those capitals $K_i$ containing a high proportion of money, as opposed to other commodities, will be reduced relative to the others; or except insofar as workers fail to recoup the loss of purchasing power. Something real lies behind these ratios; some social substance is being divided up. What is it? Marx is clear: it is value. In order to express this division as a distribution of value, price of production is analysed as a transformed form of value and profit as a transformed form of surplus-value. Expressed in the simplest possible way, the sum of prices equals the sum of values, and the sum of profits equals the sum of surplus-values.[31]

Before we turn, finally, to assess these two assertions mathematically, we ought to ask whether there is an alternative way of discussing distribution. From the outset we note that neo-Ricardian systems in general are badly suited to the job, because in them profit rates are permanently and everywhere equal, so there can be no competitive struggle. There are, however, deeper methodological objections.

The Sraffian school in general has made a lot of representing distribution between workers and capitalists as a battle over surplus product, rather than surplus-value. However, this becomes very dubious once we allow for any variation in the physical make-up of the national product. If workers buy videos and stop going to the cinema, who is to say whether the real wage in physical terms has risen or fallen? Indeed, if workers buy videos and capitalists visit the theatre, who is to say which has appropriated the biggest share of the social product? Once constructions such as the 'standard commodity' fall by the wayside, the whole project of measuring distribution of physical terms gets very arbitrary, as emerges in the problem known in economics as the 'index number problem'.[31]

Now, things improve if we use price measures, in that prices at least make unlike goods commensurable, but awkward problems remain. In 1961 British workers made £16,396 m; in 1981 £146,310 m. Are they nine times better off? Clearly not, because the money now buys less. But how much less? The orthodox solution is to compare the physical bundles of goods which could be bought with the wage in the two different years. But this puts us right back where we started, with the index number problem.

The only half-sane, and intuitively reasonable approach is to express the price of a share of the national product as a proportion of national income, as a proportion of the total price of commodities thrown into circulation. But then the issue is posed with a vengeance: what real substance does this total price represent? Clearly the total price of the commodities produced in 1982, with three million unemployed, does not represent the same thing as in 1962, when under half a million were unemployed.

The only *genuinely* invariable 'standard of measure' for assessing the share of social product which anyone or any capital appropriates is its value, for the simple reason that , abstracting from relativistic time-dilatation, an hour in 1982 had just as many minutes in it as an hour in 1962.

Only one single, accountable source of variation in labour values exists; its productivity, which even the Bureau of Labour Statistics acknowledges as the finest synthetic measure of the diverse effects of the many 'factors of production'.

More precisely, because different concrete labours are reduced in exchange to homogeneous abstract labour and because labour-power is the only commodity which appears as a direct input in every other commodity, it and only it can serve as a universal standard of measure; moreover to the extent that money can be used as a standard of measure, it is precisely and only because the money-commodity itself directly represents a determinate quantity of social labour.

However, when we approach the problem in this way, that is, when we understand that value must serve as a measure of what is appropriated in circulation, as well as what emerges from production, a question immediately arises. The total process of circulation includes not just the exchange of commodities for sale against money, but the subsequent purchase of commodities for use, with that same money. The movement of circulation is not just C–M, but C–M–C, or to be more precise still,

Figure 8

$$C'\begin{cases}C\\ \underline{\phantom{C}}\\ c\end{cases}M'\begin{cases}M-C\begin{smallmatrix}\diagup L\\ \diagdown mp\end{smallmatrix}\\ m-c\end{cases}$$

Von Bortkiewicz's presentation of Marx's 'equalities' is a very strange one, because it arrests the circulation process midway. It compares an aggregate of commodities in the form C' or c with a second aggregate in the form M' or m. Marx poses it rather differently:

'It is clear enough that the average profit can be nothing other than the total mass of surplus-value, distributed between the masses of capital in each sphere of production in proportion to their size. It is the sum total of the realized unpaid labour, dead and living, *in the total mass of commodities and money that accrues to the capitalists.*'[33]

At the very least, this is a different and more sophisticated way of putting it. For the neo-Ricardians, obsessed with the problem of numerical calculation, the issue is to compare capitals or sums of capitals entirely in their M form, with the same capitals in their C form. For Marx, the problem is to establish what share of produced value is appropriated by the different classes and sub-classes in society. The neo-Ricardians' mathematical formalizations do not permit us to answer the question Marx was asking.

I am not at all sure what will be the eventual mathematical outcome of the debate around the question as posed by von Bortkiewicz. It is a great deal more complex than most commentators have realized, as the contributions from Shaikh, Mandel and Giussani establish not least because money itself is a commodity and a component part of values in circulation. But important though this discussion is, it does not seem to me that the vindication of value theory depends on its outcome. As is explained in the introduction, the substantive issue is whether or not new value can be created in circulation, and whether or not value can be transferred from workers to capitalists in circulation. If the answer to both questions is no, the decisive component of Marx's value analysis survives intact, and in particular it vindicates the project of analysing price formation as the outcome of a competitive struggle between capitals for a share of surplus-value.

But the answer to these questions *is* no, even in von Bortkiewicz's framework, and almost (but not quite) trivially so. Total value appropriated must be equal to total value thrown into circulation, because exchange simply redistributes the same physical products to new owners. And under simple reproduction it is relatively easy to show that the total value appropriated by the capitalists is equal to the total surplus-value thrown into circulation, deviations from this rule being possible if the actual number of workers is expanding or contracting, (more generally, if the absolute mass of variable capital is changing at a different rate from the absolute mass of value in circulation), or if value is carried over from one cycle to the next.

This can be seen in the following example, derived from von Bortkiewicz's example, which displays the total circulation of commodities in the form which Marx considered the most general, namely the circuit beginning with $C'$.[34]

Let us assume that gross transfers of value take place, in a three-sector economy divided into von Bortkiewicz's sectors I, IIa and IIb (luxury goods), as follows:

Figure 9

|      | C   | V   | S   |     | Output |
|------|-----|-----|-----|-----|--------|
| I    | 300 | 120 | 80  | →   | 500    |
| IIa  | 80  | 96  | 64  | →   | 240    |
| IIb  | 120 | 24  | 16  | →   | 160    |
| Total | 500 | 240 | 160 |    |        |

The vector of surplus-value is

$$s = \begin{bmatrix} 80 \\ 64 \\ 16 \end{bmatrix}$$

We can also define a vector e, following Seton, of surplus commodities (commodities destined for capitalist consumption); it is

$$e = \begin{bmatrix} 0 \\ 0 \\ 160 \end{bmatrix}$$

Prices of production can be assigned so that these values circulate if exchanged in proportion to these prices in many different ways. We choose one such, which corresponds to an equal profit rate of 1.125, the case studied by the neo-Ricardians. This yields the prices system, with some small errors due to rounding:

Figure 10

|      | C   | V   | Profit | Output price |
|------|-----|-----|--------|--------------|
| I    | 309 | 103 | 91     | 514          |
| IIa  | 82  | 82  | 37     | 205          |
| IIb  | 123 | 21  | 32     | 100          |
| Total | 514 | 205 | 180    | 819          |

What happens to the produce of sector IIb? Clearly it is purchased by the capitalists in proportion to their profits. But it is reasonable to ask what are the values of the goods they receive. These are given by the vector

$$\begin{bmatrix} 91 \\ 37 \\ 32 \end{bmatrix}$$

which can be compared with the vector of surplus-values to show that in circulation the capitalists have gained or lost surplus-value according to the vector

$$\begin{bmatrix} +11 \\ -27 \\ +16 \end{bmatrix}$$

This vector would differ, depending on relative profit rates, if prices of production were different, showing that the surplus-value is indeed distributed differently between capitals as a function of profit rates and, consequently, as a function of a competitive struggle. Furthermore the differences are real and not just symbolic. If the luxury sector produces only Jaguar cars then the IIa capitalists have lost 27 cars, and if they push their profits up they will get them back.

We can now display a schema showing how value is transformed for each capitalist at each stage in its circuit.

We emphasize in this diagram, by putting prices and values beside each other for every form of each capital, that commodities possess a value beside their price, even after circulation. That is, if a capitalist uses money valued 120 hours to purchase commodities valued at 100 hours, then these commodities transfer 100 hours of value into production, not 120. It seems to me this is the only reasonable way to express what goes on in production, in which living and dead labour confront each other. Living labour, no matter what the price of production of variable capital, discharges its function as *labour-power*, as work measured in time. If a labourer works eight hours, these eight hours do not expand or contract with the price of food; and they cannot be properly added to the value coming from constant capital unless this too is expressed in terms of the value it acquires through production, unmodified by circulation.

It may be argued that this introduces redundancy. Not so; price, value, and use-value are all necessary to a complete analysis. But price

Figure 11

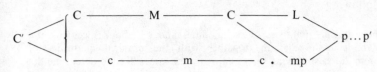

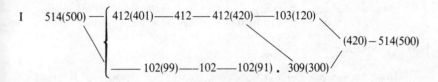

Figures in brackets are values

is the transformed form of value, which therefore comes to the fore in circulation (for example, when the capitalists calculate their profit rates, or the size of their advanced capital) rather than in production. To put it as we did earlier; the social product is ultimately appropriated in the form of value, not in the form of price. In this form, Marx's two equalities hold, and make perfect sense.

We are now in a position to assess both Steedman's logical case, and the direction of development which future formalizations of labour value theory might most fruitfully take.

## 8. Real and Metaphysical Determination

Steedman's main redundancy argument against labour values is that prices may be determined without reference to them. However, what does he mean by 'determination'? In his summary statement he writes the following:

> 'the physical quantities of commodities and of labour specifying the methods of production, together with the physical quantities of commodities specifying the given real wage rate, suffice to determine the rate of profit (and the associated prices of production); . . . the labour-time required (directly and indirectly) to produce any commodity—and thus the value of any commodity—is determined by the physical data relating to the methods of production; it follows that value magnitudes are, at best, redundant in the determination of the rate of profit (and prices of production).'[35]

However, on p.47 of his book, next to his oft-discussed diagram showing the relations of determination between prices, use-values and values, the accompanying text reads:

> 'Starting from the physical conditions of production and the real wage, one can derive values and surplus-value, showing how the values of commodities other than labour-power depend only on the (technically and socially determined) physical conditions of production, while the value of labour-power and surplus-value depend, in addition, on the real wages of the workers . . . one can also derive from the physical picture of the economy a coherent theory of profits and prices. In doing so, however, one finds that, in general, profits and prices cannot be derived from the ordinary value schema, that $S/(C + V)$ is not the rate of profit and that total profit is not equal to total surplus-value.'

The word 'determine' does not appear here; its place is taken by the word 'derive'. The two concepts are, for Steedman, identical. There is only one other reference in the text to a concept of determination which might differ from the above; this is on p.30, where he asks which of the two profit rates (according to his definition of prices, or his definition of values (will 'affect the capitalists' decisions and actions'. Elsewhere the concept of determination is unequivocal, repeated many times, and always in contexts which make it clear that when Steedman says a quantity is determined, he means it can be calculated, and vice versa.

In short, causality and calculation are for Steedman one and the same thing. This notion of causality has to be rejected on no less than four distinct grounds.

*First*, there is an inherent logical problem in such a view of determination, well known in econometrics. Suppose a set of quantities x, y, z, and so on are interrelated by a set of equations. How do we know whether x and y determine the value of z, or whether z and y determine the magnitude of x, or whether z and x determine the magnitude of y? In general there is no intrinsic basis for deciding. Thus, suppose in a Sraffian system that profits, prices and physical conditions in all but one sector of production were given exogenously. It would then be possible to calculate the necessary physical composition of the final sector of production. Can one infer that the technology of iron production is 'determined' by prices, the remaining technology, and the profit rate? In formal logical terms, the argument is identical. One requires an external, i.e. an economic argument, to explain why technology must be treated as predetermined and prices as endogenous. But no such argument is provided. It is simply 'written in' to the equations.

The *second* point is that it is not true that simply because a variable does not enter a calculation, particularly a summary or final calculation—what econometrics terms a 'reduced form'—it must be excluded from all causal mechanisms. This is easily established with an example from mechanics. Using Newton's three laws, one can write an equation for the motion of a pendulum in which the mass of the pendulum turns out to be irrelevant, because it moves with a periodicity related only to its length and the acceleration due to gravity. This does not mean the concept of mass is an irrelevancy to determining the motion of a pendulum, as you will discover if you try to build a weightless pendulum.

An even more apposite example is that of electromagnetic radiation. In the nineteenth century, Maxwell wrote down a set of differential equations explaining the relation between varying electrical and magnetic fields. In free space, the solution to these equations turns out to define the motion of light. This discovery was one of the most exciting of the nineteenth century, the foundation of all modern telecommunications and a great deal of modern physics notwithstanding subsequent advances in quantum mechanics. Nevertheless Maxwell's equations still play little or no role in the science of optics, for the simple reason that the path of a beam of light can be calculated on the basis of a number of general equations most of which in fact apply equally both to waves and particles, and involve no mention of electrical or magnetic fields. It would be absolutely absurd, however, on this basis to claim that electromagnetic phenomena are redundant in the study of light, since they illustrate all its deepest properties.[36]

However, a *third*, more telling point is this: there is no branch of science whatsoever in which any serious investigator uses a concept of causality independent of *time*. Of course, it goes almost without saying the Marx's concept of 'laws' constitutes a concept of 'laws of motion'. The study of motion and change is the essence of dialectics. But one need not be a Marxist to reject the idea that two simultaneous events can 'cause' each other. We deduce that a bullet causes death because a person is alive before being shot and dead afterwards; that a jet causes a plane to fly because the plane takes off after the jet has been started and not before. This is no less true for static equilibria where forces such as gravity, tension, pressure and so on are said to be the cause of the equilibrium. When a roof rests on a wall, we say the wall causes the roof to stay up because when the wall is removed, the roof falls. If the roof failed to fall we would not say the wall supported it. Behind all equilibrium is movement, and even equilibrium relations cannot be revealed without disequilibrium analysis. The most general study of equilibrium in mechanics, namely Lagrange's method, operates precisely by studying the effect of small perturbations on the energy of a system.

It follows that even if it were permissible to study economics by analysing the behaviour of static equilibrium models, which it is not, we could only make inference about causality by studying the effects of a disturbance to the equilibrium, and that it is entirely wrong to try and infer causality from static relations between moving objects.

There is, finally, a *fourth* and slightly distinct point which perhaps affords the deepest insight of all. Steedman's reference to the 'rate of profit which affects the capitalists' actions' contains the germ of a more correct approach to causality, if we take it to be the basis of a real study of the role of capitalist consciousness in economic movement. The difficulty with marginalism is that it seeks an explanation of consumer behaviour solely in subjective consciousness, in the secret desires of the buyers. Both Marxism and neo-Ricardianism reject this. Nevertheless, consciousness does play a definite role in economic analysis, because when one has outlined the objective laws governing its movement, one must also show how these manifest themselves in the consciousness of agents. There is, one must agree, no point in producing a completely coherent theory of price and value determination that cannot show how capitalist behaviour (and workers' behaviour) actually implements this determination.[37]

This might appear to be the post-Sraffians' strongest point; in reality it is their weakest. What does actually affect capitalist behaviour? To be sure, it is affected by price phenomena and they are not necessarily conscious of the value relations behind prices. But their behaviour is not governed by the hypothetical equilibrium profit rate predicted by the post-Sraffian models, for the simple reason that this theoretical ideal is never attained. The actual quantities affecting capitalist behaviour—individual profit rates—are not visible in a neo-Ricardian system. So what does determine capitalist behaviour for the post-Sraffians?

In section 3 we observed that, strictly speaking, a Sraffian system cannot meet new demand except through a balanced and simultaneous increase in all sectors to ensure there is no excess product.

How could such an increase take place? What form of consciousness must be assumed so that capitalists in widely different parts of the economy can co-ordinate their actions to bring about a harmonious result? Only *conscious co-ordinated planning* could achieve it. Only if each capitalist knew what every other capitalist were doing, where to obtain each part of their inputs and where to dispose of each part of their outputs, could they ensure that there was no disturbance of prices caused by fluctuations in supply or demand.

In short, the post-Sraffian concept of causality excludes the central feature of capitalism, which all contributors to this book stress—that production is private and producers are not conscious of each other's actions or the social results of their own actions. This concept of causality cannot model the consciousness of agents in a commodity economy.[38]

But this is not all. Where are the planners? There are none, so that the system takes on a profoundly idealist character. The planning agent is the equation system itself, which has incarnated itself in the real world as a causal agent. Descending like cabbalistic lightning from mathematical heaven to vulgar earth, it demands that the inner thoughts of every capitalist and every worker become miniature reproductions of its mystical inner self.

There is a striking duality between such systems and the general equilibrium systems devised by Walras in the 1930s using marginal methods. Their weakness, on which even sympathetic interpreters agree, are twofold. They have no market mechanism, and they behave unpredictably if trading goes on at disequilibrium prices. General equilibrium theory creates a *deus ex machina* in the shape of the Walrasian auctioneer, a benign but mythical figure who consults all agents concerning their inmost desires, and then announces optimum equilibrium positions, which agents then adopt and everyone lives happily ever after.

Sraffian systems encounter the same problem from the opposite side. A simultaneous equation system is neither more nor less than a Calvinist Walrasian auctioneer, austerely indifferent to agent's desires, who assigns them to their predestined role in the great eternal equilibrium on the basis of their allotted portion of technology, condemning them to live out their days forever producing and consuming the same thing at the same price.

This brings us to a final point concerning the fundamental difference in goals between Marx's inquiry and Steedman's, and its consequences for the study of transformation and social reproduction.

What is the purpose of economic inquiry into capitalism? Not, fundamentally, to take its existence for granted and explore its ideal forms, but to take its existence as fact and study its historical limits. Not to study why it can theoretically survive, but how it is actually breaking up. Not to study its ideal equilibria but its real crises. This is so, not just for moral but for scientific reasons. We can readily agree that any scientist who assumes that a theory is immutable and not subject to change and evolution is a fool and a bad scientist; but even more so someone who assumes the same thing of her or his object of study!

What, therefore, is the purpose of studying social reproduction? Marx's reproduction schemas in Volume 2 are not dedicated to the same aim as the Sraffians'. He does not begin by assuming that the economy reproduces itself, in order to find out how goods exchange. He begins by assuming that goods exchange, in order to find out how the economy reproduces itself. The purpose is to study no less than Adam Smith's 'hidden hand' — how it can be that private decisions by independent producers can lead to a coherent social effect which was not consciously planned by any of them.

*Many* inconsistences and contradictions arise from this study, because generally speaking capitalism does not reproduce itself. The problem of research is fundamentally an empirical one, to determine which of these contradictions is a pure theoretical fiction, a misrepresentation of the real world, and which is empirically true. Theory must be revised to follow reality, not vice versa as with Steedman. In this research, values, prices and profits are not deductions but *data*: *given* measurable quantities. Reproduction is not given: it is deduced. The problems, I repeat, is to show how exchange causes reproduction—not how reproduction causes exchange. Marx's own statements in Volume 2 make this clear. Thus

'The continuous supply of labour-power on the part of the working class in department I, the transformation of one part of department I's commodity capital back into the money form of variable capital, the replacement of a part of department II's commodity capital by natural elements of constant capital $II_c$ — these necessary preconditions all mutually require one another, but they are mediated by a very complicated process which involves three processes of circulation that proceed independently, even if they are intertwined with one another. The very complexity of the process provides many occasions for it to take an abnormal course.'[39]

This is very remote from the 'feedback' assumption in the form which von Bortkiewicz demands. Marx merely sets out to show that it is *possible* for an economy to reproduce the use-values used in production even though the producers do not know how this is done. In the normal course of events, this will not happen perfectly, or not at all. Hence the very careful basis on which he explains how he uses his 'abstraction' of simple reproduction:

'Simple reproduction on the same scale seems to be an abstraction, both in the sense that the absence of any accumulation or reproduction on an expanded scale is an assumption foreign to the capitalist basis, and in the sense that the conditions in which production takes place do not remain absolutely the same in different years (which is what is assumed here). But since, when accumulation takes place, simple reproduction still remains a part of this, and is a real factor in accumulation, this can also be considered by itself.'[40]

It is a far cry from saying that simple reproduction is the actual state of any economy, even an abstract one. To say that simple reproduction 'is a part of' a real economy means that a real economy is to be treated as simple reproduction plus additional elements, that is, plus some use-values which are not properly circulated, plus some use-values which are not realized, plus some use-values which are used in accumulation, plus sectors of the economy where used-up means of production are not replaced because they are obsolete — and so on.

The distinction in logical method is so emphatic that we can illustrate it as follows: suppose it were finally and conclusively proved that simple reproduction could not take place if the sum of values were not equal to the sum of prices and the sum of profits to the sum of surplus-values. *One would then have to conclude, as a Marxist, that the economy could not properly reproduce itself for this reason,* and begin to treat the transformation of value into price as a real factor in capitalist crises. Only if this prediction failed to find empirical confirmation could one finally reject value theory as unfounded.

One and only one test, a test which is remarkably and singularly absent from post-Sraffian writings can be the final arbiter of theory: the test of practice. As Albert Einstein, whose authority on such matters can hardly be questioned, remarked: 'The sceptic will say "It may well be true that this system of equations is reasonable from a logical standpoint. But this does not prove it corresponds to nature." You are right, dear sceptic. Experience alone can decide on truth.'[41]

# Notes

## Introduction

1. Marx-Engels Archiv 1, Berlin, 1928.
2. The present collection pays too little attention to French contributions to the debate on the 'transformation problem'. Let us mention in passing those of Gilbert Abraham–Froix–Edmond Berrebi, *Théorie de la Valeur, des Prix et de l'Accumulation*, Paris 1976; C. Benetti, *Valeur et Répartition*, Paris, 1974; Dostaler, *Marx, la Valeur et l'Economie Politique*, Paris, 1978; Manuel Perez, 'Valeur et Prix' in *Critiques de l'Economie Politique*, January–March 1980; Gérard Dumeuil, *De la Valeur aux Prix de Production*, Paris, 1980. Mario Cogoy, 'Das Dilemma der Neo-Ricardischen Theorie', *Beiträge zur Marxschen Theorie* 2, Frankfurt, 1974 has likewise received too little attention.
3. Let us however mention that in Chapter 49 of *Capital* Volume 3, Harmondsworth, 1981, Marx notes that the total surplus-value, i.e. *surplus labour contained* in the commodities, *produced* during the process of production is not necessarily *realised*. The identity which he establishes is between realised surplus-value and profits (there do not, of course, exist any other profits than realised ones). In other words surplus-value determines the maximum ceiling for profits. No other source of profits exists but previously produced surplus-value. More than this Marx does not establish as a law.

## Chapter Two

1. Michio Morishima, *Marx's Economics*, Cambridge 1977, p. 87.
2. Deleplace, 'Biens a Double Destination' *Cahiers d'Economie Politique*, No. 2, Paris, 1975.
3. Sraffa, p. 1.
4. Steedman, p. 161.
5. Ibid., ch. 11.
6. Ibid., p. 153.
7. Cf. Sraffa, pp. 3–4.
8. Ibid., p. 6.
9. Steedman, p. 68.
10. Sraffa, p. 90.
11. Steedman, p. 187–8, where the existence of zero prices for over-produced commodities is established and p. 204 where it is argued that Von Neumann models nevertheless constitute a good model of accumulation.

12. Ibid., pp. 163, 198.

13. Ibid., p. 187.

14. Ibid., pp. 163, 185.

15. Ibid., p. 163.

16. Ibid., p. 198.

17. Ibid., p. 127.

18. Steedman, p. 152.

**Chapter Three**

1. For a survey of previous criticisms, see Ben Fine and Laurence Harris, 'Controversial Issues in Marxist Economic Theory', *Socialist Register*, 1977. For my earlier arguments on Marx's theory of value, see 'Marx's Theory of Value and the Transformation Problem', in Jesse Schwartz, (ed.), *The Subtle Anatomy of Capitalism*, Santa Monica, California 1977, pp. 106–137. Finally, for 'The Poverty of Algebra', see *The Value Controversy*, London 1981, pp. 266–300.

2. L. Colletti, *From Rousseau to Lenin*, New York 1972, p. 83.

3. Karl Marx, *A Contribution to the Critique of Political Economy*, London, 1972, p. 86.

4. Karl Marx, *Capital*, Volume 3, Harmondsworth 1981, p. 1020.

5. Karl Marx, *Grundrisse*, Harmondsworth 1973, pp. 196–197.

6. Karl Marx, letter to Kugelmann, 11 July 1868.

7. *Capital*, Volume 1, Harmondsworth, 1976, p. 193.

8. *Capital*, Volume 3, pp. 280–281.

9. Ibid., p. 300.

10. Marx notes that this necessary distribution of social labour-time has two distinct aspects, which in turn give rise to two different concepts of socially necessary labour-time. There is in the first place the (abstract) labour-time which under given social conditions is necessary for the production of a given amount of a commodity. This quantity of socially necessary labour-time defines the total value of the commodity-product. It arises from the nature of a commodity as a value, as a bearer of exchange-value.

Second, from the nature of a commodity as use-value, as an object of social need, there is the question of the correspondence between the total quantity of the commodity-product and the social need for this product. This correspondence is expressed as a quantity of labour-time which is socially necessary to produce the appropriate amount of the product, that is an amount of product which at the regulating price fulfils the effective demand for it. In the first two volumes of *Capital*, Marx assumes that this regulating price is a direct expression of value; in the third volume he develops it into a transformed expression — the price of production.

The first type of socially necessary labour-time thus determines the unit value of a commodity, and through it the regulating price. The second type of socially necessary labour-time then determines the discrepancy between actual supply and effective demand: it therefore determines the discrepancy between market price and regulating price. (*Capital*, Volume 3, p. 774).

11. Karl Marx, *Theories of Surplus Value*, Moscow 1968, Part II, Ch. XVII, section 8 (pp. 499–507).

12. Karl Marx, 'Wage Labour and Capital', in Robert C. Tucker, ed., *The Marx-Engels Reader*, New York, 1972, pp. 174–175.

13. Steedman, pp. 13–14.

14. In my earlier paper (see note 1), I treat the derivation and structure of this problem in great detail. ('Marx's Theory of Value and the Transformation Problem', pp. 106–137).

15. Steedman, pp. 14–15. Steedman's position is not new of course, since it has always been a highly fashionable argument. Both Paul Samuelson and Joan Robinson, for instance, have long held this position.

16. *Capital*, Volume 1, p. 173.

17. For a related criticism of the neo-Ricardian conception of production, see my 'Political Economy and Capitalism: Notes on Dobb's Theory of Crisis', *Cambridge Journal of Economics*, no. 2, 1978, pp. 233–251, and the subsequent debate on these issues in the same journal, no. 4, 1980. For a detailed critique of Steedman and others, see 'The Poverty of Algebra', pp. 266–300.

18. *Capital* Volume 1, p. 291.

19. Even the facility of calculation is not at all equal. Estimation of values requires knowledge of labour flows and flows of means of production used up. Prices of production require in addition knowledge of the real wage bundle and of the stocks of capital advanced. These latter two pieces of information imply a much more detailed knowledge of the structure of the economy.

20. *Capital* Volume 3, p. 134.

21. *Capital* Volume 2, pp. 222–223.

22. M. Dobb, 'Mr Sraffa and the Rehabilitation of Classical Economics', p. 1.

23. It is interesting to note that Marx addresses this problem in connection with the theory of differential rent, not that of prices of production. It is often forgotten by Marxists that the former theory also implies price-value deviations, since it is the marginal conditions which rule price but the average conditions which determine value. As such, all the general phenomena involving price-value deviations appear here too.

24. *Theories of Surplus Value*, Part III, pp. 345.

25. Anwar Shaikh, 'Theories of Value and Theories of Distribution', unpublished PhD dissertation, Columbia University 1973, ch. IV, section 4: and Michio Morishima, *Marx's Economics*, Cambridge 1973, p. 142.

When the economy is along the von Neumann ray, the rate of profit (in a circulating capital model) is independent of relative prices. But the rate of profit is the ratio of profits to cost-prices. If the sum of prices is constant, and the ratio of profits to cost-price is the same for direct prices and prices of production, then it follows that direct profits equal transformed profits and direct cost-price equals transformed cost-price.

26. The average rate of profit is from T. E. Weisskopf, 'Marxian Crisis Theory and the Rate of Profit in the Post-War US Economy', *Cambridge Journal of Economics*, no. 3, 1979, table 2 (Full Period), p. 351. The average ratio of growth is from 'Long Term Economic Growth, 1860–1970', US Department of Commerce, 1973, chart A, fig. 3, p. 8.

27. 'Theories of Value and Theories of Distribution', ch. IV, section 4; and *Marx's Economics*, p. 64.

28. *Capital* Volume 3, p. 273. Alfredo Medio also argues in favour of viewing what I called the central industry as the industry which satisfies Marx's definition of the sphere of average composition. See Alfredo Medio, 'Profits and Surplus Value: Appearance and Reality in Capitalist Production', in E. K. Hunt and J. G. Schwartz, eds., *A Critique of Economic Theory*, Harmondsworth, 1972.

29. The relation of r to S/V can be derived graphically from *Marx's Economics*, p. 64, fig. 2.

30. Karl Marx to Friedrich Engels, 30 April 1868.

31. *Capital* Volume 3, p. 280. Marx emphasizes that this process takes place over

periods of time defined by the conditions of production in different industries. The equalization process is therefore not a 'short-run' phenomenon.

32. Anwar Shaikh, 'Foreign Trade and the Law of Value', *Science and Society*, Autumn 1979 (part 1) and Spring 1980 (part 2).

33. *The Works and Correspondence of David Ricardo*, Piero Sraffa, ed., Cambridge 1962, vol. 1, p. 34; *Capital* Volume 3, p. 356; and Paul Sweezy, *The Theory of Capitalist Development*, Oxford 1942, ch. 7.

34. *Theories of Surplus Value*, Part II, pp. 193–194. See also *Capital* Volume 3, pp. 266 and 280.

35. L. Pasinetti, *Lectures on the Theory of Production*, London and New York 1977. Pasinetti calls this process 'vertical integration'.

36. Piero Sraffa, *Production of Commodities by Means of Commodities*, Cambridge 1960, p. 8.

37. See appendix B for a formal proof of this.

38. By definition $\pi^T$ and $K^T$ are the integrated profits and capital advanced, respectively. Define the integrated profit rate as $r^T \equiv \pi^T/K^T$. Then from equation (10) in the text:

$$\pi^T \equiv \pi + \pi^{(1)} + \pi^{(2)} + \ldots$$

and

$$r^T = \frac{\pi}{K}\frac{K}{K^T} + \frac{\pi^{(1)}}{K^{(1)}} \cdot \frac{K^{(1)}}{K^T} + \frac{\pi^{(2)}}{K^{(2)}}\frac{K^{(2)}}{K^T} \ldots$$

$$= r\frac{K}{K^T} + r^{(1)}\frac{K^{(1)}}{K^T} + r^{(2)}\frac{K^{(2)}}{K^T} + \ldots$$

Thus each integrated profit rate is a convex combination of individual industry profit rates at various stages in the integration process. Insofar as the competition of capitals tends to equalize industry rates of profit, it will tend to result in individual rates $r_i$ fairly close to each other at any one moment. This in turn means that the integrated rates are likely to be very close indeed. A similar argument can be constructed for integrated wage rates.

39. $\bar{r}$ is from 'Marxian Crisis Theory and the Rate of Profit in the Post-War US Economy', fig. 1, p. 349, and $\bar{w}$ from *National Income and Product Accounts, 1929–1974*, US Department of Commerce, supplement to *Survey of Current Business*, January 1976, p. 211.

It should be noted that Leontief's total capital requirement is in units of \$10 000. Converted to these units, $\bar{w} = 0.2612$.

40. The Goldfield-Quardt test for heteroskedasticity was performed by ranking the observations by the size of the independent variable, running separate log-regressions on the first 69 and the last 69 observations, and then performing an F-test on the ratio of the respective sums of the squared residuals ($s_1, s_2$) to see if the ratio was significantly different from 1. (J. Johnston, *Economic Methods*, New York 1969, p. 219). The test indicates that there is no significant heteroskedasticity in the data.

$$s_1 = 0.84671, \ s_2 = 0.83568, \ \frac{s_1}{s_2} = 0.98698 < F_{0.95} = 1.53 \text{ (60 degrees of freedom)}$$

41. Jacob T. Schwartz, *Lectures on the Mathematical Method in Analytical*

*Economics*, New York 1961, table IIIb, p. 43.

42. For further comments on this issue, see the debate as cited in note 17 above.

## Chapter Four

1. The author is grateful for comments on an earlier version of this work from participants at a seminar on political economy at the autonomous Metropolitan University of Iztapalapa, Mexico. Particularly useful were the comments from Elizier Tijerina, Jose Carlos Valenzuela Faijo and Jaime Puyana Ferreira.

2. V. K. Dmitriev, *Economic Essays*, Cambridge, 1974; Ladislaw von Bortkiewicz, 'Value and Price in the Marxian System', *International Economic Papers* 2, 1952; L. von Bortkiewicz, 'On the Correction of the Fundamentals of Marx's Theoretical Construction in Volume 3 of *Capital*', in P. Sweezy, ed., Eugen von Bohm-Bawerk, *Karl Marx and the Close of His System*, New York, 1949.

3. Of course Ricardo's concept of classes is as far removed from the Marxist view as is that of the neo-Ricardians.

4. See G. C. Harcourt, *Some Cambridge Controversies in the Theory of Capital*, Cambridge, 1972; G. C. Harcourt and H. F. Laing, eds., *Capital and Growth*, Harmondsworth, 1971; E. K. Hunt and J. G. Schwartz, eds., *A Critique of Economic Theory*, Harmondsworth, 1972.

5. See A. Medio, 'Néo-classiques, néo-Ricardiens et Marx' in *Une Nouvelle Approche en Economie Politique?*, G. Faccarello and P. de Lavergne, eds., Económica, Paris, 1977.

6. R. Meek, *Studies in the Labour Theory of Value*, London 1973, pp. xxviii–xliv.

7. It should be noted that Meek ratifies his position in a more recent work, where moreover he says that 'the idea that profit is exclusively produced by living labour', or that it is 'a deduction from the product of labour' possesses little scientific substance. See 'Whatever Happened to the Labour Theory of Value', *Essays in Economic Analysis*, M. J. Artie and A. R. Nobay, eds., Cambridge, 1975.

8. See Maurice Dobb, *Theories of Value and Distribution Since Adam Smith*, Cambridge 1973. It should be added that Dobb is one of those many economists who include Marx in the ranks of the classical economists. See, for example, Edward Nell, 'Economics: the Resurgence of Political Economy', in *Ideology and the Social Sciences*, Robin Blackburn, ed., Harmondsworth 1979; Joan Robinson, *An Introduction to Modern Economics*, McGraw-Hill, London 1973.

9. See A. Roncaglia, 'Production des Marchandises par des Marchandises. Critique et Dépassement de la Méthode Marginaliste', *Une Nouvelle Approche en Economie Politique?*, pp. 210–221.

10. Meek expresses the same idea when he says 'I see no ideological sin in taking Sraffa's models as components of a general technical base for our analysis in which we need only specify whatever additional institutional data is needed.' 'Whatever Happened to the Labour Theory of Value?', p. 256.

11. Sergio Latouche, 'Quelques Repères pour Analyser la Signification Historique de la Théorie du Professeur Piero Sraffa', *Cahiers d'Economie Politique* no. 3, Amiens, 1976.

12. See Paolo Giussani, 'A propos de la Théorie Marxiste de la Valeur: une Critique de Sraffa', *Communisme* no. 24, September–October 1976.

13. See Pierangelo Garegnani, 'La Realidad de la Explotación I, II y III' and 'Fórmulas Mágicas y Polvo de Arsénico', *Debate sobre la Teoría Marxista del Valor de Pasado y Presente* no. 82, Mexico, 1979, pp. 30–64 and 177–190.

14. Lucio Coletti, 'Valor y Dialéctica en Marx', *Debate sobre la Teoría Marxista*, pp. 75–83.

15. Claudio Napoleoni, 'El Enigma del Valor' and 'El Marx Inútil de Lippi', *Debate sobre la Teoría Marxista*, pp. 15–29 and 133–138.

16. We consider completely erroneous the views of Altvater, Hoffman and Semmler that Sraffa developed a theory of the 'distribution of the net product which presents itself as an alternative to neo-classical theory' and which is explained fundamentally by the 'relation of social forces'. See 'El Valor de Marx' in *Debate sobre la Teoría Marxista*, pp. 97–98.

17. This returns us to the Ricardian hypothesis which treats wages as a part of circulating capital. From this it is equated to a quantity of commodities of short-term durability. That is, the wage is not represented as a sum of money with which certain commodities can be bought.

18. Sraffa, p. 11.

19. 'El Valor de Marx', p. 98.

20. David Ricardo, 'An Essay on the influence of a low price of corn on the profits of stock'.

21. Adam Smith, *The Wealth of Nations*, Harmondsworth, 1970.

22. David Ricardo, *Principles of Political Economy and Taxation*, London, 1972, p. 27.

23. Ricardo, 'Absolute Value and Exchange Value', in P. Sraffa, ed., *The Collected Works of David Ricardo*, Volume 4, Cambridge.

24. This does not mean Sraffa has a theory of income distribution. This question, which is in general an important one, is not important for Sraffa because he is interested only in the relation between prices and the level of the various distributional variables, whatever may be the factors which determine them and affect their variation.

25. Sraffa, p. 18.

26. Ibid.

27. Ibid.

28. Sraffa, p. 23.

29. Obviously the concrete system he starts from comprises only fundamental branches.

30. H. G. Johnson, review of *Production of Commodities by Means of Commodities*, *Canadian Journal of Economics and Political Science*, Vol. 28, 1962, pp. 464–465.

31. R. F. Harrod, 'Compte Rendu du livre de P. Sraffa, *Production of Commodities by Means of Commodities, Une Nouvelle Approche en Économie Politique?*

32. 'Prelude to a Critique of Economic Theory', *Collected Economic Papers*, Oxford, 1965, vol. 3, p. 9.

33. Remember that for Sraffa, the notion of prices can only be elaborated correctly outwith any restrictive hypothesis on final demand. Equally the influence of final demand on the formation of long-term prices is excluded. These are obtained taking produced quantities as given, that is, prices are determined independently of quantities. The theory of prices of production is radically different from the 'symmetrical' theory of A. Marshall. See P. Sraffa, 'Sulle Relazioni fra Costo e Quantità Proddotto', *Annali di Economia* 1925, vol. 2, no. 1, pp. 277–328. Interesting also is 'The Laws of Return under Competitive Conditions', *The Economic Journal*, December 1926, vol. 36, pp. 535–550.

34. Harrod, 'An Essay in Dynamic Theory', *The Economic Journal*, 1938, p. 18.

35. J. Hicks, *Value and Capital: An Enquiry into Some Fundamental Principles of Economic Theory*, Oxford, 1939.

36. See Jean Cartelier, *Surproduit et Reproduction*, Paris, 1976.

37. Harrod, 'Compte Rendu...', p. 11.

38. See Carlo Benetti, *Valeur et Repartition*, Grenoble et Paris, 1974, pp. 128–129.

39. Ibid., pp. 128–129.

40. 'El Sistema de Sraffa y la Cortica de la Teoría Neoclásica de la Distribución', in *Teoria del Capital y la Distribución*, Ed. Oscar Braun, Madrid, p. 375.

41. F. van de Velde refers to the fact that when the wage forms part of advanced capital, the relation between profit rate and wage rate is inverse, but not linear. See 'Travail et Salaire. Marx-Sraffa', *Cahiers du CEREL* Centre d'Etude et de Recherches en Epistemologie, Lille.

42. H. Denis, *Cours d'Histoire de la Pensée Économique*, Paris, 1972–73, p. 127.

43. For more details, see C. Benetti, Suzanne de Brunhoff and J. Cartelier, 'Elements pour une Critique Marxiste de P. Sraffa', in *Cahiers d'Economie Politique*, Amiens, 1976; c. Benetti and J. Cartelier 'Prix de Production et Etalon', in *Économie Classique — Economie Vulgaire*, Grenoble-Paris, 1975.

44. Luigi Pasinetti, *Lectures on the Theory of Production*, McGraw-Hill, 1978.

45. Benetti, de Brunhoff and Cartelier, p. 33.

46. Sraffa himself confounds them when he says 'We shall also hereafter assume that the wage is paid *post factum* as a share of the annual product, thus abandoning the classical economists' idea concerning a wage "advanced" from capital'. See Sraffa p. 10.

47. 'In every country where the capitalist mode of production prevails, it is the custom not to pay for labour-power until it has been exercised for the period fixed by the contract, for example, at the end of each week. In all cases, therefore, the worker advances the use-value of his labour-power to the capitalist. He lets the buyer consume it before he receives payment of the price. Everywhere the worker allows credit to the capitalist.' K. Marx, *Capital* Volume 1, Harmondsworth, 1976, p. 278.

48. K. Marx, *Grundvisse*, Harmondsworth, 1973, p. 95.

49. *Grundvisse*, p. 96.

50. Sraffa, p. 33.

51. N. Kaldor, 'A Model of Economic Growth', *The Economic Journal*, 1957; L. Pasinetti, 'Rate of Profit and Income Distribution in Relation to the Rate of Economic Growth', *The Review of Economic Studies*, 1962, p. 267.

52. D. M. Nuti, 'Vulgar Economy in the Theory of Income Distribution', *Science and Society*, vol. 35, no. 1, Spring 1971, pp. 27–33.

53. Thus, for example, Harcourt suggests that 'Bhaduri, J. Robinson and Nell adhere to Marx's theory of exploitation, realised in the form of relative negotiating strengths, to explain the distribution of rent considered as a surplus left over from wage-earners and those who receive profits.' Harcourt, 'Some Cambridge Controversies in the Theory of Capital', quoted by Frank Roosevelt, 'Cambridge Economics and Commodity Fetishism', *The Review of Radical Political Economics*, 1975, p. 21.

54. Thus, for example, one of Marx's 'correctors' says 'magnitudes... are determined in terms of value or measured by the quantity of labour contained in each one of these magnitudes.' Claudio Napoleoni, *Lecciones sobre el Capítulo Sexto (inédito) de Marx*, Mexico 1975, p. 183.

55. Thus Napoleoni, 'Lecciones', p. 195, says that 'we must establish a system of equations such that if values alone are known, that is *quantities of labour*, the system will jointly determine prices and the profit rate.' Von Bortkiewicz himself admits the possibility that units of value can be measured in terms of labour time. In this respect he says, 'In Tugan-Baronovsky's value schema he uses units of labour time for the calculation instead of units of money... This usage is acceptable.' 'Contribution to a correction...', p. 224.

56. See Claudio Napoleoni, 'Lecciones...', p. 199.

57. Ibid., p. 200.

58. *Ibid.*, p. 203.

59. See Marina Bianchi, Editorial *La Téoria de Valor desde los Clásicos a Marx*, Madrid, 1975.

60. 'El Valor de Marx', p. 102. On the neo-Ricardians' incomprehension of money, see Hans Georg Backhaus, 'Dialectique de la Forme Valeur', *Critiques de l'Economie Politique*, Paris, no. 18, Paris, 1975, October–December 1974; Pierre Salama, *Surla Valeur*, David Yaffé, 'Value and Price in Marx's Capital', *Revolutionary Communist* no. 1, London, 1975.

61. For an excellent presentation of the Marxist method see Roman Rosdolsky, *The Making of Marx's 'Capital'*, London, 1978.

62. In this respect Bernstein says that 'whether the Marxist theory of value is exact or not is without importance for the proof of a labour surplus', and that 'the labour theory of value is above all wrong in that it appears systematically as the actual means by which the worker is exploited by the capitalist.' E. Bernstein, *Evolutionary Socialism: The Premises of Socialism and the Tasks of Social Democracy*, New York, 1963.

63. Garegnani, 'La Realidad de la Explotación I, II y III', *Debate sobre la Teoría Marxista*, p. 57.

64. 'Capital did not invent surplus labour. Wherever a part of society possesses the monopoly of the means of production the worker, free or unfree, must add to the labour-time necessary for his own maintenance an extra quantity of labour-time in order to produce the means of subsistence for the owner of the means of production, whether this proprietor be an Athenian καλόδκ̈αλαθόδ, ["Handsom and Good"], an Etruscan theocrat, a *civis romanus*, a Norman Baron, an American slave-owner, a modern landlord, a Wallachian boyar, or a capitalist.' K. Marx, *Capital* Volume 1, p. 344.

65. See Georg Lukacs, Marxismo Ortodoxo y Materialismo Historico, Mexico.

66. See Garegnani, 'Fórmulas Mágicas...' pp. 189–190.

67. Sraffa, p. 6.

68. *Ibid.*, p. 3.

69. *Ibid.*, p. 11.

70. Roosevelt, p. 21–23.

71. In Marxist value terms, Sraffa's surplus includes both V and S, while Marx's surplus includes only S.

72. K. Marx, 'Wages, Price and Profit', *Selected Works*, p. 226.

**Chapter Five**

1. Piero Sraffa's *Production of Commodities by Means of Commodities* is the basis of the neo-Ricardian school's development, but his contribution has probably been exaggerated, since many of his conclusions can be found in the 1904 works of V. K. Dmitriev and L. von Bortkiewicz. The model expounded by J. von Neumann (see, for example, J. von Neumann, 'A Model of General Economic Equilibrium', *Review of Economic Studies*, 1945–6) has also been influential. Marx's criticisms of the Ricardian school appear in *Theories of Surplus Value*, volume 3, ch. 20. For the critique of Ricardo himself see *Theories of Surplus Value*, volume 2 and in particular pp. 373–469.

2. *Capital*, volume 1, Harmondsworth, 1976, p. 165.

3. The neo-Ricardian theoreticians have some trouble distinguishing their own prices from those of neoclassical general equilibrium theory. The latter would, unlike the former, be the only indices of rational resource allocation. If the prices of a linear

system like Sraffa's are not compatible with the redistribution of the social product through bilateral exchange, then of necessity they are indices of a pure allocation of resources, whether or not rational, and not an expression of the commodity character of production. Bob Rowthorn has noted, opportunely enough, that neo-Ricardian theory is compatible with general economic equilibrium in 'Neo-classicism, neo-Ricardianism and Marxism', *New Left Review*, no. 86, London, 1974.

4. On the normalisation question see the last volume of Stamatis, *Sraffa und Sein Verhaltnis zu Ricardo und Marx*, Gottingen, 1983.

5. The difficulties encountered in trying to introduce money are well represented in Luigi Pasinetti's attempt in *Structural Change and Economic Growth*, New York, 1975, pp. 156–175.

6. *Theories of Surplus Value*, volume 3, p. 144.

7. One must however be careful of the current view that linear systems based on the input–output technique are the generalisation either of the *Tableau Economique* or of Marx's volume 2 reproduction schemata. Marx's schemata are based on a study of the direct bilateral exchanges needed for reproduction on the basis of already given values. The linear input–output systems make abstraction of this, and therefore cannot be used to study the real conditions for economic equilibrium.

8. It is superfluous to make clear that I do not believe system (16) is an exact representation of production using labour-power as a commodity. Labour-power cannot secure a rate of profit. However the reason it cannot is derived from the theory of labour-values alone. From the neo-Ricardian standpoint, full internal coherence would require a system of this type.

9. As distinct from the values of common commodities, the value of labour-power is a function of *two* variables: the value of the wage-commodities and the quantity/quality of these same goods. The 'historical and moral' element of the wage of which Marx speaks in *Capital*, Volume 1, means exactly that the rage is in its turn a function of the values of consumer goods, that is of productivity in those industries which produce the goods which workers consume. That transforms, finally, the value of labour-power into a function of a single variable.

10. Ian Steedman's *Marx After Sraffa*, London, 1977, summarises the neo-Ricardians' criticisms of Marx. Many other neo-Ricardian theoreticians have avoided formulating direct criticisms of Marx, not least Sraffa himself. Steedman's assertion, quoted in the text, is the pivot of the book.

11. Brody, *Prices, Proportions and Planning*, Budapest, 1970.

12. It is obviously implicit that at the same time $S_I + S_{II} + \dots + S_{N+1} = \pi_0 + \pi + \dots + \pi_N$.

13. George Stamatis, pp. 404–440, constructs all possible examples on the basis of a system analogous to (26).

14. Sraffa, Appendix B.

15. Marx explains the level of the general rate of profit in a manner apparently analogous to Smith's in Chapter 10 of *Capital*, Volume 3. But there are enormous differences. The point of departure is not an arbitrary spectrum of profit rates, indeed the profit rates obtained when commodities are sold at their values or at prices proportional to values, and these are directly established by conditions of production. In this situation — and in no other — equalisation or demand and supply is possible. Secondarily, Marx clarifies that the movement of capitals from sectors of higher organic composition towards those of lower composition is precisely that of a purchase and sale of commodities — not a 'movement of resources' or a pure monetary transfer — and must therefore alter the very phenomenon it has generated.

16. An example of what is said in the text is furnished by the treatment of fixed capital

around the Okishio theorem offered by John Roemer, 'Continuing controversy on the Falling Rate of Profit: Fixed Capital and Other Issues', *Cambridge Journal of Economics*, volume 4, 1979. Roemer identifies in a totally arbitrary manner the criterion of choice of technique of Marx, which Marx attributed to individual capitalists, with the neoclassical criterion of perfect competition. He does not recognise that within each individual sector the competing capitalists struggle directly to conquer growing quotas of produced value and therefore to lower each other's individual rate of profit. For a treatment of the problem of the choice of techniques and the falling rate of profit see Shaikh. 'Political Economy and Capitalism: Notes on Dobb's Theory of Crisis', *Cambridge Journal of Economics*, volume 3, 1978; and P. Giussani, *Competition and the Falling Rate of Profit, the Anti-Okishio Theorem*, unpublished, Milan, 1983.

17. See Eatwell, 'Mr Sraffa's Standard Commodity and the Rate of Exploitation', *Quarterly Journal of Economics*, volume 89.

18. See Pasinetti, *Lezioni di Teoria della Praduzione*, Bologna, 1975

## Chapter Six

1. Ladislaus von Bortkiewicz, 'Value and Price in the Marxian System', *International Economic Papers 2*, 1952. Von Bortkiewicz's treatment of gold production was criticised in J. Winternitz, 'Values and Prices: a solution of the So-Called 'Transformation Problem'', in *The Economic Journal*, June 1948. See also: Paul M. Sweezy, *The Theory of Capitalist Development*, New York, 1968, Piero Sraffa, *Production of Commodities by Means of Commodities*, London 1960, and Ian Steedman, *Marx after Sraffa*, London, 1977.

2. Marx's general theory of money is developed in *Contribution to a Critique of Political Economy*, London, 1971, ch. 2, and in its original version (the so-called *Urtext*: Marx-Engels-Gesamte-Ansgabe II/2, Berlin, 1980), and in *Capital*, Vol. I, ch. 3. Marx explicitly states that his theory of money is relevant to conditions of commodity production in general, including pre-capitalist commodity production (and therefore also post-capitalist commodity production) and does not limit itself to the capitalist mode of production only.

3. 'That the latter (money) is in actual fact nothing but a special expression of the social character of labour and its products, which however, as antithetical to the basis of private production, must always present itself in the last instance as a thing, as a particular commodity, alongside other commodities.' Karl Marx, *Capital*, Volume 3, Harmondsworth, 1981, p. 743.

4. The owner of gold does not 'sell' his commodity, which therefore has no price. He 'barters' it against, say, wheat. The owner of wheat thereby effectively sells his commodity against gold.

5. Marx states that commodities cannot enter the circulation process without having a price, (*Contribution...*, pp. 86–107).

6. What about paper money, which has hardly any intrinsic value, whose production hardly costs any socially necessary labour? For Marx, paper money is money which 'represents the money commodity' (under present circumstances gold), regardless of government decisions or regulations. Governments are of course free to print bank notes in any quantities they desire. Banks are equally free, under the constraint only of the central banks' practical regulations, to advance as much credit (that is bank money) to their customers as they wish. But neither governments nor banks can suspend the operations of the law of value. If to produce one ounce of gold takes as much average socially necessary labour-time as to produce twenty tons of steel, you can impose a

price of $35 for twenty tons of steel only if, simultaneously, $35 enables you to actually buy an ounce of gold. If you have to pay in fact $350 for an ounce of gold (whether at the mint, the central bank or on the free market), the price of twenty tons of steel will also rise towards $350, simply because now a banknote of ten dollars now represents not 1/3.5th ounce of gold, but only 1/35th ounce of gold. But this depends not only on the quantity of paper and bank money put into circulation, but also on the relative increases or decreases in the productivity of labour of gold mining on the one hand, and industry and agriculture on the other. In other words, it depends on the relation between the intrinsic value of gold and the intrinsic value of other commodities measured in the labour-time necessary for their production, as well as on the curculation velocity of paper and bank money, on the phase of the business cycle, and so on.

7. When we talk about the value of gold, we always mean its intrinsic value, that is the quantity of social labour necessary for its production, measured in labour-time, and never its purchasing power. This purchasing power can only be deduced from the evolution of the general price level, which is precisely a relation between the value of the commodity gold and the average value of all other commodities.

8. 'Gold must be in principle a *variable* value, if it is to serve as a measure of value, because only as reification of labour-time can it become the equivalent of other commodities, but as a result of changes in the productivity of concrete labour, the same amount of labour-time is embodied in unequal volumes of the same type of use-values.' *Contribution*.

9. I myself also made the mistake, in *Late Capitalism*, London, 1973, of using gold production as a 'department III' of production, confusing gold in general with its particular (and minor) role of luxury good.

10. Rumour has it that the next gold bonanza is starting to take place in Brazil. This remains to be seen. Note that, according to the *International Herald Tribune* of 6 April 1983, Brazilian gold production has increased from 4.4 tons in 1968 to 30 tons in 1982, half of which is in the new supposedly bonanza area of the Madeiras-Topajos, in the Amazon basin.

11. 'In August 1862, Messers Hartley and Reilly arrived at Dunedin with 1.047 oz gold, which they had found by cradling and washing the sands on the beaches of the Clutha River, between the sites of the present towns of Clyde and Cromwell [in New Zealand]. As soon as this became known the excitement was so great that men left lucrative employment and comfortable houses to follow the life of a digger. Prices of agricultural produce and food of all descriptions went up, and the demand for teamsters to take goods and tools to this new Eldorado was so great that £120 per ton was paid for the carriage of goods from Dunedin ... The demand for sawn timber was also so great that boards were stripped from drays and wagons and sold, the usual price for an empty gin-case being £5. (New Zealand Official Year-Book 1908).

12. A basic reason for apartheid and racist political, civil and labour laws in South Africa is to create a segregated labour market, which has largely insulated for more than half a century the black miners' wages (a significant part of the cost of production of gold) from the ups and downs of the general level of wages in that country, not to mention wages in the imperialist countries, which, during that period, bought practically all the gold produce in South Africa. In fact, according to Francis Wilson, in *Labour in the South African Mines, 1911–1969*, Cambridge, 1972, on the basis of 100 = the average black miners' wages in 1936, black miners' wages were actually in 1969 a bit below those of the 1911 index, 108 as against 111. In the latter nineteen-seventies and the early nineteen-eighties, this trend was reversed, as a result of the new gold boom, the relative shortage of labour-power for the mines given the low wage level

compared to that of black workers in industry and building and the pressure in the independent black states against providing cheap labour-power for South African mines. As a result of these changes, black South African miners' real wages increased by 230% between 1969 and 1983 (*The Economist*, 23 June 1983).

13. Between 1933, when the price of gold was fixed at $35 an ounce by the US authorities, and 1980, when the free market gold price rose to $500 an ounce, the cost-of-living index in the USA has multiplied by six, but productivity of labour had increased by twice as much in industry and agriculture as in gold mining. 12 multiplied by 35 gives us 420 as the purchasing power of gold, of which the gold price is the reciprocal. Marx's theory of money hasn't done so badly in offering a basis for explaining the empirical facts.

14. 'With a given development of the production of social labur (as on the one hand the mastering of mechanical or chemical obstacles becomes easier and on the other the relative distance of gold and silver producing countries becomes less important) *the discovery of alternative gold and silver deposits must weigh even more decisively in the scales.*' Urtext of *Zur Kritik...*, MEGA II/2, p. 44.

15. The gold bonanza area attracts *both* labour and capital, be it only because gold digging rapidly requests capital investment. In his book *After the Gold Rush — Society in Grass Valley and Nevada City* (Stanford University Press 1981), Ralph Mann describes how 'by 1850, mining operations had already left gold pans and one-man rockers behind: sluices and long toms (a kind of large rocker) worked by organized companies of miners, dominated the diggings. Coyoteing demanded even more planning and cooperative effort, and new knowledge and technology. Miners had to learn to map the courses of the ancient underground stream beds where the deposits lay, to sink shafts that would not cave in, and to get workers, tools, and fresh air to the bottom of them. Miners also had to raise capital for the expensive work of digging and equipping shafts before any returns were possible... Men arriving at the coyote mines alone and with little cash had to go to work for those with enough of a stake to pay wages' (p. 12). In other words: whatever the specificity of gold and gold production, under capitalism it tends to separate capital and wage labour rapidly, like any other branch of production. Even if gold miners' wages are initially above social average, profits (surplus value) accrue only to the owners of capital.

16. 'Cloth breeches reached 30 pesos, laced boots as much, a black cape, 100 pesos, a quire of paper 10 pesos, an *azumbre* (2 litres) 20 pesos, and a horse 3000, 4000, and even 5000 ducats, which prices persisted for a number of years' (one peso at that time equalled more or less 4 gr of gold) F. L. Gomara, *Historia de las Indias*, cited in Michele and Bernard Gazxier, *Or et Monnaie chez Martin de Azpilcueta*, Paris, 1978, p. 5.

17. Braudel and Spooner, 'Prices in Europe from 1450 to 1750', in *Cambridge Economic History*, Cambridge 1967; Pierre Vilar, *A History of Gold and Money*, London, 1976, pp. 104, 115–116, on gold production, pp. 117–118 and 123–133 on the amalgamation process and the social relations of production in the Potosi silver mines.

18. See *Capital*, Vol. 3, ch. 14, for the countervailing forces braking the tendency of the average rate of profit to decline. For the concrete explanation of the 'upward' turning points of long waves through a combination of these counteracting forces, see *Late Capitalism*, ch. 4, and Ernest Mandel, *The Long Waves of Capitalist Development*, Cambridge, 1980.

19. Engels Ref: p. 367. Herr Eugen Dühring's Revolution in Science (Anti-Dühring) Part III, London 1969, Chapter IV (Distribution). 'From the moment when society enters into possession of the means of production and uses them in direct association for production, the labour of each individual, however varied its specifically

useful character maybe, is immediately and directly social labour. The quantity of social labour contained in a product has then no need to be established in a roundabout way, as daily experience shows in a direct way how much of it is required on the average. Society can calculate simply how many hours of labour are contained in a steam-engine, a bushel of wheat of the last harvest, or a hundred square yards of cloth of a certain quality. *It could therefore never occur to it still to express the quantity of labour put into the products, quantities which it will then know directly and in their absolute amounts, in a third product, and in a measure which besides, is only relative, fluctuating, inadequate, though formerly unavoidable for lack of a better, rather than express them in their natural adequate and absolute measure, time.*

20. Throughout this contribution, I consider gold and paper currencies (banknotes) as identical, assuming paper currencies to be convertible into gold. The problems of inconvertible, constantly depreciating, inflationary paper currencies — moneys with forced course as Marx called them — are outside the realm of this study, as they were outside the realm of the third volume of *Capital*. But they can be easily reduced to Marx's commodity theory of money, on the basis of chapter II of *Contribution to a Critique of Political Economy*.

21. Marx explicitly states that prices differ from values for that reason. But this confirms that when he identifies the sum of values and the sum of prices of production in the third volume of *Capital*, he does make abstraction of money, that is he does not refer to prices in the monetary sense of the word. The important point for him to stress is the fact that value, that is the law of value, regulates the movement of prices, and therefore also the deviations of monetary prices from values.

22. Ernest Mandel, Introduction to *Capital*, vol. 2, Harmondsworth, 1979.

23. A striking confirmation of this thesis of Marx is offered by the way the *international* capitalist system depends today upon the South African *apartheid* regime. In their above-quoted book, Lanning and Mueller indicate that around 1920, South Africa's so-called 'marginal mines' — which constituted roughly one-half of the Rand's gold mining industry — 'had been kept in production only because the mining companies held down wages of Africa mineworkers... In real terms, black wages were 13% lower in 1921 than they had been in 1916. But without a segregated (segmented) labour market, such a decline of real wages could have been impossible. And without such decline, there would have occurred a drastic reduction of gold output, which would have been a real catastrophe for the international capitalist economy!

24. I have insisted on the importance of the time schedule for the transformation problem in previous writings, for instance in my introductions to the second and third volumes of *Capital*. Independently from me, but basing himself on partially similar reasoning, Professor Michel de Vroey of Louvain University, has arrived at similar conclusions ('A restatement of the Marxian Theory of Value', working paper no. 8005, Institut des Sciences Économiques, Université Catholique de Louvain, June 1980), published also as 'Value Production and Exchange' in *The Value Controversy*, London, 1981.

## Chapter Seven

1. See, for example, Morishima and Catephores in 'Le Problème de la Transformation: un Processus Markovien' in *Valeur, Exploitation et Croissance*, Economica, 1980. We have also dealt with this in a book and several articles: P. Salama, *Sur la Valeur*, Paris 1979.

2. Note that successive corrections often leave chapter 10 out of their treatment, biasing their mathematical solutions.

3. Von Bortkiewicz reproduces Marx's error when he considers a single coefficient of transformation for each department. Each department is composed of several branches, with different organic compositions. This leads to treating the products of these branches as if they exchanged at their values.

4. We have developed this in our book. See also D. Yaffe: '*Value and Price in Marx's Capital*', Revolutionary Communist No. 1, London 1975, and P. Salama 'Transformación Mathemática o Metamórfosis del Valor en Precios de Producción', in *Críticas de la Economía Política*, Mexico, 1978, no. 20, where we show that this conception flows from a confusion between Ricardo's theory and Marx's, sometimes to the point of presenting them in a unified way.

5. *Capital*, Vol. 1, Harmondsworth, 1976, p. 126.

6. 'The commodity is an immediate unity of use values and exchange values, that is to say of two opposites. It is thus immediately *contradictory*. This contradiction must develop as soon as we cease, as we have up until now, analysing the commodity now as a use value, now as an exchange value, and consider it in its totality, in its real relation to other commodities. But the real relation between commodities is their exchange.' K. Marx, *Value Studies*, A. Dragstedt, ed., London, 1976, p. 40. Also quoted by Yaffe, p. 39. This paragraph was originally at the end of the first chapter of volume 1 of *Capital* but was removed in the third edition.

7. This point will be further developed in what follows.

8. What is important at this stage of the analysis is this 'something' in common and not the common quantity of something.

9. Coletti, from *Rousseau to Lenin*, New York, 1972. This view is not neutral. It has been the subject of a debate between Rubin and the 'idealists' on one hand and the 'mechanists' on the other in the Soviet Union just after the revolution. See Lomis Baslé, *L'Élaboration de L'Économie Politique du Socialisme*, State Thesis for Paris 10, 1979, p. 128.

10. *Capital* Volume 1, p. 128.

11. *Ibid.*

12. R. Rosdolsky, *The Making of Marx's Capital*, London, 1971.

13. Bachaus, 'Dialectique de la Forme Valeur', *Critiques de L'Economie Politique* (*CEP*) no. 18, 1974, p. 8, which continues, 'The fact that the 'object in general' as such, that is, value as value, cannot be expressed at all but only 'appears' in a deformed form, as a 'relation' between two use values, is hidden from the reader.' (p. 9).

14. As Fausto rightly stresses: 'what does one analyse when one analyses the simple form of value?' An actual exchange? In fact, actual exchange is not analysed here — this is properly the subject of ch. 2 of the first section. Fausto, 'On the Value Form and Fetishism', *CEP*, no. 16, Paris 1981.

15. We could permit ourselves an ironical inversion of the footnote in Morishima and Catephores, p. 165; Marx's contribution to mathematical economics has always been underestimated or ignored, giving rise to the annoying tradition which ensures that the aptitudes for formalisation of the Marxist economists are always more limited than those of the orthodox economists', remarking that the use of mathematics in economics, without methodological preliminaries is perilous, when as in this precise case it is not transformed by a simple school exercise.

16. Fausto.

17. *Ibid.*

18. 'Now, however, we have to perform a task never even attempted by bourgeois economics. That is, we have to show the origin of this money-form, we have to trace the

development of the expression of value contained in the value-relation of commodities from its simplest, almost imperceptible outline to the dazzling money-form.' *Capital* volume 1, p. 139.

19. Marx, *Theories of Surplus Value*, London, 1969, volume 2, p. 200.

20. *Capital* volume 1, p. 148.

21. *Ibid*., p. 150.

22. *Ibid*.

23. J. L. Dallemagne, 'Le Mythe de la Stagflation', in *l'Inflation Capitaliste*, Paris, 1972, p. 163. We should add that a very interesting discussion on the status of money has developed in France in the last ten years or so, with the above work of Dallemagne with the (unpublished) thesis by Cartelier, and more recently the book by Benetti and Cartelier, *Marchands, Salariat et Capitalistes*, Paris 1980, discussed by Guibert in *CEP* no. 13 and by Fausto, op. cit. The critical presentation of this discussion is beyond the scope of this study.

24. *Capital*, volume 1, p. 202.

25. 'Nevertheless the coat, in relation to the linen, cannot represent value, unless value for the latter simultaneously assumes the form of a coat', unless, in other words, it appears that 'the coat, just as it is, expresses value and is endowed with the form of value by nature itself', Rosdolsky, p. 124 and Marx, *Capital*, volume 1, p. 143.

26. There is a certain similarity between money and labour-power. Both, though they are commodites, are very specific kinds of commodities. They are commodites and they are not commodities. Here we cannot develop this point. We note, however, that a very interesting discussion has broken out on the status of labour-power. Is it a commodity or not? Does it have a value or not? See Benetti and Cartelier.

27. We can thus understand why in Marx's work section 1 of Chapter 1 analyses commodity and value without dealing either with wage-earners or surplus-value. Those who consider that Marx's most important discovery was exploitation have often forgotten his exposure of fetishism, and present exchange value as equivalent to value.

28. Aglietta, 'La Dévalorisation de Capital, Étude des Liens entre Accumulation et Inflation', Cahiers de l'ISMEA, 1980, p. 387.

29. See my *Sur la Valeur* and 'Transformación Matemática'.

30. *Capital* volume 3, Harmondsworth, 1981, p. 274.

31. K. Marx, *Grundrisse*, Harmondsworth, 1977, 3rd edition, p. 761.

32. P. Sweezy, *The Theory of Capitalist Development*, New York, 1968, p. 110, notably when he writes: 'Obviously this would not be a position of equilibrium. The capitalists would all want to go into the production of wage goods [with a low organic composition] in order to share in the higher rate of profit obtainable there. And such a migration of capital out of some industries and into others would clearly upset the whole schema [of value]. A position of equilibrium must be characterised by equality in the rates of profit yielded by all the industries in the system'. Note that numerous economists take a similar position.

33. It is true that one finds this kind of erroneous reasoning in Marx, in contradiction with his more common positions: 'Capital withdraws from a sphere with a low rate of profit and and wends its way to others that yield higher profit... this provokes a relationship between supply and demand such that the average profit is the same in the various difference spheres, and values are therefore transformed into prices of production.' *Capital* volume 3, p. 297.

34. *Capital* volume 3, p. 280. See also p. 297.

35. It is understood that the sum of individual values necessarily corresponds to the sum of market values, since several commodities are considered. For more detail see *Capital*, volume 3, pp. 283–285.

36. This opinion is not widely known. It is generally considered that exchange on the market produces this average value, thus mixing up market value and market price. See Rosdolsky's interesting remarks on pp. 88–95.

37. Marx, ibid., p. 285. We should add that there is sometimes confusion in the French version between market value and market price. These confusions seem to be the result of a bad translation of the first edition, as a note on p. 200 [of the French edition: translator] indicates. But sometimes it is very clear, for example: 'If demand falls, for example, and with it the market price, this can lead to a withdrawal of capital and thus a reduction in the supply. But it can also lead to a fall in the market value itself as a result of inventions.' p. 292 (English edition) p. 209 (French edition). 38. This distinction is rarely made. On this point see *Capital*, volume 3, p. 296, for example, and its developments dealing with rent. The importance of this distinction was drawn to our attention by A. Cot and C. Gauchet.

39. For example the work of d'Andreff in *Profit et Structures du Capitalisme Mondial*, pub. Calmann-Levy, 1976; of Christian Palloix, *Procès de Production et Crise du Capitalisme*, Paris 1977.

40. P. Salama, L'État Capitaliste comme Abstraction Réelle', *CEP* nos. 7 and 8, Paris, 1978.

## Chapter Nine

1. See 'Positive Profits with Negative Surplus Value', *Economic Journal*, March 1975.

2. See *Marx After Sraffa*, pp. 150–162.

3. The article's scope is strictly limited. In particular, there is no intention of developing a Marxist theory of joint production. It should be noted that the refutation of Steedman's arguments concerning 'negative values' is totally independent of this. I intend to show that Steedman's arguments are wrong. If they are, then this remains true irrespective of the nature of the correct Marxist treatment of joint production.

4. On this whole question, see *Capital*, vol. 3, Harmondsworth, 1981, ch. 10.

5. *Capital* volume 1, Harmondsworth, 1976, p. 129.

6. Steedman, 'Positive Profits with Negative Surplus Value: A Reply', *Economic Journal*, September 1976, p. 607.

7. *Marx After Sraffa*, p. 151.

8. E. Wolfstetter, 'Positive Profits with Negative Surplus Value: A Comment', *Economic Journal*, December 1976.

9. *Marx After Sraffa*, pp. 137–149.

10. Ibid., pp. 142–144.

11. Ibid., pp. 144–146.

12. *Capital* volume 1, p. 314.

13. Ibid.

14. Ibid., p. 311.

15. The only modification necessary is the insertion of the machines of different age not on an equal basis but in different proportions. Another very simple case would be that in which a single capitalist (say an absolute monopolist) uses the same means of production over the years.

## Chapter Ten

1. Ian Steedman, *Marx After Sraffa*, London 1977, p. 29.

2. Ibid., p. 49.

3. Ibid., p. 49.

4. 'It has been shown that the proximate determinants of the rate of profit, the rate of accumulation, the prices of production, the social allocation of labour, etc., are the physical conditions of production, the real wage and the capitalist drive to accumulate. The next step is then to investigate the social, economic, political, technical, etc., determinants of those proximate determinants... Such study can no doubt draw on much of Marx's work, as one source amongst the many which will be needed. *But it will involve no reference to Marx's value magnitudes*, which are mere derivates of the things to be explained.' Ibid., p. 207, emphasis in original. This is a complete scientific project involving the reconstruction of political economy, and though it shares the mathematical system of Sraffa it is not the same project. See Sweezy, 'Marxian Value Theory and Crises', *The Value Controversy*, London, 1981, p. 21, who quotes the following remark of Joan Robinson: 'Piero has always stuck close to pure unadulterated Marx and regards my amendments with suspicion.' Robinson, 'The Labour Theory of Value', *Monthly Review*, December 1977, p. 56n.

5. Though value theory is not refuted but confirmed by a proper study of joint production, as Farjoun shows in this volume, joint production nevertheless plays a special role in Sraffian theory which is irrelevant to value theory, and very unsatisfactory in general. Its real purpose is the basis of a strange treatment of fixed capital in which capitalists 'produce' their unused fixed capital and resell it to themselves annually. This is very doubtful since it is at best an accounting transaction and certainly not a real sale; for example the capitalists do not have the option of buying someone else's unused capital instead of their own. Is the entire universe in a permanent frenzy of exchange by virtue of merely existing? This aside, 'genuine' joint production where outputs emerge in fixed proportions is extremely rare, and is confused by the Sraffians with multiple production in which the same factory can produce many different things but there is a choice of what to make. Even in the case of coking and oil fractionation, to which the Sraffians refer in support of their case, study shows that in practice refineries and coking plants can and do vary the proportions of outputs by using different admixtures of varying grades of crude oil or coal, so that in reality virtually all industries can independently control the quantity of every product sold. This is not to say that multiple production is not deserving of study; but it is not what the Sraffians are talking about.

6. A less trivial example is the famous correspondence between Bertrand Russell and the German logician Frege. Frege devised the first complete formalisation of mathematical set theory. Russell sent him a note expressing a very deep paradox in Frege's concise notation, a paradox which turns out to be the archetype of an entire class of logical paradoxes including the famous 'liar' paradox. Frege had unwittingly produced a system in which this could be very concisely expressed, so that when he read Russell's one-line note, he is said to have exclaimed that his life's work was ruined. Yet his system remains the foundation of most modern mathematics and, had it been junked because of this paradox, mathematics as we know it would not exist. This is not to say there are not inherent limitations in the Frege–Russell approach, which derived from the 'corrections' introduced by Russell. But these limitations derive from the attempt to reduce all mathematics to logic, rather than the paradox itself. See Andrzej Mostowski, *Thirty Years of Foundational Studies*, Oxford, 1966.

7. Piero Sraffa, *Production of Commodities by Means of Commodities*, Cambridge, 1960, preface.

8. Steedman, p. 18.

9. It is, of course, possible to exhibit systems in which, for example, a vector of profit rates replaces the single uniform rate, as Steedman does on p. 180. The point is,

however, that when this is done there are no longer the same number of equations as variables and neither prices nor profits can be uniquely determined. See note 20 on Morishima's treatment.

10. K. May, 'Value and Price of Production: A Note on Winternitz's Solution', *Economic Journal*, December 1951, Francis Seton, 'The Transformation Problem', *Review of Economic Studies*, vol. 24, 1957, pp. 149–160.

11. Sraffa, preface.

12. Steedman, p. 184, where he says 'If there are constant returns to scale and if wages are paid in advance...' and adds in his footnote 'Both assumptions will be made throughout this chapter, the former being essential to the argument, the latter merely a convenience.'

13. Steedman, p. 50.

14. Karl Marx, *Grundrisse*, Harmondsworth, 1977, pp. 137–39. See Rosdolsky, *The Making of Marx's Capital*, ch. 4, London, where there is an excellent discussion of this and related passages.

15. Space does not permit a full discussion of the relation between this mechanism and the role of money, which Mandel deals with at greater length. It should be clear with a little thought, however, that the mechanism is possible precisely because goods exchange against a third commodity, money, and not against each other. In a barter or semi-barter society, supply and demand variations would call forth *independent* movements in the ratios of exchange of each commodity against each other commodity so that a price vector in the normal sense would cease to exist.

16. Market price also, of course, diverges from price of production. Value, price of production and market price are three distinct entities, both conceptually and actually.

17. 'Marx's Theory of Value and the "Transformation Problem"', in Jesse Schwartz, ed., *The Subtle Anatomy of Capitalism*, Santa Monica, California, 1977.

18. See, for example, Steedman, p. 128, where he discusses the falling rate of profit under the assumption that all capitalists will adopt the technology which gives optimum profits for society as a whole. He continues 'some writers have been tempted to confuse this straightforward argument by asserting (correctly) that decentralized, individual decisions need not always lead, in aggregate, to the achievement of the commonly pursued objective... This 'argument' is just silly. For unless the previously adopted technique is no longer available, it is being asserted that, after the change, capitalists are no longer maximising the rate of profit attainable with the given wage! Even if a new invention should lead many capitalists mistakenly to adopt it, as soon as it is found to be less profitable than the previously used technique, all capitalists will revert to the latter. With a given real wage, the rate of profit can be lowered only by technical *regress*, never by technical progress.'

19. 'It has been said that competition equalises profit rates between the different spheres of production to produce an average rate of profit, and that this is precisely the way in which the values of products from these various spheres are transformed into prices of production. This happens, moreover, by the continual transfer of capital from one sphere to another, where profit stands above the average for the time being... This movement of capitals is always brought about in the first place by the state of market prices, which raise profits above the general average level in one place, and reduce it below the average in another.' *Capital*, Volume 3, p. 310. Even more explicitly, 'Market value, (and everything that was said about this applies with the necessary limitations also to price of production) involves a surplus profit for those producing under the best conditions in any particular sphere of production. Excluding all cases of crisis and overproduction, *this holds good for all market prices*, no matter how they might diverge from market values or market prices of production. The concept of market price means

that the same price is paid for all commodities of the same kind, even if these are produced under very different individual conditions and may therefore have very different cost prices.' *Capital*, volume 3, p. 301 (our emphasis). See E. Mandel, *Late Capitalism*, London, 1973, where the role of technological rents as a mechanism of the law of value was first systematically developed.

20. Sraffa, pp. 82–83. An alternative approach is outlined in the final chapter of Morishima, *Marx's Economics*, Cambridge, 1973 — building on the work of J. von Neumann, Steedman uses some of this work in chapter 13 on the determination of labour allocation. The approach uses linear programming methods to determine which of a large number of possible processes will be used under the assumption that society as a whole will try to maximise its rate of profit. However, this does not escape my central point which is that many different techniques of production *simultaneously* in use; furthermore it introduces weird assumptions such as that discussed by Farjoun in this volume, namely that excess products are sold at zero prices. Finally, with the introduction of the completely arbitrary idea that a society of private producers strives consciously to maximise its average rate of profit, all prospect of modelling real economic mechanisms under commodity production are thrown to the winds.

21. Among many reasons for labour-time as the foundation of value is one which receives less allowance than it ought, labour-power is virtually the only commodity whose use-value has strictly speaking, a two-dimensional magnitude, one component being the *time* dimension, the other the number of labourers. If we study speed of any economic change — for example, the rate of new investment in new processes — labour time is the only way we can relate the speed of this process to the rate of creation of new value. Neither 'price' nor 'physical quantities' can do this properly, because neither has a time dimension. See section 8 of this piece and also Mandel's comment in footnote 24.

22. There is a considerable discussion on Marx's analysis of the relation between supply, demand and the formation of market (social) values from individual values, for which see Rosdolsky, pp. 89–93. In the calculations which follow, I treat only Marx's 'intermediate' case in which market value is the average of individual values. The alternative cases can be analysed into the model using the same essential method, but two complications present themselves. First, some assumption must be made (on the basis of empirical observation) as to what relation must exist between supply and demand (i.e. some assumption on the level and rate of change of unrealised commodities seeking realisation) to determine which case applies. Second, if market value is not the average of individual values, then some labour must be counted as more or less productive than the average and the total labour time of society no longer adds up to the total new value created; as with skilled labour, the reduction of concrete to abstract labour then involves quantitative as well as qualitative changes. An alternative, which I prefer, is to treat market value as always being the average of individual values, and deal with Marx's other two cases (which he himself regards as exceptional) as forming prices of production which include a component of rent as well as average profit.

23. Nor does it make the clock accurate, even though as the logical Charles Dodgson remarked, it will be right twice a day.

24. There is a specific reason for separating out the effects of turnover in this way. The model keeps track of the quantity of goods and values tied up in production, and distinguishes this clearly and from the outset from the quantity turned over. This 'minor' distinction is rarely made although it can be done even in the framework of a simultaneous equation model. One consequence is to systematically obscure the discussion on profit rate. Marx calculates profit as the capitalists do, on capital advanced and not on capital turned over. On this basis his derivation of rising organic

composition is a lot clearer. If one takes the total labour of society as approximately constant (i.e. abstracts from population growth) and assumes that a proportion of it is each year invested and not immediately turned over, then the stock of dead value tied up in production must, ceteris paribus, increase faster than living value. Of course, advances in productivity will then reduce the values of these stocks but the mechanism will be distinctly different from that assumed in most discussions on the question, because these stocks of fixed capital are not devalued gradually through cheaper replacements, but suddenly and abruptly in the crisis phase of the business cycle, when society discovers their new values through a general surplus of unrealised value seeking realisation. Because value tied up in fixed capital does not seek realisation directly (i.e. the products of these factories), the cheapening of the elements of constant capital is by no means as simple as it appears in models where constant capital is assumed to circulate completely in each production period. See Marx's Letter to Engels, April 30, 1868, in *Letters on 'Capital'*, K. Marx, F. Engels, London, 1983.

25. We write our price-value multipliers in this way in order to emphasise Marx's concept that the transformation process involves *transfers of value* from one sector of the capitalist class to another. The quantities represent the proportion of value transferred in or out of a given capital, per unit of value sold. Marx's proposition that total value equals total price then boils down to the equation $\Sigma \mu_i = 0$.

26. See for example, the series of studies reviewed and often presented in the *Bulletin of the European Productivity Association*, Paris, 1956–61 and the series published by the Bureau of Labour Statistics under the general rubric 'Case Study Data of Productivity and Factory Performance' in the 1950s. There is a considerable bibliography in Zoltan Roman, *Productivity and Economic Growth*, Budapest, 1982. The surge of interest in inter-firm productivity comparisons in the fifties and sixties had died away, partly because firms are unwilling to divulge what is clearly sensitive commercial information in more competitive times. See, however, W.E.G. Salter, *Productivity and Technical Change*, Cambridge, 1969. Note that the quantity 'specific productivity' we have defined above is not identical in magnitude to labour productivity since it includes a contribution from constant capital, i.e. from dead labour.

27. US Bureau of Labour Statistics, *Relationship Between Productivity Measurements*, undated. The BLS is simply replying to the charge that, by considering only the productivity of labour it is considering only one 'factor of production'. It is virtually compelled to admit that in comparative studies, labour presents itself as the real basis of all so-called factors of production: Marx's entire point in a nutshell, confirmation of his view that in controversies amongst bourgeois economists, the statisticians turn out to be right against the theoreticians ninety-nine times out of a hundred.

28. 'As long as we were dealing with capital's value production and the value of its product individually, the natural form of the commodity product was a matter of complete indifference for the analysis, whether it was machines or corn or mirrors… Insofar as the reproduction of capital came into consideration, it was sufficient to assume that the opportunity arose within the circulation sphere for the part of the product that represented capital value to be transformed back into its elements of production, and therefore into its shape as productive capital, just as we could assume that worker and capitalist found on the market the commodities on which they spent their wages and surplus-value. But this purely formal manner of presentation is no longer sufficient once we consider the total social capital and the value of its product. The transformation of one portion of the product's value back into capital, the entry of another part into the individual consumption of the capitalist and working classes, forms a movement within the value of the product in which the total capital has

resulted; and this movement is not only a replacement of values, but a replacement of materials, and is therefore conditioned not just by the mutual relations of the value components of the social product but equally by their use-values, by their material shape.' *Capital*, volume 2, Harmondsworth, 1978, p. 470.

29. 'The "social need" which governs the principle of demand is basically conditioned by the relationship of the different classes and their respective economic positions; in the first place, therefore, particularly by the proportion between the total surplus-value and wages, and secondly, by the proportion between the various parts into which surplus-value is itself divided (profit, interest, ground-rent, taxes, etc.)' *Capital*, volume 3, p. 282. 'Demand and supply, on further analysis, imply the existence of various different classes and segments of classes which distribute the total social revenue amongst themselves and consume it as such, thus making up a demand created out of revenue'. p. 296.

30. Most clearly in his summary statement: 'that [Sraffa's] critique is in no way destructive of the project of providing a materialist account of the capitalist mode of production; nor is it in the least inconsistent with the attempt to build a fully articulated social, political and economic account of particular capitalist social formations. More specifically, many aspects of Marx's political economy, because they are independent of his reasoning in terms of value magnitudes, are unaffected by the Sraffa-based critique.' Steedman, p. 206. The point is that value magnitudes supply the hinge, the buckle, the pivotal point which relate class analysis to economic analysis, and cannot be prised loose from the frame without destroying the edifice.

31. See in particular Marx's letter to Engels of April 30, 1868 (quoted above) in which the whole argument is summarised very clearly and concisely.

32. 'If we find that the cost of base-year purchases at current prices is greater than the value of current purchases at current prices; while the cost of current purchases at base-year prices is also greater than the cost of base-year purchases at base-year prices; then we are unable to say whether the standard of living has increased or not, since the current quantities were not available in the base year, and the base year quantities are not available now. This is the index number problem.' G. Bannock, R. E. Baxter and R. Rees, *The Penguin Dictionary of Economics*, Harmondsworth, 1977, p. 211.

33. *Capital*, volume 3, p. 274, my emphasis.

34. 'But precisely because the circuit $C' \ldots C'$ presupposes in its description the existence of another industrial form $C(= L + mp)$ (and mp comprises other capitals of various kinds, e.g. in our case machines, coal, oil, etc.) it itself demands to be considered not only as the *general* form of the circuit, i.e. as a social form in which every individual industrial capital can be considered (except in the case of its first investment) hence not only as a form of motion common to all individual industrial capitals, but at the same time as the form of motion of the sum of individual capitals, i.e. of the total social capital of the capitalist class, a movement in which the movement of any individual industrial capital simply appears as a partial one, intertwined with the others and conditioned by them... $C \ldots C'$ is the basis of Quesnay's *Tableau Economique*, and it shows great discernment on his part that he selected this form in opposition to $M \ldots M'$ (the form fixed on and isolated by the Mercantile System), and not $P \ldots P'$. *Capital*, volume 2, p. 179.

35. Steedman, p. 202.

36. Indeed Kuhn, *The Structure of Scientific Revolutions*, Chicago, 1962, remarks that optics is one of the few sciences whose basic techniques have remained virtually static and untouched by the continuous revolutions in its foundations. From time to time post-Sraffians attempt to place themselves in a Kuhnian framework, arguing that they are participating in a 'scientific revolution' following the discovery of

inconsistencies in Marx. It is hard for anyone with a background in the natural sciences to stifle a sense of outrage at this idea: Kuhn's entire work is devoted to explaining how science progresses through inconsistencies between theory and *empirically observed fact*, to which virtually no-one on the post-Sraffian side of the debate makes the slightest reference. It is difficult to see what conceivable relation can exist between observed reality and Steedman's closing remark which I quoted in footnote 17, since every single capitalist observer now concedes that the rate of profit world has been systematically declining *in fact* since the late 1960s, far faster than can be accounted for by changes in the real wage.

37. Hodgson, *Capitalism, Value and Exploitation — A Radical Theory*, Oxford, 1981, p. 95–97, acknowledges that the post-Sraffian system does not have an adequate causal theory, but falls back on the argument that neither has Marxism. We have just seen that Marxism does have a causal theiry: the argument is therefore in the post-Sraffian court.

38. This is yet another reason why Steedman is entirely wrong to consign Marx's concept of fetishism to a *separate* department of political economy from value theory, or even relegate it to philosophy, outside of political economy altogether. The concept of fetishism is integral to Marx's value theory because it expresses the precise fact that the form in which economic laws come into the consciousness of economic agents is not transparent; they are not immediately conscious of the laws which nevertheless govern their actions. This does not mean they are like headless chickens with no consciousness at all, or a consciousness imparted to them by the tabloid newspapers. Crucial determinants of their consciousness are also the expression of laws; the *same* laws. As Marx progresses from volume 1 to volume 3, from abstract to concrete, he also demonstrates the way in which capitalists perceive economic categories, while still showing that, even on the basis of their false perceptions, they can be the agents of the law of value *because their consciousness is also a function of the law of value*. If the disciples of von Neumann had troubled themselves to study his contributions to cybernetics, they would have found out that formal theory is perfectly content with systems, such as cellular automata, in which individual components of the system possess 'consciousness' distinct from the aggregate effects of their interaction, and nevertheless governed by the same law as those same aggregate effects.

39. *Capital*, volume 2, p. 571.

40. *Capital*, volume 2, p. 472.

41. Albert Einstein, *Uber die Allgemeine Gravitationslehre*, in *Ideas and Opinions*, New York, 1960, p. 355.